Directing Shakespeare in America

RELATED TITLES

Anecdotal Shakespeare: A New Performance History,
Paul Menzer

Performing King Lear: Gielgud to Russell Beale,
Jonathan Croall

Shakespeare in Our Time: A Shakespeare Association of America Collection, edited by Suzanne Gossett and Dympna Callaghan

Shakespeare on the Global Stage, edited by Paul Prescott and Erin Sullivan

Shakespeare's World of Words, edited by Paul Yachnin

Directing Shakespeare in America

Current Practices

Charles Ney

THE ARDEN SHAKESPEARE
LONDON • NEW YORK • OXFORD • NEW DELHI • SYDNEY

THE ARDEN SHAKESPEARE
Bloomsbury Publishing Plc
50 Bedford Square, London, WC1B 3DP, UK
1385 Broadway, New York, NY 10018, USA

BLOOMSBURY, THE ARDEN SHAKESPEARE and the Arden Shakespeare
logo are trademarks of Bloomsbury Publishing Plc

First published 2016
Reprinted 2017, 2019

Copyright © Charles Ney, 2016

Charles Ney has asserted his right under the Copyright, Designs and
Patents Act, 1988, to be identified as author of this work.

For legal purposes the Acknowledgements on p. xiii constitute an
extension of this copyright page.

All rights reserved. No part of this publication may be reproduced or
transmitted in any form or by any means, electronic or mechanical,
including photocopying, recording, or any information storage or retrieval
system, without prior permission in writing from the publishers.

Bloomsbury Publishing Plc does not have any control over, or
responsibility for, any third-party websites referred to or in this book. All
internet addresses given in this book were correct at the time of going
to press. The author and publisher regret any inconvenience caused if
addresses have changed or sites have ceased to exist, but can accept no
responsibility for any such changes.

A catalogue record for this book is available from the British Library.

A catalog record for this book is available from the Library of Congress.

ISBN: HB: 978-1-4742-3984-4
PB: 978-1-4742-3983-7
ePDF:978-1-4742-3986-8
eBook: 978-1-4742-3985-1

Typeset by Fakenham Prepress Solutions, Fakenham, Norfolk NR21 8NN
Printed and bound in Great Britain

To find out more about our authors and books visit www.bloomsbury.com
and sign up for our newsletters.

CONTENTS

List of Illustrations x
Acknowledgements xiii

Introduction 1

Part I Core Beliefs about Directing Shakespeare

1 Text and Context 7
   British influences on US practice 7
   Other studies 10
   Recent developments 16

2 The Directors and their Aesthetic Values 25
   Shakespeare as contemporary 33
   Endless possibilities 37
   Complexity in Shakespeare 41
   The invisible director 45
   The interpretive director 48
   The language and text director 55
   The original practice director 64
   The physical and visceral director 68
   Mixing approaches 74
   The inclusive director 79

Part II Preparations for Rehearsal and Production

3 Developing an Approach 89
Given circumstances 94
Images 95
Critical scenes/central issues 95
Questions of interpretation 97
Point of view 100
Following an Elizabethan model 101
Concepts 103
Challenges and limitations of concepts 105
Examples of context approaches 106

4 Research and Analysis 115
Research 118
Analysis 123

5 Preparing the Production Text 129
Consulting different editions 133
Punctuation 133
Cutting 134
Transposing scenes 140
Replacing, emending and adapting 142

6 Working with Designers 145
Preparing for design meetings 149
Talking with designers 154
Attitudes about working with designers 157
Two contrasting views on design approach 162
Ground plans 162

7 Casting 165

Desirable qualities for Shakespeare 168
Racial diversity in casting 173
Cross gender casting 176

Part III Rehearsing the Production

8 Beginning Rehearsals 181

First day 184
Working with actors 186
Goals, atmosphere, energy 192

9 Table Work 197

Everyone at the table versus scene-by-scene 201
Meaning and comprehension 204
Punctuation, scansion, language analysis 206
Story 208
Getting the company on the same page 209
Event, structure, energy shifts 210
Developing layers 212
Going back to table work 214
Image chains 214

10 Staging the Play 217

Moving from table work to staging 221
Blocking 223
Sketching a structure or frame 225
Organic blocking; improvising the staging 230
Designs and blocking 234
Transitions 235
Additional advice on staging 238

11 Speaking Shakespeare's Language 241

Qualities and objectives 244
Phrasing and word choice 249
Rhetoric and language structure 253
Stresses and operatives 254
Rhythm and pacing 255
Physical language 258
Later rehearsals 259

12 Middle Stage Rehearsals 261

After the first week 266
Character issues 274
Subtext and motivation 278
Shaping 281
Run-throughs 282
Giving notes 286
Rehearsal schedules and time management 289

Part IV Finishing the Production

13 Tech and Dress Rehearsals 297

Possibilities 300
Problems/challenges 301
Original practice tech/dresses 302
An opportunity for improvement and change 305
A description of tech for *The Merchant of Venice* 307
Moving on 308

14 Adding the Audience 309

Number of previews 312
Using and assessing previews 313

Opening 320
After opening 323

Conclusion 327
Interviews Conducted 331
Notes 335
Select Bibliography 341
Index 343

LIST OF ILLUSTRATIONS

FIGURE 1 *King Lear*, directed by Robert Falls, Goodman Theatre, 2006, Stacy Keach as Lear with the company. Photograph by Liz Lauren 12

FIGURE 2 *Hamlet*, directed by Elizabeth LeCompte, The Wooster Group, 2007, Scott Shephard as Hamlet. Photograph © Paula Court 13

FIGURE 3 *The Taming of the Shrew*, directed by Kate Buckley, Oregon Shakespeare Festival, 2007. Vilma Silva as Kate and Michael Elich as Petruchio. Photograph by Jenny Graham 15

FIGURE 4 *Macbeth*, directed by Jim Warren, American Shakespeare Center, 2014. Patrick Midgley, Jonathan Holtzman and Gregory Jon Phelps as the Weird Sisters. Photograph by Lindsey Walters 16

FIGURE 5 *Pericles*, directed by Mary Zimmerman, Goodman Theatre, 2006. Ryan Artzberger as Pericles, Naomi Jacobson as Lychorida and Glenn Fleshler as Sailor. Photograph by Liz Lauren 19

FIGURE 6 *Othello*, directed by Lisa Wolpe, Boston Court Theatre, 2008, Lisa Wolpe as Iago. Photograph by Maxine Picard 23

FIGURE 7 *Julius Caesar*, directed by Amanda Dehnert, The Oregon Shakespeare Festival, 2011. Vilma Silva as Caesar with Anthony Heald, Kevin Kenerly, Frankie J. Alvarez, Brooke Parks. Photograph by Jenny Graham 26

FIGURE 8 *Timon of Athens*, directed by Barbara Gaines, Chicago Shakespeare Theater, 2012. Ian McDiarmid as Timon. Photo Credit: Liz Lauren 90

FIGURE 9 *Hamlet*, directed by Darko Tresnjak, Hartford Stage, 2014. Floyd King as First Gravedigger. Photograph by T. Charles Erickson 116

FIGURE 10 *Henry V*, directed by Bonnie J. Monte, The Shakespeare Theatre of New Jersey, 2007. Jack Wetherall as the Chorus. Photograph by Gerry Goodstein 130

FIGURE 11 *Cymbeline*, directed by Mark Lamos, Lincoln Center, 2007. John Cullum as Cymbeline, Michael Cerveris as Posthumus and Martha Plimpton as Imogen. Photograph by Paul Kolnik 146

FIGURE 12 *A Midsummer Night's Dream*, directed by Daniel Sullivan, Free Shakespeare in the Park, Public Theater, 2007. Keith Randolph Smith, Tim Blake Nelson, Jay O. Sanders, Jesse Tyler Ferguson, Ken Cheeseman, Jason Antoon. Photograph by Michal Daniel 166

FIGURE 13 Avery Glymph, Rachel Mewbron, Sean Fri, Dan Jones and Matthew Pauli in the Shakespeare Theatre Company's 2014 production of *The Tempest*, directed by Ethan McSweeny. Photograph by Scott Suchman 182

FIGURE 14 *Romeo and Juliet*, directed by David Ivers, Utah Shakespeare Festival, 2011. Christian Barillas as Romeo and Magan Wiles as Juliet. Photograph by Karl Hugh 198

FIGURE 15 *As You Like It*, directed by J. R. Sullivan, Oregon Shakespeare Festival, 2007. Danforth Comins as Orlando and Tod Rjurstrom as Charles the Wrestler. Photograph by David Cooper 218

FIGURE 16 *Much Ado About Nothing*, directed by Benjamin Curns, American Shakespeare Center, 2014. Photograph by Lindsey Walters 242

FIGURE 17 *Richard III*, directed by Brian Kulick, Classic Stage Company, 2007. Michael Cumpsty as Richard III. Photograph by Joan Marcus 262

FIGURE 18 *Troilus and Cressida*, directed by Rob Melrose, Oregon Shakespeare Festival, 2012. Photograph by Jenny Graham 298

FIGURE 19 Photograph of the audience at American Players Theatre, Spring Green, Wisconsin. Photograph by Carissa Dixon 310

ACKNOWLEDGEMENTS

I want to first thank Jim O'Quinn at *American Theatre* whose support and guidance years ago led me to realize I really did have the potential for a book with this project. I also thank him for opening up a new way of thinking about writing for the theatre.

Of course this book wouldn't exist without all of the directors I interviewed. I especially want to thank them for their time and many contributions to this study. They are individually named throughout and also appear in a list at the back. My deepest thanks for giving me the most incredible education in directing Shakespeare that one could ever have.

I wish to thank Cassandra Knobloch for her proofreading and many hours reviewing the first rough drafts. I also thank John Fleming and Richard Sodders, two colleagues and department chairs, who always supported my efforts and my many travels. Additionally John Fleming helped by commenting on some of my earliest drafts. Jim Volz provided invaluable advice in the middle of what became a decade long project.

I also thank the Shakespeare Theatre Association for embracing my efforts and letting me attend their annual conferences where I interviewed several directors. The staff of the Folger Library and the staff at the Performing Arts Library at Lincoln Center have been exceptionally supportive with their assistance and advice. I want to thank my assistants who helped me transcribe hours of interviews throughout the past decade: Melissa Utley, Robert Wighs, Megan Sullivan and Debbie Swain.

I owe the staff at Bloomsbury Arden Shakespeare my deepest gratitude for their invaluable assistance and guidance, especially Margaret Bartley, Emily Hockley and Kim Storry.

Finally, I wish to thank my wife Michelle and my daughters Rachel and Cameron for supporting me on this incredible journey. They were there to help transcribe the very first interviews when an unexpected hospital visit led to a tense deadline. They have been there for me ever since, encouraging me to finish.

Introduction

Directing Shakespeare in America: Current Practices examines the present landscape for directing Shakespeare in the US. It provides a snapshot picture of the field through an examination of the beliefs, methods and productions of many types of directors, from artistic directors at preeminent theatres to freelance directors working in a variety of situations. Ultimately, it intends to be a framework in which to view an individual director's work.

At present, a comprehensive study of contemporary Shakespeare directors in America does not exist. *Directing Shakespeare in America* concentrates on a considerable base of US Shakespeare directors and theatres. There are more than 200 theatres in the US that devote a substantial portion of their repertoire to producing Shakespeare's plays.[1] Over the last decade, I have spoken with over sixty artistic directors and directors about their work. *Directing Shakespeare in America* compares many aspects of their craft as they discuss issues and concerns in directing Shakespeare's canon. They disclose their interpretation of the text, how they manage the various stages of production, and how they go about supervising rehearsals – including sharing specific exercises and tactics. In addition they discuss their thoughts on current trends in the field.

This book includes such notable figures as Michael Kahn, Oskar Eustis, Barbara Gaines, Daniel Sullivan, Des McAnuff, Mark Lamos, Mary Zimmerman, Darko Tresnjak, Kent Thompson, Tina Packer, David Esbjornson, Bill Rausch, André Bishop, Fred Adams, Brian Kulick, David Frank and Lisa Wolpe. They represent work at this country's leading Shakespeare theatres, including The Public/Shakespeare in the Park, Chicago Shakespeare Theater, the Old Globe (San Diego), Shakespeare Theatre Company (DC), Oregon Shakespeare Festival, Utah Shakespeare Festival, American Shakespeare Center, Classic Stage Repertory, Shakespeare & Company, American Players Theatre, Shakespeare Theatre of New Jersey, Los Angeles Women's Shakespeare Company and Judith Shakespeare Company.

Directing Shakespeare in America is an eclectic blend of advice on staging Shakespeare's plays. Subjects covered include researching and analyzing, preparing the production script, casting, collaborating with designers, handling heightened language, staging, rehearsing, orchestrating a production's pacing, shaping the storytelling and managing run-throughs, technical/dress rehearsals and previews. In addition, these directors discuss the challenges of finding connections with contemporary audiences, deciding where to situate their productions in regards to its world and appearance, translating multiple layers of meaning into action, answering stylistic issues and achieving collaboration with actors and the production team.

Each director believes passionately in her own approach and ideas about directing Shakespeare. Yet methods for achieving a director's goals reflect principles often unrecognized by the director, by those who work with them and by audiences. It is a contention of this study that these values in a director's work can be made more apparent when compared and contrasted with other directors' approaches. Not only can we learn about the craft of directing and about American Shakespeare production practices, but we may be able to decipher cultural attitudes towards Shakespeare as well.

This study uses the words of each director to impart advice. I found it important to conduct live interviews in order to get to know each director's personal style. In most instances, I have witnessed at least one production directed by them.[2] Over the course of ten years, I compiled many interviews. As transcribed, these constituted over 1,000 pages of single-spaced raw data. I have assembled the directors' collective answers under each production task and organized comments chronologically in the order in which they are carried out on a typical production. Quotes are further subdivided and organized into four sections. Part I serves as an introduction to each director. It reviews career highlights and then presents each director's major beliefs, their aesthetic sensibilities, value systems, and how they impact a director's approach and production choices. These statements suggest a framework in which to evaluate the subsequent comments. Parts II, III and IV divide the various tasks into the major phases of production. Thus Part II considers preparations for production and rehearsal, Part III focuses on the rehearsal period and Part IV reviews finishing the production work. If there are duplicate answers, I have elected to choose the ones that have the clearest and most interesting points of view. *Directing Shakespeare in America* offers, then, a variety of opinions and intends to be a sourcebook of directing methods. It is a guide through every stage of directing a Shakespeare production.

In early December 2014, I submitted comments to each director for approval. I offered them an opportunity to clarify and update their statements. Many of the directors took advantage of this. As some of the interviews were several years old, directors were able to provide recent material on how their work has developed. In addition, I added three new interviews with directors at the January 2015 Shakespeare Theatre Association conference.

It is my hope that *Directing Shakespeare in America* will be of interest to anyone who wants to learn more about directing Shakespeare in the US. A specific advantage is that the reader can examine what the collective base of directors in the study has to say on any given topic. It will appeal to students seeking to learn about craft and the profession. Scholars can analyze directorial attitudes as well as production choices and performance interpretations of the text. Practitioners can discover what other directors are thinking and practicing. Shakespeare enthusiasts who want to know more about what directors think, as well as how they influence and shape productions, will find a wealth of information on that topic. And the neophyte can develop a greater clarity and understanding concerning the whole process.

PART ONE

Core Beliefs about Directing Shakespeare

1

Text and Context

British influences on US practice

While this is a study of US Shakespeare directors, it is important to acknowledge English directors and teachers who have been significant throughout the history of directing Shakespeare in America. They include B. Iden Payne, Margaret Webster, Tyrone Guthrie, Peter Brook, John Barton, Patrick Tucker and Cecily Berry.

B. Iden Payne 'proselytized' his ideas about performing Shakespeare to theatre organizations and universities throughout the US. His beliefs were heavily influenced by fellow Brit William Poel, founder of the 1895 Elizabethan Stage Society. Poel, living at a time when directors were coming to the fore, believed Victorian staging conventions, with extensive scenery, lengthy scene changes and excessive cuts, marred Shakespeare's intentions. He espoused the use of what was known about Elizabethan theatrical practices when mounting Shakespeare's plays. He also believed in moving the stage action quickly – both in the textual delivery and through the use of rapid scene changes.

Payne began a life-long association with Carnegie Mellon University in 1914. Like Poel, he argued for simpler, more efficient staging methods. However, unlike Poel, he was not as interested in recreating the distinctiveness of Shakespeare's stage as in uncovering the characteristics of dramaturgy embedded in the text that were fundamental to the staging of the plays. He continued the practice of excising text he thought would be difficult for modern audience sensibilities to comprehend, while ensuring the verse and meter were not affected. He also argued for a scheme to employ parts of the stage through the use of 'zones' appropriate to the staging of specific kinds of scenes. He applied this method regardless of whether the production was on a proscenium stage or on a recreation of an Elizabethan stage. More important was the fact his system supported the swift shifts in scenic action dictated by Shakespeare's dramaturgy. Beginning in 1930, he began lecturing on his ideas about Shakespearean production at several universities, most often in summer programmes from Carnegie Mellon to the University of Washington. Frequently he demonstrated his system through his direction of Shakespeare plays.[1] According to Noel Craig, Payne helped found the Oregon Shakespeare Festival and the Old Globe, the first two US Shakespeare theatres in 1935.

Margaret Webster's productions on Broadway still hold performance records for the longest Shakespeare runs. The daughter of two British actors, she was born in New York, but raised in England. Her debut as a Broadway director was with a production of *Richard II* starring Maurice Evans in 1937. Over the next couple of years, the pair produced *Hamlet*, *Twelfth Night* and *Henry IV Part 1* – all on Broadway. Her 1943 *Othello* with Paul Robeson ran for 296 performances and remains Broadway's longest running Shakespeare production. It was the first Broadway production to feature an African-American actor in the title role. A 1941 *Macbeth* with Evans set a record for longest run of that play with its 131 performances and a national tour that extended the run to 225. Her 1945 production of *The Tempest* was also the longest Broadway run of that play at 124 performances. Ironically, many scholars and practitioners know little about her or her achievements.[2] I believe this is due, in large measure, to the field's gender prejudices of the time. According to Webster's biographer, Evans confessed that he wanted Webster to direct *Richard II* because he would have more control over the project by hiring a young, relatively inexperienced director: 'Although I knew exactly how I wished the play to look and be performed', he admitted, 'it would be a serious mistake to occupy the director's post myself besides playing the leading role'.[3] In addition, the actress who played Desdemona, Uta Hagen, disliked Webster's non-method based approach at a time when the US theatre was beginning to be dominated by American versions of Stanislavski. These factors have contributed to many overlooking Webster's remarkable record of achievement.

In the 1950s, Tyrone Guthrie brought his idea for a classical theatre – a three-sided non-proscenium, open, classless democratic space – to the Stratford Festival Theatre, and then again later to the Minneapolis Guthrie Theater. He felt such spaces would be more conducive to playing Shakespeare and reignite the ritual aspects of ancient Greek theatre.[4] He argued that it was not his job to coach or develop the actors. Rather he believed the director must act like the conductor of an orchestra to craft the pacing and rhythm – the scene's architecture – in Shakespeare's scenes. That architecture he considered to be the most important element.[5]

Many directors I spoke with were profoundly affected by Peter Brook's work, particularly his *A Midsummer Night's Dream* that toured the US in the early 1970s with its bold and innovative staging that shattered all preconceptions about that play. They consider Brook's production a watershed moment. As Libby Appel told me, 'Were any of us not completely just mesmerized, but also changed in all of our thinking of work when Peter Brook's *A Midsummer Night's Dream* happened? *The Empty Space*? Suddenly drama meant something totally different'.

John Barton's *Playing Shakespeare*, which first came out in a 1982 television series and spurred a follow up book in 1984, has had a significant impact on the development of a generation of actors, directors and teachers, who, in turn, are passing the information on to younger enthusiasts. Having realized the limits of method acting with the classics, and in particular Shakespeare, Barton's work was disseminated at a time when US actors and training programmes were hungry for ideas on how to play this material. Similarly, Patrick Tucker (Barton's assistant before forming his own company, the Original Shakespeare Company) and Cecily Berry (the voice director at the Royal Shakespeare Company and author of *The Actor and the Text*) also influenced direction through their workshops and writings. Chicago Shakespeare Theater's artistic director Barbara Gaines brought in all three to give a series of workshops that would advance the training of her company.[6] Kate Buckley, an assistant director at the time, referred to these workshops as fundamental to her thoughts on performing Shakespeare.[7]

While the US has co-opted Shakespeare as our own, there have been a few Americans who have been influential to British Shakespeare. P. T. Barnum's desire to purchase and bring Shakespeare's birthplace to the US spurred fundraising that led to the inception of the Shakespeare Memorial Theatre.[8] More recently, Sam Wanamaker has had a tremendous impact on London Shakespeare with his relentless pursuit of a theatre built near the site of the original Globe. And Joseph Papp argued the enormous advantages of using diversity in casting Shakespeare's plays.[9]

Other studies

Whereas a comprehensive contemporary study of American Shakespeare direction does not exist, there have been several that have looked at directors working in North America.

Ralph Berry's landmark *On Directing Shakespeare* is an interview book of Shakespeare directors. Most of the interviews are of British directors. Michael Kahn is the sole American director in the book. Berry argues that the director's choice of setting constitutes the frame for the production and dictates subsequent decisions regarding the visuals. By choosing the 'renaissance' setting, Berry believes, a director avoids anachronistic problems with clothing and props. His 'modern' production paradigm has the advantage of making the text appear relevant to audiences who may find it antiquated. Such a production will inevitably have discrepancies between text and staging choices, between swords and AK-47s, between crowns and CEO suits. Yet this approach can lead to inventive choices by a director who finds effective equivalents to royalty and archaic references in a contemporary world. By 'period analogue' Berry means the choice of any period other than renaissance. He makes a distinction between choosing a period-look based entirely on the visuals ('décor') and choosing a period because it suggests an inherent criticism found within the text ('concept'). The 'eclectic' approach is one that is not interested in history and thus avoids settings and costuming that might identify the actor as of a particular nationality or living within a given period. It's motto is 'keep the options open' allowing for a multiplicity of interpretations.[10]

While one can question aspects of Berry's paradigm definitions, according to freelance director Ethan McSweeny (almost four decades later), 'By and large, those are the four ways you can approach the plays. The different ones propel you to different things'.[11]

In *Rescripting Shakespeare*, Alan Dessen reviews modifications he has witnessed directors make to the text and analyzes choices that call into question the playwright's given circumstances. He defines 'rescripting' as 'the changes made by the director in a received text in response to a perceived problem or to achieve some agenda'. Motives for directors to rescript include to '(1) streamline the playscript and save running time by cutting speeches or entire scenes, (2) eliminate obscurity (in mythological allusions, difficult syntax, and archaic words), (3) conserve on personnel by eliminating figures completely … (4) sidestep stage practices appropriate to the Globe that

FIGURE 1 King Lear, *directed by Robert Falls, Goodman Theatre, 2006, Stacy Keach as Lear with the company. Photograph by Liz Lauren.*

might mystify today's playgoer or actor, and occasionally (5) cancel out a passage that might not fit comfortably within a particular agenda or "concept"'. He also sees two production paradigms: 'pure' Shakespeare versus transposed or 'Designer's Theatre'. By 'pure' he means 'play the Quarto or Folio Version with as few trappings as possible'. 'Transposed' refers to productions that are placed in other periods and 'Designer's Theatre' denotes settings that Dessen suggests are innovative scenic milieus. For Dessen, these last two are conjoined to a production that has an 'agenda' or 'concept'.[12]

The study that looks at the largest number of American directors is Nancy Taylor's *Women Direct Shakespeare in America: Productions from the 1990s*. It is a critical examination of eight female directors and their productions of Shakespeare from a feminist performance theory perspective. Taylor examines preparation, decisions about approach, rehearsal methods as well as 'views on representing women in

FIGURE 2 Hamlet, *directed by Elizabeth LeCompte, The Wooster Group, 2007, Scott Shephard as Hamlet. Photograph © Paula Court.*

Shakespeare's plays' in the work of Jayne Koszyn, Lisa Wolpe, Tina Packer, Ellen O'Brien, Abigail Adams, Melia Bensussen, Barbara Gaines and JoAnne Akalaitis.[13] In particular, she examines the directors' work for how they 'have interpreted and staged female subjectivity, particularly with romantic or sexual relationships between men and women'.[14]

A comprehensive study of thirty-one international directors can be found in *The Routledge Companion to Directors' Shakespeare*. Edited by noted British scholar John Russell Brown, it reviews 'the most acclaimed productions of the last 100 years in a variety of cultural and political contexts'. Prominent Shakespearean scholars have contributed chapters focusing on the director's 'theatrical vision and methods of rehearsal and production'. Of the thirty-one directors, only four are North American: Orson Welles, Joe Papp, Julie Taymor (US) and Robert LePage (Canadian). Taymor and LePage are the volume's only living North American practitioners.[15]

In addition, there have been several interview books with US directors, some of whom direct Shakespeare. An excellent example is Jason Loewtih's *The Director's Voice, Volume 2*. Loewith refers to the 'extraordinary' diversification of the American theatre since 1988's Volume 1 – both in terms of audiences and types of productions: 'The fragmentation of the audience is perhaps the most significant [influence on directors], and the one that resonates most profoundly in this digital age, when every individual can curate his or her cultural experience on a moment-to-moment basis'. As a consequence, directors understand they 'can no longer speak to a single audience'.[16]

Of the twenty-one directors covered, four have considerable experience with Shakespeare: Michael Kahn, Bartlett Sher, Julie Taymor and Oskar Eustis. Two share ideas that suggest additional revisions to Berry's production categories above. Michael Kahn discusses the central objective of setting a play in a given period: 'I don't think it's about the period. It's about how you illuminate this point about this play'.[17] Bartlett Sher believes every theatre production is '*autonomous*' and subject to its own rules: 'If you have that as a point of view, you learn to pursue an idea through a piece, and make your own set of laws for how that idea works … I don't start with any idea of what a work is going to become. I just pick elements that I'm going to juggle in the poetics of the piece, and figure out how they go together. Then I have something that only makes sense to itself'.[18]

Two additional books are from the practitioner's point of view. The first, *A Lifetime of Shakespeare: Notes from an American Director of all 38 Plays* is a chronicle of Paul Barry's direction and the issues he has confronted when directing Shakespeare's plays. His authority comes from his considerable background in directing the entire thirty-eight-play canon.[19] In *Directing Shakespeare: A Scholar Onstage*, Sidney Homan argues that the two disparate approaches to the plays can intersect. He discusses concepts for plays and offers advice on cutting, interacting with actors, approaching the set design,

FIGURE 3 The Taming of the Shrew, *directed by Kate Buckley, Oregon Shakespeare Festival, 2007. Vilma Silva as Kate and Michael Elich as Petruchio. Photograph by Jenny Graham.*

achieving theatrical presence, and making adaptations.[20] Both Homan and Paul Barry do not consult other directors.

I asked Fred Adams, who has witnessed countless directors come and go at Utah Shakespeare Festival, to come up with his categories of directing. He named three. 'There are directors who simply come and recreate what they saw some other director do with the piece'. There is another kind of director who cobbles together a 'really clever' production by ignoring the text and Shakespeare's setting, often making cunning choices that call attention to themselves. He refers to those choices as 'tricks' that actually get in the way of the audience receiving the story. For Adams, the most valued category of directors are those 'who bring a freshness, not out of concept, but out of working with the actor, to discover the reasons, the motivations, the resources, the background, the history behind the character'.[21]

Recent developments

A major change since *On Directing Shakespeare* was published is the birth of the original practice movement. Just as Poel's Elizabethan Stage Society was a rebellion against the excesses of Victorian Shakespeare productions, Original Practice is a revolt against today's visually oriented, technologically complex theatre production systems. Devotees believe there are values in the original texts and theatrical practices that are lost when transposing a play to another period or using visually oriented contemporary theatre methods. For instance, in the Elizabethan theatres, there were no lighting differences between audience and stage. Both parts of the theatre were lit by natural light for outdoor theatres and by candlelight for indoor theatres. Many devotees translate that fact into contemporary performances on Elizabethan facsimile stages with uniform lighting throughout the space. The American

FIGURE 4 Macbeth, *directed by Jim Warren, American Shakespeare Center, 2014. Patrick Midgley, Jonathan Holtzman and Gregory Jon Phelps as the Weird Sisters. Photograph by Lindsey Walters.*

Shakespeare Center uses the aphorism 'We do it with the lights on' to market a distinction between their approach and those of other theatres. If the performance is outdoors, daylight becomes the only lighting source before the sun sets.

Other characteristics include the use of Elizabethan costumes to avoid disconnect between the text and the clothing. However, some original practice directors employ present day clothing, arguing that the Elizabethan theatre's costuming was also contemporary. The original practice movement holds great reverence for source texts, with some advocates favouring the First Folio techniques of Tucker and his Original Shakespeare Company. In the late 1990s, he pioneered original practice methods in several productions at London's Globe. In essence, supporters believe the original texts hold performance clues in the First Folio's punctuation, spelling, capitalization, parenthetical phrasing, rhyme schemes and shared lines. Some believe Shakespeare was referring to an original practice with his 'the two hours traffic of our stage' line in *Romeo and Juliet*. Productions must move the text and action rapidly forward, they argue. Pauses should be eliminated unless dictated by a short verse line in the folio.

What we currently know of Elizabethan rehearsals is that there were very few of them – perhaps as few as one. And there were no directors. Consequently some original practice adherents implement a reduced role for the director. Others have experimented with unrehearsed Shakespeare, the actors learning their lines and performing with no rehearsal. Actors are given more ownership over their choices. In a more recent development, directors have experimented with the Elizabethan practice of actors receiving only their role's parts and the cue immediately before it – the last few words of the previous line. They must listen carefully for their cue, which sometimes Shakespeare gives several times in a speech. Ralph Alan Cohen points to *The Merchant of Venice* when Shylock says, 'I'll have my bond', as an example. 'The Jew says, "And my bond". And it is the cue for the next thing that Solanio has to say. He says it about five times in the same speech. Well it cues, in original practices at least, when they're doing that rehearsal. If you've got any brains at all you'd realize, "Wait a second, I would in fact be responding."'[22] Those responses can be lost today when actors receive the complete text and rehearse it numerous times to prepare their reactions.

Although original practice directors share a similar philosophy, interpretations on how to apply Elizabethan theatrical practices can vary. Joanne Zipay – a director who works with expanded concepts of gender – explains, 'Everybody has different ideas about original practices. We're all approaching it differently. But there has to be an essential connection with the language'.[23] Most original practice companies have enormous respect for received texts.

Another transformation over the last couple of decades is a frequent reference to a production's 'context' by directors. This term seems to have replaced a previous generation's use of 'concept' as the goal of a production. For directors, 'context' can have several meanings. It is possible to analyze a director's production choices for their: (1) societal, cultural, political resonances; (2) relationship to Shakespeare's language, imagery and texts; (3) historical placement; (4) location, setting and environmental influence; and finally (5) the specific community the production is born from and/or intends to address.

Several directors express an interest in the social, cultural and political significance of Shakespeare's text as it resonates in a contemporary setting. (See Figure 1: *King Lear*.) As Libby Appel points out: 'We are all products of our time, not only the culture, in terms of the political times we're in, but the artistic aesthetic of the times'.[24] For a director like Lisa Peterson, that means her productions must somehow relate to Americana in some way. 'Usually, I try to find an American context. And I don't mean just picking a period, because sometimes I think that can be limiting, but thinking about the play's issues through a contemporary, American lens. Because that's the world I'm living in as I work on that play, I think it's essential that we use Shakespeare's plays to reflect on our lives

FIGURE 5 Pericles, *directed by Mary Zimmerman, Goodman Theatre, 2006. Ryan Artzberger as Pericles, Naomi Jacobson as Lychorida and Glenn Fleshler as Sailor. Photograph by Liz Lauren.*

now'.²⁵ Robert Falls told me that a production must not be set any further back than ten years from the present time.²⁶ Some argue that it must be placed in the here and now. Bill Rauch explains: 'I feel like societal context, cultural context is hugely significant in our lives. Certainly in interpreting a Shakespeare play'. As an example, he points to his production of *Measure for Measure* in which the actors started with 'their own ethnic/racial identity'.²⁷ In a recent email, Rauch added:

> I have had big break throughs in recent years getting to the heart of Shakespeare plays through an aggressive commitment to specificity. Because the themes in any Shakespeare play are so epic and so deep, it can be tempting to keep a production open-ended to the degree that choices become general washes and the work can be, well, boring. In a well-intentioned effort to achieve timeless depth, the

danger can be that there are no flashes of real insight. For me as an artist, the more culturally specific I have gone in the work, the more that the full force of the writing's humanity is unleashed.[28]

Context can also refer to the director (and theatre's) relationship to Shakespeare's text. (See Figure 2: Wooster Group's *Hamlet*.) Directors contend that Shakespeare's story, his language or his imagery is the most important circumstance for a production. 'What story is it that we are telling? And if we make this choice, what story does that tell?' Stephanie Shine queries.[29] Paul Mullin states, 'We do this to tell a story. We look at what he wrote on the page. We can put it in a strange place, and we can put people in other kinds of clothing, and we can do all of these things, but we must tell the story by using his words, and making those words plain, and telling the story in a plain way, plain text, matter of fact'.[30] Another relationship to the text is to the language. Kent Thompson remarks, 'I approach a Shakespeare play first and foremost through the language and through the text. Figuring out ways to animate the language and to excavate the language and to make it come alive is primary in my directing work'.[31] Shakespeare's language is equally important to Mark Lamos who expresses in several chapters his distinct ideas about speaking the verse, staying on thought, using pauses, properly stressing and accenting syllables, and shaping the play's rhythms.[32] Still another possible text relationship is to the imagery. According to John Neville Andrews, 'You look at the text, and you see the words, and its so image driven, that what we really need to do is make sure you've got the imagery really bold and vivid. Once you've got that, and there's clarity, you can do pretty much whatever you want with Shakespeare'.[33] Julie Taymor adds, 'One of the reasons I adore Shakespeare is because it's all in the text. So some people say, 'Then why do you do it visually?' Well, I believe profoundly that the images we hear in the language can be supported by images on the stage without being redundant. Our audiences don't listen as well as they see, and it supports the language to have the imagery be as poetic as possible. You need to match the power of the language with the power of movement and your imagery on stage'.[34]

Context can mean historical placement. (See Figure 3: *The Taming of the Shrew*.) Rauch shared an observation put forward by Lue Morgan Douthit, OSF Director of Literary Development and Dramaturgy: 'anytime we're doing a Shakespeare, there are up to four time periods that we are dealing with: (1) the historical setting of the story; (2) the historical period in which it was first produced; (3) the historical period that the director has chosen; and (4) the historical period in which the audience is living. Depending on the production, you may get all four of those time periods at play'.[35] Oskar Eustis argues, 'As an historical materialist (which I am), I don't believe we can ever separate ourselves from history. There is no pure truth. We're always contingent. We're always in history. The history of the way the western world has unfolded in the last 400 years has made Shakespeare the most revered author that we have. Our job, then, is to place ourselves in relationship to that reverence'.[36] Kate Buckley's position, while embracing a relationship to history, has another perspective: 'The playwright is very specific, with a certain culture, a certain code of ethics, certain honour codes. So I am much more dedicated to staying true to what he gave us, and then riffing inside of that world, than creating a whole new world'.[37]

The production's physical environment is another kind of context that can greatly influence the director's choices. A theatre's specific location can be an integral part of determining solutions. By far, the largest number of US Shakespeare theatres can be found outdoors, many in a festival atmosphere. They celebrate Shakespeare's work in environs that foreground a relationship with nature. Some are large permanent structures such as The Public's Delacorte Theater in New York's Central Park, Oregon Shakespeare Festival's Elizabethan Stage, The Old Globe's Lowell Davies Festival Theatre and American Players' Up-the-Hill Theatre. At the other end of the spectrum are temporary, once a year structures set up for a season of one, two or three productions. Indoor theatres come in all sizes and all styles: a reconstructed Blackfriars, a small warehouse space, a deep thrust, a large proscenium. (See Figure 4: *Macbeth*.) Still another type of theatre is site specific with each new production adapted specifically to a given locale. This is one of the missions of New York Classical Theatre where a recent production of *Henry V* had the audience take part in the journey from England to France on boats that moved the audience from Manhattan to Governor's Island. Still another category of environmental context is the specific design for a production. Here one notices trends. Whereas there used to be open stage designs for Shakespeare, a strain of the last decade locates all the action in a room that can contain the many scene locations required by the text. For instance, Mary Zimmerman's *Pericles* was set in a Shaker Hall (see Figure 5: *Pericles*), and Rauch's *Measure for Measure* was in a non-descript institutional setting. (See cover photo.) Both productions transformed their room to depict separate locations with lighting, projections, furniture, props and costumes. Any design solution for a play can provide an environmental context that dictates the behaviour and other production choices if an essential feature of the production is the setting.

Finally, context can refer to the specific community that the production targets (audience) or employs (production personnel) or both. Productions can be racially oriented such as the work of the African American Shakespeare Company. They can be gender based as Los Angeles Women's Shakespeare Company and Judith Shakespeare Company's productions are – 'expanding the presence of women in classical theatre'.[38] (See Figure 6: *Othello*.) They can also be aimed at various populations of school children; most of the major Shakespeare theatres have a touring programme or an onsite school performance programme. There are companies creating productions in prisons using inmates to produce, act and design, as Shakespeare Behind Bars does. In addition,

FIGURE 6 Othello, *directed by Lisa Wolpe, Boston Court Theatre, 2008, Lisa Wolpe as Iago. Photograph by Maxine Picard.*

there are theatres and productions aimed at gay, urban, rural and religious populations. The theatrical communities in which American directors of Shakespeare operate are numerous and varied.[39]

A characteristic of some context productions is that directors routinely reject 'received tradition' in how they interpret characters and production choices. There is a lively debate between directors and audiences as to what constitutes a traditional production of Shakespeare. According to Des McAnuff, 'tradition goes back only four productions. Generally people mean "convention" when they use the word "tradition"'.[40] Oskar Eustis echoes this sentiment, 'When people say, "Are you going to do Shakespeare traditionally?" what they mean is, "Are you going to do Shakespeare the way I saw it in the 1950s or 1960s", depending on when they grew up. Of course the Shakespeare that they mean by "traditional Shakespeare" is as far removed from the original practice of Shakespeare as anything Peter Sellars is doing at the Taper'.[41] Rauch recognizes a problematic history of manipulating Shakespeare's text and changing production styles through the ages: 'Like a painting that is being restored, you often have to scrape off the layers and layers of brown gunk of other productions – decades and sometimes even centuries past – in order to reveal the intensity of colour that exists in Shakespeare's extraordinarily vibrant original choices'.[42] I have come to believe 'traditional Shakespeare' denotes the way of performing Shakespeare when someone was first introduced to a production and liked it.

Throughout this book directors discuss their ideas and methods about directing Shakespeare. Considering a director's production context can be a relevant means of assessing each director's work. It also can account for the diversity of approaches and styles that can be found in the productions occurring in the US today.

2

The Directors and their Aesthetic Values

I am never more moved than I am when hearing masterful artists allow Shakespeare's words to flow through them – they are, indeed, cartographers of the soul. The shift that I witness when human beings devote themselves to that poetry, that prose – these plays being so richly knit into the human experience of being alive on the planet, in relationship with the cosmos and all life – and the tender, aching questions of mortality and Spirit, posed in each Shakespearean story – open my heart and mind. The writing is so eloquent that actors must of force become more present, more conscious, more aware of humanity's sacred strivings when handling these rich, mystical, textual rosaries. This work, for me, offers a greater range of thought and feeling than almost anything else that I have encountered in the wide world of the theater.

LISA WOLPE

FIGURE 7 Julius Caesar, *The Oregon Shakespeare Festival, 2011. Directed by Amanda Dehnert, Vilma Silva as Caesar with Anthony Heald, Kevin Kenerly, Frankie J. Alvarez, Brooke Parks. Photograph by Jenny Graham.*

As the reader will soon discover, directors have very different ideas about directing Shakespeare. What is it that guides them and dictates their choices? I believe their aesthetic values influence their choice of method as well as the agenda they choose to follow when working on Shakespeare. Here aesthetic value refers to the artistic and philosophical opinions, as well as directorial beliefs, about Shakespeare and the direction of his plays.

For example, a given director believes in doing little or no preparation for rehearsal. He reads with each actor in order to decide whom he will cast. His extensive background in voice work can be seen in the way he works with actors on releasing physical tension in order to reveal a richer voice and uncluttered thoughts. Physical ticks are indicators of tension or confusion that must be addressed. He does not block or stage *per se*, but lets the production evolve as he works intimately with the actors on their physical and vocal manifestations of character. Run-throughs do not happen until quite late in the process. His attitude to the director's function is 'working as an equal'.

Another director does extensive research, examining other texts and scholarly references. She spends hours looking at paintings from relevant periods that will serve as the basis for an amalgamation of period to be used in her upcoming production. In addition, she works a solid week at the table, discussing meaning and language issues. She has specific ideas about the blocking and elaborate choreography necessary to impart the visual story. She stages and is ready for a run-through by the end of the second week. She favours frequent run-throughs. Her approach to directing is 'dictating'.

How the director works with actors is also an indicator of values. The second director does not give the individual actor's growth much attention. Rather the visuals in telling the story receive primary focus. That director regularly adjusts the actors' positions and blocking to achieve this focus. The first director keeps the actors and their development a primary focus. In both instances, the director's aesthetic values are indicators of the methods he or she will use to achieve rehearsal goals.

Frequently a director's personal style can be so distinctive and impressionable that it can actually disguise the methods used to create changes in the production. According to one study, there is a tendency of directing novices to imitate the style of directors they most admire.[1] But it is rarely the style that leads to actual change in rehearsal. Rather, the style helps the director sell the solution to the company, to the designers, or to the producer. With experience, budding directors will discover the actual techniques that cause changes to occur.

As theatre artists, directors are diverse – thinking and working in incongruous ways from each other. They do not share the same beliefs about their role within the production process. They subscribe to values about theatre and performance that are often in conflict with those of other directors, and they use a multitude of methods to accomplish their aims.

What can account for the differences? Humans are imperfect and inconsistent. They are also illogical at times, favouring one approach in one instance, and an opposite one in another. Consider that the particular circumstances of a given situation might dictate a different approach from what a director might usually do.

Many directorial belief systems appear to be based on theoretical underpinnings. Much of practice is based on achieving end results as well as realizing and maintaining a productive working environment. Thus the conditions of the production might create a disparity for the director between theory and practice. Any director worth their salt in the profession will adapt and improvise to keep producers, leading actors and other important figures on the production team content.

The reader may also bring their own biases to a review of director comments: 'directors should never dictate', or 'directors must always be strong leaders', or 'never violate Shakespeare's text'. This analysis suggests there is more that can be learned by setting those judgements aside.

* * *

I have separated director comments into categories. The first part of this chapter presents directorial ideas and opinions about Shakespeare and the nature of his works. The next section discusses multiple views of the director's purpose or function.

Echoing an assertion made by Jan Kott,[2] the directors in 'Shakespeare as a Contemporary' contend that the texts must be germane to the present – what Appel calls 'the artistic aesthetic of the times'. Gaines maintains that the plays are 'living organisms that constantly change' as we change. Esbjornson claims 'a Shakespeare production should attempt to be relevant'. These directors believe the images and words and ideas in Shakespeare's text metamorphose and find new resonances within the ever-changing present.

'Endless Possibilities' takes this idea to the next level. It investigates the concept that in rehearsal the meaning in Shakespeare constantly shifts beneath a director's feet. Serban calls that landscape 'slippery' – we cannot quite ever fully grasp it. 'One has to accept that the unknowable will not be totally known'. Kulick has a similar observation that each new rehearsal discovery suggests yet another way to perform the text. When you think you have found the room you are in, there is a door into another room and ultimately there are 'all these rooms with all these doors [that] stretch to infinity'. Anyone who has seen multiple productions of the same play can attest that productions can take place in many rooms, each one capable of containing a Shakespeare play. Monte adds that as artists, our work is a lifelong pursuit of knowledge, to know as much as we can about what it means to be human – an objective that will always remain beyond our full grasp – just as defining or seeing the definitive production of any of Shakespeare's plays.

'Complexity in Shakespeare' notes the text's density. Kahn's insight that earlier readings of characters when he was younger lack the intricacy that he currently finds in the text. Several directors, including Gaines, Lamos and D. Sullivan, allude to an increasing awareness of their sophistication with Shakespeare as they gain more experience and return to redirect the same play. MacLean also finds 'complicated and multi-faceted' characters, while Zimmerman, in directing the 'problem plays', deciphers many different hues in various moments throughout those plays. 'There's too much variety and richness and contrariness in the play[s], just as there is in life in each of us'. She cautions that the plays cannot be portrayed as all one tone.

The two directors in 'The Invisible Director' avoid a strong directorial stamp in their work. J. R. Sullivan borrows Lao Tzu's phrase 'erase the traces' and applies it to directing a production with a goal to 'simply let it be what it is' so that the true essence of the piece shines forth: 'It doesn't matter about the artist. It's just a thing of such beauty or meaning, impact, purpose that we just are transported'. D. Sullivan looks for a 'transparency' in the work/production, 'that you are looking straight through to the sense of it'.

The interpretive director has an opposite perspective. Rauch sees himself as interpreter of the text, but not 'auteur'. He argues that 'you *better* be pushing yourself as an artist to explore the outer reaches of your imagination. You have to be, to match the power of the work and to *dare* be worthy of interpreting this work'. He believes in creating 'dynamic … twenty-first century' productions that are 'mined' for various points of view: 'political, class-dissecting, psychological, philosophical and spiritual insights' which are only a few of the 'infinite points of entry'. McAnuff contends: 'Theatre is a place where you want to encounter, not just emotions, but ideas, insight into our own times … if theatre seems simply there to amuse, or if it seems narcissistic, then I am probably impatient with that'. Peterson shares her process as an interpretive director. She reads the play repeatedly, until she finds her 'inner voice' and her 'own point of view'. That then becomes her guide as she develops her production. Tresnjak enjoys all kinds of productions interpreted or otherwise with one caveat: each production must 'illuminate the text beautifully'. He cautions that novel interpretations should never mean that the director's craft suffers.

'The Language and Text Director' focuses on the language as the primary vehicle for production. 'It begins and ends with the language as far as I am concerned', Woronicz attests. Thompson identifies the 'spoken word' as the target for his work on the production. Lamos, like Woronicz, has enormous respect for Shakespeare's language. Characters think as they speak. 'There is no thinking *off* the line. No thinking *before* the line'. Similar to music, there are no real pauses. He finds that the many varied rhythms are always pushing onward: 'Verse-speaking, in my work, is the muscular core of the production, and everything else about the production flows out of its rhythmic certainty'. Metropulos also has a director's ear on the language's musicality. Ivers believes Shakespeare's language is 'extraordinarily muscular' and pulsating and dynamic. It must also be 'classical enough and colloquial enough and clear enough'. Buckley says the First Folio technique 'has moulded everything about my work with text'. After many years of working with those precepts, she admits she is now less prescriptive about technique and more concerned about 'service to the playwright' in adhering to a production's setting, culture, imagery and atmosphere. Mullins advises: 'tell the story by using [Shakespeare's] words, and making those words plain, and telling the story in a plain way'. By 'plain' he means without an interpretive slant as Shakespeare's characters signify what they want; there is no subtext.

Closely aligned with the Language and Text Director is the Original Practice Director. In addition to language, they are also interested in Elizabethan staging practices and recreating those for audiences today. They seek to unearth characteristics embedded in the text that would not be there without those stage practices. Cohen views the director's job as serving the audience and 'the room': specifically the Blackfriars Theatre where he directs. His mission is to explore the dynamics of that space. Warren's purpose is not only serving as a director archaeologist, but also to 'create community, story, journey, environment' that with his audience should be 'experienced … *together*'. Shine chooses to focus on the story that Shakespeare wrote; she sees no reason to compete with his genius. She also argues for making her actors the central figures: 'Actors are given the responsibility and freedom to realize that they're the most important thing', she says. The notion of actors taking back the text from directors seems to be a common characteristic of original practice adherents.

As 'The Physical and Visceral Director', McSweeny believes the production 'emanates from an instinctual and emotional place'. For Sevy, a production must have 'vitality' and the actors must be 'so committed' it seems as if the production is 'living'. In embodying the production, 'everything fits' to Shakespeare's 'vigorous' text. Stephen Burdman produces what he terms 'panoramic theatre' based on engendering a physical and immediate reaction from his audience. He combines aspects of promenade and environmental theatre that are site specific, and moves the audience from location to location to experience each new scene. He believes 'the deeper the audience's involvement, the greater their emotional experience and commitment to the show'. Douglas confesses that his directorial work is about achieving 'authentic communication ... first experienced in the [actor's] body and then realized via the text'. This leads to a decidedly physical approach. The work requires the actor to bravely 'access and be willing to reveal *self*'. Furthermore, he believes Shakespeare's language supports actors entrée to their deepest selves 'in communicating infinite heights and depths'.

'Mixing Approaches' explores a comparison of director statements that contain two or more dissimilar methods. Reporting on changes he's witnessed over his career, Neville-Andrews sees a less scholarly approach to text than there used to be. He celebrates a combination of imagery that is 'bold and vivid' with a clarity of language that is now a part of the Shakespeare environment. Conlin also desires a 'physically expressive' performance married to 'a strong sense of the language'. Tina Packer and David Frank, both raised in England, share a desire to conjoin the best of that country's technical skills for speaking Shakespeare's language with a physical spontaneity found in the US. This is epitomized by Viola Spolin's improvisation work for Frank,[3] and by a free physical/vocal instrument for Packer.[4] They search for greater specificity as well as connection to text and to partner in the moment-to-moment behaviour based performances.

The directors in 'The Inclusive Director' argue the need for expanding traditional points of view as to what constitutes Shakespeare in this country. They examine issues of race, gender, perceived sexuality and access. Timothy Bond discusses his experiences with Shakespeare as a person of colour, arguing for an 'inclusive approach' to casting. Choices can be racially insensitive: 'It is simply embracing our diverse culture as Americans, as global citizens'. Joanne Zipay and Lisa Wolpe provide two examples of expanding traditional notions of gender casting. Zipay works to feature women in lead roles, but continues to experiment with men in pushing traditional boundaries of gender. Wolpe is noted for her all female productions in Los Angeles, but also is interested in serving all communities, including trans-gendered and 'any shading or variation of gender – and sexual preference'. Finally, Oskar Eustis points out how some populations do not have a basic literacy of Shakespeare and the problems which that can engender: 'You get excluded from a certain kind of cultural discourse that ultimately is the cultural discourse that runs the country', he contends. While there has been an increasing awareness of inclusion issues, there are still productions that do not recognize insensitive casting choices or that hold on to colour blind approaches that were in vogue a generation ago.

Shakespeare as a contemporary

Libby Appel, Artistic Director Emerita

Oregon Shakespeare Festival
Ashland; 11 June 2004
Revised 4 January 2015

Libby Appel was artistic director of Oregon Shakespeare Festival from 1995 until 2007. During her tenure, she directed *The Tempest*, *The Winter's Tale*, *Richard III*, *Henry VI, Part 1*, *Henry VI, Parts 2 and 3*, *Richard II*, *Macbeth*, *Henry V*, *Hamlet*, *Henry IV, Part 2*, *Measure for Measure*, *King Lear*, *The Merchant of Venice* and many other contemporary and classical plays. Ms Appel was also artistic director at Indiana Repertory Theatre from 1992–6; dean and artistic director for the School of Theater, California Institute of the Arts; and head of the acting programme at California State University, Long Beach. My interview with Ms Appel was in Ashland where I saw her productions of *Henry VI Part 1* and *Henry VI Parts 2 and 3*.

We are all products of our time, not only the culture, in terms of the political times we're in, but the artistic aesthetic of the times. If you think about it, Angus [Bowmer]'s[5] desire to go back to the roots of what Shakespeare actually wrote is an early twentieth century change from the seventeenth, eighteenth and nineteenth centuries – Colley Cibber and all of those people who completely tore up the text. They were the first postmodernists there were, and made them to go their way. But then came Ur Shakespeare texts at the end of the nineteenth century, beginning of the twentieth century. Angus was a product of 'Let's do Shakespeare straight'. That's why those early productions with John Gielgud and [Laurence] Olivier were done kind of straight. Olivier was the one who changed it around. I sound like I'm preaching to you. I'm not. I'm just trying to say that I'm aware that Angus was as much in his fashion as I am a minimalist. I'm a part of the world that I live in now, and it's as much a fashion. Who knows what it's going to be like twenty years from now. People think Angus had the answer. Of course he didn't have the answer. He was just in his own generation of the way things were being done at that time.

Barbara Gaines, Artistic Director

Chicago Shakespeare Theater; 3 June 2004
Revised with new material 17 January 2015

Barbara Gaines founded Chicago Shakespeare Theater in 1986 and has been its artistic director ever since. In 2008, the theatre received the Tony Award for Outstanding Regional Theatre. Ms Gaines has directed over thirty Shakespeare productions at CST. She has garnered Chicago's Jeff Jefferson Awards for Best Production (*Hamlet*, *Cymbeline*, *King Lear* and *The Comedy of Errors*) and for Best Director (*The Tale of Cymbeline*, *King Lear* and *The Comedy of Errors*). She has received the Honorary Officer of the Most Excellent Order of the British Empire (2004) in recognition for her contributions to British-American cultural relations and an Honorary Doctorate of Letters from the University of Birmingham UK. She is a member of the Shakespearean Council of Shakespeare's Globe Theatre in London. I interviewed Ms Gaines before attending her production of *King John*. Since then I have returned several times to see the work of Terry Hands, Darko Tresnjak and Marti Maraden.

There is absolutely nothing stationary in Shakespeare. His works are living organisms that constantly change as we grow, as we age, as the world changes.

I never feel that I 'know' the canon even though I've been studying it since I was twenty. I've directed a handful of his plays three times and I'm consistently shocked about what I learn every day in rehearsal ... shocked that I didn't see a certain connection or understand a phrase or a character. What, was I blind – or even worse not paying attention? With my own maturity, the language, situations and entire marrow within the plays have shifted dramatically.

He breathes in a different dimension for me now and I've come to understand that as we grow and go through the slings and arrows that life tosses at us all – his work keeps expanding. Hopefully we do too. Peter Brook once said to me: 'We are all searching, we are all struggling'. Certainly, I feel that my capacity for empathy has grown, as my older judgemental self shrinks. Life is just too complex to be so woefully opinionated. Even though my perspectives keep shifting as life washes over me, I find that understanding people is as mystifying now as it always was. The main thing that's shifted within me is that life is so much more precious and I want to uncover the mysteries of human behaviour so they can be shared by many hearts ... entertainment is of prime importance but so is enlightenment.

David Esbjornson, Freelance Director

The Public Theater/New York Shakespeare, Delacorte Theater
New York City; 9 August 2004
Revised with new material 6 January 2015

Past credits include artistic director of Seattle Repertory Theatre (2005–9) and artistic director of New York's Classic Stage Company (1992–9) which received the Lucille Lortel Award in 1999. He is well known for his productions of Tony Kushner, Edward Albee and Arthur Miller's plays. On Broadway Esbjornson has directed *Driving Miss Daisy* (2010), *Bobbi Boland* (2003), *The Goat, or Who is Sylvia?* (2002) and *The Ride Down Mt. Morgan* (2000). World premieres include *Angels in America: Millennium Approaches*, *In the Blood* and *Homebody/Kabul* (Part 1). In 2011, he directed Shakespeare in the Park's *Measure for Measure* and in 2004, *Much Ado About Nothing*. Regional theatre credits include the Geffen Playhouse, The Guthrie, Signature Theater, Cleveland Play House, Mark Taper Forum, Berkeley Repertory Theatre, Eureka Theater Company, the WPA Theatre and resident director at the O'Neill Playwrights Conference and the Iowa Playwrights Festival. I interviewed Mr Esbjornson outside of the Delacorte Theater in Central Park where his production of *Much Ado About Nothing* was just finishing its run.

I believe that someone given the opportunity to direct Shakespeare has a responsibility to put him or herself on the line and strive for an interpretation that invites discussion and even debate. Just as with a new play, a Shakespeare production should attempt to be relevant. Some will argue that it is enough to get the original story across and that a director should simply stay out of the way. On a certain level I can understand this position because there is nothing more important than to present the text clearly to a modern audience. It takes skilled actors and endless hours of investigation to unlock the details and secrets in the language. This task is the first responsibility of the director, and if the language isn't handled well, it doesn't matter what else you do.

Shakespeare's world was volatile even by today's standards. Religious war, the Irish rebellion, threats from Spain, the plague, torture and executions, national poverty and the dangerous whims of Queen Elizabeth were part of everyday existence. Shakespeare's plays arose from this uneasy environment. Just like our contemporary writers, Shakespeare is a product of his time. His plays are filled with contradiction, unspeakable loss, personal and political struggle as well as his own profound questions about life. What makes working on Shakespeare so rewarding is that all of these things exist simultaneously in the material, and a director can choose to emphasize what matters to him or her at any given moment.

Endless possibilities

Andrei Serban, Freelance Director

Head of MFA Acting, Columbia University
New York City; 12 August 2004
Revised with new material 17 January 2015

Director of the Oscar Hammerstein II Center for Theatre Studies at Columbia University's School of the Arts, Andrei Serban studied at the Theatre Institute in Romania. He worked with Peter Brook at his International Theatre Institute in Paris and Persepolis. His Shakespeare productions include *Julius Caesar*, *Twelfth Night*, *Cymbeline*, *The Merchant of Venice*, *Hamlet* and *Pericles*. His *Fragments of a Greek Trilogy* won several Obie awards and toured to over twenty international festivals. His *The Cherry Orchard* won a Tony Award for Best Revival. Other awards include the Romanian Star (highest Romanian national order), Elliot Norton Award (Boston), George Abbott Award (New York) and the Robert Brustein Award (2009). He has also directed for Shakespeare in the Park/Public Theater, the Guthrie Theater, American Repertory Theater, Yale Repertory Theatre, American Conservatory Theater, Circle in the Square Theatre, La MaMa Experimental Theatre Center, the Royal National Theatre (London), the Comedie Francaise (Paris) and Schauspielhaus Bochum. His background in the American theatre is chronicled in *The Magic World Behind the Curtain* (Ed Menta, 1995) as well as in a photographic survey, *My Journeys* (2008). Our interview took place at Lincoln Center.

Shakespeare is slippery. When you feel like you caught the meaning, he whispers 'Oh! That's not it!' At least there is a germ of what it could be. But one has to accept that the unknowable will not be totally known. There is a mystery of the man as well, not only in the work. Facing this larger than life situation, it helps us to get away from the clichés, from the habits of what we think we know. It brings some healthy humility in this recognition. Shakespeare in fact relates to us all, touching our deepest essence, the hidden truth. There are no words to define truth; there is only the feeling. It's like being in front of an old cathedral or a great painting: there is that moment of suspense when everything stops and one experiences a state of wonder.

There is a potential Socratic-like wisdom to all of his plays that is neither left nor right, but it's something from above. It's like a messenger from above who tells us, illuminates us to have wisdom and compassion. It's saying both: 'Apparently there's nothing new under the sun', and at the same time 'Look at everything with a new attitude and you will discover life again'.

Brian Kulick, Artistic Director

Classic Stage Company
New York City; 17 June 2004
Revised with new material 19 January 2015

Brian Kulick has directed *Timon of Athens*, *Twelfth Night* (with Jimmy Smits and Julia Stiles), *The Winter's Tale*, *Pericles* (with Jay Goede and Miriam Laube), *Much Ado About Nothing*, *Hamlet*, *Richard II*, *Richard III* (with Michael Cumpsty) and *The Tempest* (with Mandy Patinkin). In addition, he has staged many other classical plays, including Anne Carson's adaptation of *An Orestia*. Kulick was also creative director at The Shakespeare Society, artistic associate at The Public, associate artistic director at Trinity Repertory and artist-in-residence at Mark Taper Forum. He has worked on several new works, including those by Nilo Cruz, Tony Kushner, Charles Mee and Han Ong. He has directed at ACT, Berkeley Repertory Theatre, Mark Taper Forum, McCarter Theatre, New York Theatre Workshop, Playwrights Horizons, The Public/New York Shakespeare and Trinity Repertory Company. He is a member of the MFA directing faculty at Columbia University.

A Shakespeare text is deceptive. You enter it, look around and think, 'What a lovely room'. You suddenly notice a door, you open it and discover another room with another door to another room with another door and pretty soon you realize that all these rooms with all these doors stretch to infinity.

You're not in a room, or a house, or a factory but a veritable palace of meaning. One that, like some living creature, keeps growing while you are rummaging around inside of it

We can only speculate about how they spoke these extraordinary lines, or what exactly was the scale of behaviour when they played Lear. Ours is a broken tradition. An entire generation between when English theatre was banned and when it was finally allowed to reopen its doors passed away. This was just enough time to lose a direct link to the traditions and practitioners of the Elizabethan period. But this lacuna is actually a very important, generative, thing. It's allowed each generation to come back to Shakespeare and his theatrical world and try to reimagine it; each generation has to figure out for themselves what Shakespeare is to them; which means, with each generation we get a new view of Shakespeare. It's foolish to think that we can do Shakespeare the way Shakespeare was done. We'll never really know, but this not knowing keeps us searching. It keeps our understanding dynamic rather than static. I sometimes wonder when we put on a play of Shakespeare's, say *Hamlet*, if we should actually say, 'written by Shakespeare and Time'. Or, perhaps to be more exact, 'by Shakespeare and the twenty-first century'. Time has become a very serious co-author of these works and keeps insidiously reshaping them.

Bonnie Monte, Artistic Director

Shakespeare Theatre of New Jersey
Madison New Jersey; 11 August 2004 and 24 January 2008
Revised 25 January 2015

Bonnie Monte has been artistic director of Shakespeare Theatre of New Jersey since 1990. Prior to that, she was casting director at Manhattan Theatre Club and associate artistic director at Williamstown Theatre Festival. She has directed over forty productions, including *Twelfth Night, King Lear, As You Like It, Henry V, Antony and Cleopatra* and *A Midsummer Night's Dream*. She has supervised numerous other Shakespeare productions and regularly directs Shakespeare LIVE! a touring company to schools throughout the surrounding area. She has adapted/translated several original productions: *Pride and Prejudice, The Triumph of Love, Enrico IV, Artists and Admirers, The Blue Bird* and *Around the World in Eighty Days*. She received the Person of the Year Award (National Society of Arts and Letters), the Women of Achievement Award (New Jersey General Assembly) and one of the twenty-five Most Influential People in the Arts in New Jersey (Star-Ledger).

The great privilege of being a theatre artist, and therefore the great responsibility and demand that you must meet is that, as a theatre artist we have the amazing job and privilege of being the people chosen by the larger tribe to tell the story of humanity. It is our job to be around our whole lives and to study what it means to be human. To find incredibly effective ways of taking what we think that means, putting that into two and a half hour sound bites, so to speak. That in our lifelong pursuit of this intelligence, this knowledge, we are able to condense that down into two and a half hour digestible chunks for the rest of humanity. In doing so, we must become in essence Renaissance men and women in a sub-cultural select. I would use the word pride. While we are often derided or given short shrift or made fun of, we are probably more knowledgeable about things than most people on earth. We must be because we are forced to examine the heart and soul of every kind of human being that exists. Both professionally and spiritually. Aura wise. Karma-ly. We have to know as much as we can. We have to be like devouring animals that eat up every piece of knowledge and visual stimulus that we can. *And to be able to do that as your work?!*

… THE DIRECTORS AND THEIR AESTHETIC VALUES 41

Complexity in Shakespeare

Michael Kahn, Artistic Director

The Shakespeare Theatre Company
Washington, DC; 14 September 2004 and 18 July 2008

Michael Kahn has a distinguished career as a director of Shakespeare as well as an artistic director for Shakespeare theatres. Before developing The Shakespeare Theatre Company, he was artistic director of the American Shakespeare Theatre in Stratford, Connecticut from 1969 to 1976. His anti-war *Henry V* and *Othello* went on from AST to have successful Broadway runs. He became artistic director of the Shakespeare Theatre at the Folger in 1986 shortly after it was separated from the Folger Shakespeare Library. In addition to his background with Shakespeare theatres, he has been producing director of the McCarter Theatre and artistic director of The Acting Company. He received Tony nominations for *Whodunnit* and *Showboat*, and has directed for many regional and New York theatres. He served as the Richard Rodgers Director of the Drama Division at Julliard from 1992 to 2006, and since 1968 has been a member of the faculty. I interviewed Mr Kahn after seeing his production of *Macbeth* in 2004 and again in 2008 after opening his *Antony and Cleopatra*.

My excitement now is to try to put on stage the complexity of Shakespeare's idea of character and the world. I remember when I first started. I did a *Measure for Measure* for Joe Papp where I decided Angelo was a comic Tartuffian villain and just a hypocrite, period. When I came back to the play several times, I finally understood that Shakespeare gives us a much more complex portrait of a man who is trying to be good in a very difficult situation, but who is also repressed. All of a sudden, his libido takes over and he cannot handle it and so he becomes tyrannical. Shakespeare allows him to be forgiven in the play. What does all of that mean? It's Shakespeare's ambiguous, or quite frankly, very modern approach to character. When I was going to college in the 1950s and 1960s, we were still reading scholars that were influenced by the definition of character as immutable. The complexity and ambiguity of Shakespeare is what I'm more interested in putting on stage now rather than my big concept, or one- or two-colour take on characters. I learned it through several productions of *Henry V*. I learned it through *Measure for Measure*. I learned it through pretty much all the plays.

I have things I believe in, in terms of the rhythm of an act that I'm not sure I was as aware of before or had the same understanding. I hope in certain cases my skills are better. I mean I've been doing this for a while. On the other hand, when you do it for a while, you're also more aware of what the problems are. So on some level it's easier. On some level it's harder because you have more questions because you know what the questions are. When you're young, you have a lot of bravado and hopefully some talent. When you've been doing it for a while, you hopefully still have talent, but probably less bravado, and more awareness of the difficulties and where the potholes are. I just don't like to have them anymore. You can't cover them up. You've got to work on them so they're filled in and solid. I don't think it's gotten easier. There are certain things that you know that you just have to do and that you didn't know about.

Calvin MacLean, Artistic Director

Illinois Shakespeare Festival
Normal, Illinois; 26 June 2004

Cal MacLean is artistic director at the Clarence Brown Theatre and head of the Department of Theatre at the University of Tennessee-Knoxville. Prior to that he was artistic director of the Illinois Shakespeare Festival. He has directed numerous professional productions in Chicago where he also had a long association with the Famous Door Theatre. While there he received Joseph Jefferson citations for direction and outstanding production: *Lonesome West*, *Living*, *Conquest of the South Pole*, *Salt of the Earth* and *Ghetto*. *Ghetto* was acclaimed as one of the best Chicago productions in 1999 and earned MacLean the first Michael Maggio Award for Outstanding Direction of a Play. His Shakespeare productions include *As You Like It*, *Two Gentlemen of Verona*, *Cymbeline*, *Measure for Measure*, *King John*, *Romeo and Juliet* and *King Lear*. He was head of the graduate directing programme at Illinois State University for fifteen years. In 2012, he directed *Kiss Me Kate* and *Sweeney Todd* starring Dale Dickey with the Knoxville Symphony Orchestra. I conducted this interview on his front porch.

I'm really interested in, not the ideas about the play, but the ideas *in* the play. I find Shakespeare to be endlessly interesting in terms of his investigation of what makes people tick, what their emotional life is and what it is to be a feeling human being. Whether it's a simple comedy like *Twelfth Night* or if it's *King Lear*, there's always an investigation of these themes, the idea that the characters in the play are dealing with cosmic forces, or forces well beyond their field of view. I'm also fascinated, increasingly as I get older, in Shakespeare's playful language: the wit games and the inventiveness of the language.

I like the story [to be] clear, but the people in the story as complicated and multi-faceted as human beings are. I prefer physical stillness – well spoken, clear. When spoken clearly, Shakespearean language is not that difficult to grasp, even for an audience of children. I think that if you get the action right, the character thinking right and the verbal syntax right, any of his plays come to life quite easily.

Mary Zimmerman, Freelance Director

Pericles, Goodman Theatre
Chicago; 15 June 2006
Revised 6 January 2015

Mary Zimmerman has received numerous awards, including a Tony award for her direction of *Metamorphoses* (2002), over twenty Joseph Jefferson Awards (Chicago) and a MacArthur Fellowship (1998). She is particularly known for her stage adaptations of the classics: *Journey to the West, The Odyssey, The Arabian Nights, The Notebooks of Leonardo de Vinci, Metamorphoses* and *Eleven Rooms of Proust*. She is an artistic associate of the Goodman Theatre and a member of the Looking Glass Theater Company. Since 2007 she has opened a new production annually for the Metropolitan Opera. In 2013, she adapted and directed a version of Disney's *The Jungle Book* that premiered at the Goodman Theatre and the Huntington Theatre. Her direction of

Shakespearean productions include *All's Well That Ends Well* (Goodman Theatre) *Measure for Measure* and *Henry VIII* (Shakespeare in the Park/ Public Theater), *A Midsummer Night's Dream* (Huntington Theatre) and *Pericles*, which originally opened at The Shakespeare Theatre (DC) with a subsequent run at the Goodman Theatre. She is a professor of performance studies at Northwestern University. I interviewed Ms Zimmerman at her home just outside of Chicago.

I have done the undone and underdone plays. I really do like doing them because people come in with a great excitement as though a new Shakespeare play has just been unearthed. *Pericles* felt that way. No one knew that play. They came in with excitement and low expectations thinking, 'This must not be very good. It's not done very often. It's a problem play. And yet it will be interesting to see'. Audiences don't have fetishes about these undone plays in the way they do about so many of the great, iconic parts of the canon. An ideal form of those plays may exist in a lot of people's heads that come to see them, and then, immediately the production in front of them diverges from that in some way and they are upset. They have *Hamlet* or *Lear* in their heads in a certain way: No one has in their head a *Henry VIII* or *Pericles*.

The so called problem plays turn out remarkably to be not problems – if you just take them on their own terms and not apply the modernist approach that 'Everything must be unified. Everything must come to a single point. The wild contradictions within it must be dissolved. It all must be thematically related to itself at every moment'. Just loosen up your feeling about that and take it scene-by-scene. *Now* this character is taken seriously. *Now* this character is not taken seriously.

Like Marina in *Pericles*, she's in a dangerous situation, but it's really not dangerous to her because these brothel keepers are very benign. Shakespeare lets us know this by giving them a scene before Marina's entrance. They talk about their retirement and how they're going to make their way when they're old – like anybody else on earth. You just have to accept them on their own terms. Don't decide that *Measure for*

Measure is totally comic or totally cynical or totally romantic. It has all those strings in it and they're contradictory. You *can* laugh in the jail scene when Claudio seems to turn, wheedling with Isabella, and ask her would it be so bad to sleep with the Duke. It doesn't mean you don't take Isabella's predicament seriously or that it can't be moving later on. It only means that you see and understand Claudio's point of view. It's the same with *Pericles*. People think, 'If it's funny, it won't be moving. If it's moving, it won't be funny'. 'It has to be dark'. 'It has to be light'. But it can actually be all of them without much struggle. Exactly like life.

I don't think it's good to paint any of these plays with one single brush that washes over all and says, 'Ah ha! The key to this play is that it will be this 'x', and every single thing corresponds to that x'. There's too much variety and richness and contrariness in the play, just as there is in life in each of us. Deciding to make it singular in tone, to decide Shakespeare wasn't serious about this play or he *was* deadly serious about this play is a mistake.

The invisible director

J. R. Sullivan, Associate Artistic Director

Utah Shakespeare Festival
New York City; 1 December 2007
Revised 3 January 2015

J. R. Sullivan was artistic director of New York's The Pearl Theatre Company from 2009 to 2013. From 2002 until 2009, he was associate artistic director at the Utah Shakespeare Festival. Before that, he was founder and producing artistic director of the New American Theatre, Rockford, Illinois producing twenty-two seasons and directing over 150 productions. Shakespearean directing credits include *Twelfth Night* (Pearl Theatre), *Henry V, Othello, King Lear, The Merchant of Venice, Hamlet, All's Well That Ends Well, Macbeth, Henry IV Part 1, The Richard II, Richard III* (Utah Shakespeare Festival) and *As You Like It* (Oregon Shakespeare Festival). He has directed at the Arden Theater, Milwaukee Repertory Theater, American Players Theatre, Studio Theatre (Washington, DC), Delaware Theatre Company and Chicago's Steppenwolf Theatre, Touchstone Theatre and Light Opera Works. He also produced and performed his one-man show, *An Evening with Ben Hecht*. I interviewed Mr Sullivan in a Manhattan Starbucks one winter afternoon.

Lao Tzu has this phrase about erasing the traces, which I take to mean erasing those things that tell you too much about it as a construction, and simply let it be what it is. There's something magnificent in an artwork like Beethoven's *Ninth* or Michelangelo's *David*, or something truly is transporting, has that quality. It doesn't matter about the artist. It's just a thing of such beauty or meaning, impact, purpose that we just are transported. That's the thing that we are all going for. That's the thing that we all see occasionally in the theatre. That's the thing that we all saw once or twice when we were very young that keeps us going to the theatre. Because we know it can happen.

I am for the kind of direction that erases the traces, so that you are not aware of me, and not aware of the actor as a personality in life so much as that character in that situation. And allowing that that may take a little while to happen in a play, that doesn't come right away, but that it can happen in the process of a performance. It all for me begins back in the rehearsal room. And if we successfully erase the traces, then the true genius of all of this is present. It's the writing of Shakespeare himself. His work is still astounding as far as its understanding of what it means to be a human being. And I'd like to get out of the way of that.

Daniel Sullivan, Freelance Director

The Public/Shakespeare in the Park
Urbana, Illinois; 4 March 2008
Revised with new material 3 March 2015

Daniel Sullivan is a former artistic director of Seattle Repertory Theatre from 1981 to 1997, where he directed over sixty productions and started a new play programme. He directed the Broadway productions of *The Merchant of Venice* starring Al Pacino and *Julius Caesar* starring Denzel Washington. Other Shakespeare credits include South Coast Repertory's *Hamlet, A Midsummer Night's Dream* and *The Taming of the Shrew*, the Old Globe's *Julius Caesar, Cymbeline, Romeo and Juliet, The Merry Wives of Windsor* and *Othello*. Shakespeare in the Park productions include *The Merry Wives of Windsor, A Midsummer Night's Dream, Twelfth Night, The Merchant of Venice, The Tempest, King Lear* and *Cymbeline* (2015). He is the recipient of a Drama Desk Award for Most Promising Director (*Suggs* 1972) and the Tony Award for Best Direction (*Proof* 2001). He has directed original premieres for Wendy Wasserstein, Herb Gardner, Donald Margulies, Jon Robin Baitz and Charlayne Woodard. He holds the Swanlund Chair at the University of Illinois' Krannert Center for the Arts where I interviewed him on a frigid winter afternoon.

I look for a kind of transparency in the work: that you are looking straight through to the sense of it. I've always believed that if actors understand the text deeply, sense will be communicated, no matter how complicated, no matter how antique that sense might be. And I hope (maybe I should say 'insist') that all of the actors have the same technical approach to the material. If the actor doesn't understand poetic scansion, doesn't understand the rhythm of the language, I simply won't cast that person. It's something you can't learn in four or five weeks of rehearsal.

In the training of actors, I think we need more of an insistence on the technicalities of scansion. Many actors don't understand that meaning is imbedded in the placement of emphasis in an iambic pentameter line. Take a look at Hamlet's most famous soliloquy: 'To be or not to be that is the question'. Most contemporary interpretations put the emphasis here: 'To be or not to be THAT is the question'. But scansion tells us the stress falls on'… that IS the question'. The first interpretation tells us 'THAT' is the big question. But when the stress falls on IS (and it does), it tells us that the idea of choosing life or death was current in the intellectual life of that time and that Hamlet, home from the University, would have puzzled this through before: if the life is madness, why do we not end it? That IS the question. So in knowing where the rhythm falls in this single line of poetry, Hamlet's history of learning is opened up for us. Scansion, far from being technical drudgery, is a way of discovering meaning and subtext.

The interpretive director

Bill Rauch, Artistic Director

Oregon Shakespeare Festival
Ashland, Oregon; 2 August 2007 and 17 June 2008
Revised 15 January 2015; new material 16 February 2015

Bill Rauch has been Oregon Shakespeare Festival's Artistic Director since 2007. At OSF he has directed *A Comedy of Errors*, *The Two Gentlemen of Verona*, *Romeo and Juliet*, *Measure for Measure*, *King Lear* and *Cymbeline*. Other classical pieces there include *Medea/Macbeth/Cinderella*, *Hedda Gabler* and *The Clay Cart*. Rauch directed the Broadway production of *All The Way*, which won numerous awards including two Tony awards for Best Play and Best Actor (Bryan Cranston). Classical productions staged for Cornerstone, where he was artistic director from 1986 to 2007, include *As You Like It*, *Romeo and Juliet*, *Peer Gynt* and *A Midsummer Night's Dream*. Cornerstone often adapted Shakespeare to specific contexts – even changing the words at times to make the piece more potent in its community based productions. Rauch has worked at many regional theatres such as Yale Repertory Theatre, Mark Taper Forum, South Coast Repertory, Guthrie Theater, Arena Stage, Long Wharf Theatre, Great Lakes Theater Festival and Lincoln Center Theatre. He is a recipient of the Margo Jones Award as well as the Los Angeles Weekly Drama-Logue, Seattle Critics Choice and Helen Hayes awards for direction. He has received Emmy and Ovation nominations and the 'Leadership for a Changing World' Award.

I feel like I'm an experimentalist. I feel like I'm an innovator. But ultimately, I do feel my job, as director, is *interpreter of the text*. I don't feel like I'm an auteur as the director. I don't feel like it's mine ... I feel like everything I'm doing is in service to the vision of William Shakespeare. But with that said, I think what Shakespeare wrote is so passionate and so shocking. He plumbs the depths of despair and the heights of joy, and every contour of the human experience. So you *better* be pushing yourself as an artist to explore the outer reaches of your imagination. You have to be, to match the power of the work and to *dare* be worthy of interpreting this work.

[The next five paragraphs are from a draft of 'Shakespeare at OSF: A Framework' which Rauch shared with me dated 20 December 2014.]

[W]e want all decisions relating to our Shakespeare productions to be made with intention ... and with a full understanding of the context in which we aspire to create the most dynamic and engaging twenty-first-century American productions for our audiences.

We at the Oregon Shakespeare Festival are committed to Shakespeare the populist. Too often in contemporary American society, Shakespeare is seen as medicinal high culture reserved for the elite. We strive for productions that tap into the spirit of the man who wrote plays for nobility *and* groundlings crammed together in a teeming mass of shared humanity. We celebrate the Shakespeare whose work was performed in frontier towns and on riverboats as the heart of nineteenth century American popular culture, the Shakespeare who invented words, the Shakespeare who slammed together street jargon and erudite classical references into startling poetry, the Shakespeare whose work can be mined for its political, class-dissecting, psychological, philosophical and spiritual insights, to name but a handful of the infinite points of entry into the work of this most human of artists.

Shakespeare captures a full range of the human experience in every play he wrote, in part a product of the tumultuous time and place in which he lived. The renaissance brought to London a new mix of cultures, religious disruption and tremendous shifts in thought and innovation. We in turn are living in a time and place of tremendous innovation, conflict of ideas, as well as religious and cultural clashes.

In order to harness the energy of writing that grew out of the particular chaos of Elizabethan and Jacobean England, our current American productions should capture the fullest possible range and complexity of our own era's and country's cultures onstage.

[W]e endeavour to reflect the diversity of our own country in casting all of Shakespeare's plays. On occasion, a production might choose to explore one or more specific cultures; past examples include a *Measure for Measure* set in a 1970s largely Latino urban neighbourhood [see cover photo], a *Comedy of Errors* set in the Harlem Renaissance, or a *Troilus and Cressida* with production parallels to the Iraq War.

Too often when it comes to expressing time and location, we as artists tend to focus on design elements and particularly costumes. We invite OSF's creative teams to thoroughly explore the parameters of period and setting through as many prisms as possible. For instance, even a production set in a historically distant era will be affected by current gender politics or racial and ethnic dynamics in how the characters interact with one another and how the audience receives those interactions. And most importantly for our language-based theatre, what is the specificity of approach to speaking the text? Artistic choices about interpreting language are equally or perhaps more vital than any casting or design element in determining a production's success.

Des McAnuff, Artistic Director and Robert Blacker, Dramaturg

Stratford Festival
Stratford, Ontario; 12 July 2008 and 7 October 2008
Revised with new material 31 March 2015

Des McAnuff is a former artistic director of La Jolla Playhouse and has directed numerous Broadway productions. They include *The Jersey Boys*, *The Farnsworth Invention*, *Guys and Dolls*, *Jesus Christ Superstar*, Billy Crystal's

700 Sundays, *Dracula, the Musical*, *How to Succeed in Business* (1995), The Who's *Tommy*, *Big River* and the upcoming *Doctor Zhivago*. His productions and his directing have received Tony Awards. He is also the recipient of London's Olivier for best director. From 2008 to 2013 he was artistic director of the Stratford Festival. Mr Blacker has worked most of his career with Mr McAnuff serving as his dramaturg and head of literary services for La Jolla Playhouse, and then 'dramaturge' at the Stratford Festival during McAnuff's tenure. Blacker's credits include eight years as artistic director of Sundance Theatre Labs where *I Am My Own Wife*, *The Laramie Project*, *Light in the Piazza* and *Spring Awakening* were incubated. He teaches playwriting and Shakespeare studies in the graduate programmes at Columbia, Iowa and Yale. This interview was recorded in two parts. In the first session, at the Stratford Festival, Des McAnuff and Robert Blacker discuss how they work as director and dramaturg on Shakespearean text. This session was unexpectedly interrupted. A second interview was arranged with Des McAnuff several months later in New York City.

It is not enough to hold a mirror up to the world we live in. I think it is important to take responsibility for attempting to actually change the world. Tyrone Guthrie described the theatre as the oldest social, moral and political platform in the history of Western Civilization. The theatre is a place where you go to encounter, not just emotions, but ideas, insight into life in general and specifically, insight into our own times. As a playgoer and especially as a theatre artist, I am not terribly patient with drama that is intended only to amuse.

Shakespeare is the actor's best friend. It may take a certain amount of time for an actor to come to trust that but it's a rare talent that doesn't take to Shakespeare. Generosity has become more and more important to me over the years. I look to work with people who are hungry to explore and discover, and those that have respect and sensitivity about the work that is going on in the rehearsal room. It has become important to collaborate with people who respect the creation of the whole.

When actors discover the power that they can endow a Shakespearean character with, they have a tendency to become deliciously fanatical about playing that role. The greatest revelation, however, comes from the knowledge that real life on Shakespeare's stage can only be created when there is a matrix of points of view from a whole host of characters. There is a glorious simulation of human life that takes place in formal and organized ways, like a great symphony, but that life exists in the space between the characters. When we learn that, we come to appreciate each other, not just selflessly, but because we're utterly dependent on the members of the rest of the troop and can only succeed ourselves when everyone succeeds.

I couldn't begin to tell you what discoveries will be made next in the collaborations I enter into because quite literally I haven't encountered them yet. What I can say is that there needs to be a real sense of freedom in the room. There needs to be emotional safety for everyone. We all need to check the challenges and problems from our day-to-day lives at the door. We want to start every rehearsal and performance day in a childlike state or at least we want to get as close to that as we possibly can.

On the other hand, knowledge is not to be feared. It is vitally important to explore every line of the text rigorously so that ultimately that information can be jettisoned as well. Ultimately, it is about thinking, feeling and listening.

Lisa Peterson, Freelance Director

Oregon Shakespeare Festival
Ashland; 14 June 2008
Revised with new material 17 January 2015

Lisa Peterson, is a former resident director at the Mark Taper Forum and former associate artistic director at La Jolla Playhouse. Shakespeare credits include *Antony and Cleopatra* at Berkeley Repertory Theatre, *Love's Labours Lost*, *The Winter's Tale*, *All's Well That Ends Well* and *King Lear* at California Shakespeare Theater. She has worked at New York City's Ensemble Studio Theater, the Drama Dept., the Vineyard and New York Theater Workshop where she received two Obie awards for *An Iliad* and *Light Shining in Buckinghamshire*. Regional credits include work at Actors Theatre of Louisville the Guthrie Theater and Sundance. She has directed off Broadway at Playwright Horizons, Soho Playhouse, 59E59 Theater and won a Seattle Critic's Choice Award for Best Director of a Musical. She built her career doing new plays in New York and Los Angeles. At the time of our interview, she had just finished *Othello* at Oregon Shakespeare Festival, and was in the planning stages of *A Midsummer Night's Dream* at Hartford Stage. I met with her at a local coffee shop.

The first thing I do is read the play over and over. While I am reading, I am listening to my inner voice and hunting for my point of view. With a new play, I don't worry as much, initially, about my personal point of view. When I'm directing the premiere of a new play, I have to understand the world, the style, the tone and the playwright's intentions. That comes from talking to the playwright as well as reading the play. With Shakespeare, I have to have a door that's my door in, nobody else's door. The only way that I can find that door is just to read the play as many times as it takes for me to have a little echo sound inside myself.

Sometimes my big idea can seem very small at first. I'm remembering when I did *Love's Labour's Lost*. That was only my second Shakespeare and it wasn't a play that I had chosen for myself. It was offered to me and I took it. It took me a number of readings with *Love's Labour's Lost* to find my particular way in, that idea that could grow into a design and a production concept. With *Love's Labour's Lost*, the initial seed of an idea was something as silly as: 'These ladies – the princess and her friends – they are camping'. That's interesting to me. I like camping.

So with *Love's Labour's Lost,* I started to think, 'Camping, hmm, when did camping become popular?' Trying to imagine the world in which it would be fun to see these women setting up a tent. I researched camping. I discovered that in America in the late 1920s, early 1930s, camping became what it is still now, a pastime. So I ended up setting the play in the early 1930s in the countryside. I just needed a little entry point.

Darko Tresnjak, Artistic Director

The Old Globe Shakespeare Festival
San Diego; 5 and 6 July 2004

Darko Tresnjak received the 2014 Tony Award for Best Direction of a Musical for *A Gentleman's Guide to Love & Murder*. He became artistic director at Hartford Stage in 2011 where he has directed *The Tempest*, *Twelfth Night*, *Macbeth* and *Hamlet*. He made his London debut with *The Merchant of Venice*, a production that originated at New York's Theatre for a New Audience. As artistic director for the summer Shakespeare festival at the Old Globe, he staged *Pericles*, *Antony and Cleopatra*, *Two Noble Kinsmen*, *The Winter's Tale*, *The Comedy of Errors* and *Coriolanus*. He left Old Globe after the 2009 season and directed *Titus Andronicus* for Stratford Shakespeare Festival and *Twelfth Night* for Oregon Shakespeare Festival. He has directed at many regional theatres including The Public, Theatre for a New Audience, Chicago Shakespeare, Williamstown, Blue Light, Vineyard, Goodspeed, Westport and Long Wharf theatres. He is the recipient of the Alan Schneider Award for Directing Excellence, TCG National Theatre Artist Residency Award and the Boris Segal Directing Fellowship. I sat down to talk with Tresnjak outside the Old Globe outdoor stage. We then later continued our conversation in a coffee shop.

I don't think that the director's voice is the first thing that audiences attach themselves to: 'is it going to be widely original? Is his voice going to be different?' I believe that both veteran theatre-goers and novices appreciate the story being lovingly told, moment to moment, work being taken care of rigorously.

Nothing upsets me within the aesthetic parameters of what it's trying to do if it's successful and if there's a consistency of vision. The production design, concepts, settings can be wildly different as long as I feel that the choices are rooted in the text, as long as it illuminates the text beautifully.

A number of years ago, there was a book that came out. I think the title was *What Peter Sellars Did to Mozart*. It was an attack on the productions of Mozart that Peter Sellars was doing. A few years later when you think about it ... well, what did Peter Sellars do to Mozart? It's not as if people have stopped listening to Mozart or seeing his operas. You may not have liked it, but he did nothing. And it's not like any director can permanently damage Shakespeare. You might not like a production. You might find it offensive, but life goes on. It's one production. There will be another one coming down the long road that you will like somewhere else. So in that sense I don't understand why people get so uptight.

I agree with the notion of directing as a craft. Sometimes the sculptor takes a back seat to the notion of directing being all about wildly original choices no matter what, a certain kind of insecurity and nervousness and at times perverseness that doesn't illuminate the text. I am hoping that what is coming in terms of Shakespeare productions is a greater wedding of craft/originality – an originality that illuminates the text.

The language and text director
Henry Woronicz, Freelance Director
Utah Shakespeare Festival
Cedar City, Utah; 29 June 2004
Revised 25 January 2015

Henry Woronicz spent eleven seasons at Oregon Shakespeare Festival as a director and resident actor, playing Petruchio, Peer Gynt, Henry VIII and Cyrano de Bergerac. From 1991 to 1995 he was artistic director there. Since then, he has been a freelance director and actor. At the Utah Shakespeare Festival he has directed *Titus Andronicus*, *As You Like It* and *Coriolanus*. Leading roles include Prospero, Antonio (*The Merchant of Venice*), Duke (*Measure for Measure*) and the title roles in *Henry V*, *Richard III* and *Macbeth*. He has also acted on Broadway in *Julius Caesar* with Denzel Washington, and played Leontes in *The Winter's Tale* at American Repertory Theater. Other acting credits have been at the American Players Theatre, Actors Theatre of Louisville and Indiana Repertory Theatre. He has numerous film and television credits as well. I sat down with Henry outside of the Adams Theatre, where the outdoor season was about to open with his production of *The Taming of the Shrew*.

There are some people who see the director's role as the primary creator, the mover. Because I worked as an actor, which is really an interpretive artist, I always think of the work that I do as a director as interpretive. I'm being given a script by this guy, who on any given day was much smarter than you in terms of his perceptions about things. So, you try to do that script justice. You try to make it heard, to get the themes out. I think your role, as an interpretive artist, is to respond to what resonates for you in the script. I think how I would approach *Hamlet* at thirty would be different than how I would approach directing it at fifty-five or sixty. You see different things in the play, and I think your job is to bring the play out of its shell. But it starts with the play for me. It doesn't start with 'I have to do something new with this'.

And underneath all that is the challenge of doing the plays well and not be so reverential that they're museum pieces because that turns people off. So you've got to find a way to do them well and do them justice, and at the same time make them feel modern.

When I see a Shakespeare production I first tune into how they're using language. Can the actors speak the language? Do they know how it works? Do they know what the form is? Then that reflects on the director's understanding of the form, making sure that the language is the main muscle of the production. That's what drives it through. A lot of directors don't understand that because they might be more interested in a concept or the external elements of the play. I've heard famous directors say, 'Don't worry about the language, just give me power, just give me speed', or something like that. It begins and ends with the language as far as I am concerned.

Kent Thompson, Artistic Director

Alabama Shakespeare Festival
Montgomery; 18 June 2004

Since 2005 Kent Thompson has been Artistic Director of the Denver Center Theater Company where he established two programmes for new plays, the Women's Voices Fund and the Colorado New Play Summit. Shakespearean productions at Denver include *A Midsummer Night's Dream, Othello, King Lear* and *Measure for Measure*. Other productions for Denver Center include *Eventide, Dusty and the Big Bad World, Plainsong* and Irving Berlin's *White Christmas*. From 1989 to 2005 he was artistic director of the Alabama Shakespeare Festival where he frequently directed and produced Shakespeare. The National Endowment on the Arts (NEA) selected his *Macbeth* to tour to thirteen military bases in 2004. Thompson founded the Southern Writer's Project at Alabama Shakespeare in 1991 and developed many new plays there. He has been on numerous peer review panels, including TCG, NEA, The Pew Charitable Trusts, The Fulbright Scholars Program, The Wallace Funds, The Doris Duke Foundation and The Andrew W. Mellon Foundation.

I approach a Shakespeare play first and foremost through the language and through the text. Not in necessarily a hugely literal or academic way, although I know all of those things like scansion, and I know a lot about the First Folio and Neil Freeman's work.[6] Figuring out ways to animate the language and to excavate the language and to make it come alive is primary in my directing work.

I believe that language is a powerful and effective communicator, and that poetry is a particularly potent way to communicate. That doesn't mean I don't cut it and do all sorts of horrendous things to it, according to other people. But I am very much into the spoken word. I had a southern Baptist minister/preacher for a father, a well-known really good preacher. I come from the southern storytelling tradition where stories tend to be more linear. But also there is a very strong oral, spoken sense of words and colouring words. A lot of my love of Shakespeare probably derives from that.

Shakespeare is a living playwright and he is writing about human beings. I mean that in the sense that when people get too trapped in either the mechanics or the indulgences of verse or text, or Shakespeare as a kind of high art form, I think they lose a lot of both the low art form of Shakespeare and a lot of the humanity. That it's fundamentally about people caught in situations that we need to see happen in real time and we need to be emotionally engaged by.

Mark Lamos, Freelance Director

Lincoln Center Theatre
New York City; 15 May 2008
Revised with new material 15 January 2015

I caught up with Mark Lamos at Metropolitan Opera House where he was casting *Adrienne Lacouvreur* several months after his *Cymbeline* closed at Lincoln Center. Currently he is artistic director of the Westport Country Playhouse. His background includes seventeen seasons as artistic director for Hartford Stage where he directed fourteen Shakespearean plays, classics, musicals and new plays, some of which transferred to New York. As a freelance director he has many New York credits including Broadway, New York Shakespeare Festival, Roundabout Theatre, Lincoln Center Theater, Primary Stages, Signature Theatre and Playwrights Horizon. His regional work has been at the Guthrie Theater, Yale Repertory Theatre, Old Globe Theatre, The Kennedy Center, American Conservatory Theater and Ford's Theatre. He has received Lortel Awards as well as nominations for the Tony and Drama Desk awards. In addition he regularly directs opera for the Metropolitan Opera, New York City Opera, as well as at major opera houses around the country.

Let's begin with the speaking of verse. There are many philosophies – perhaps too many – about this essentially simple action. Iambic pentameter, in Shakespeare's hands, is the most economical way of expression imaginable. Poets reduce thoughts to essentials. So when an actor is speaking verse, he is saying something elemental and direct. He is thinking *as* he speaks; sometimes in fact thought and speech are simultaneous. There is no thinking *off* the line. No thinking *before* the line. (And not thinking prior to making an entrance, since there is no subtext in Shakespeare.) Shakespeare writes as speech the 'pause' that a modern dramatist would present as a stage direction: 'He pauses, trying to work out what she's said', for instance. Shakespeare doesn't need that. We hear the character thinking his way to the ultimate point he's going to make. This can feel absurd to a modern actor, but of course it's the way we all talk. Just sit and listen to chatter at a dinner party, or at a Starbucks. Spoken English is unstoppable; it flows. Conclusions are arrived at, not foregone – often long after mouths are opened and talking. The forgone conclusion is the death of any soliloquy, any interaction on a Shakespearean stage. Even Iago's soliloquies to us in which he explains what he's going to do need to be thought of as inventions, thought by thought, until he arrives – with us in collusion, almost – at the concluding thoughts.

The lack of pauses in Shakespeare is also significant for me. There are no pauses in music, right? Or at least very few. And a Shakespeare play is first and foremost an auditory event. The speaking of the verse gives the play its definition through an ever forward-moving rhythm. Verse speaking, in my work, is the muscular core of the production, and everything else about the production flows out of its rhythmic certainty. Speech evolves and then action follows. I've come to learn this, and it serves my work with the actors and the text.

Penny Metropulos, Associate Artistic Director

Oregon Shakespeare Festival
Ashland; 11 June 2004
Revised 24 January 2015

Penny Metropulos has directed productions in nineteen seasons at the Oregon Shakespeare Festival. They include *The Comedy of Errors* (a Western Musical adaptation), *Henry IV Part 1*, *Antony and Cleopatra*, *As You Like It*, *The Tempest*, *A Midsummer Night's Dream*, *Timon of Athens*, and *The Merry Wives of Windsor*. Other directing credits include Chicago Shakespeare Theater (*Cyrano de Bergerac*, *The Madness of King George* – Jeff Award,

The Two Gentlemen of Verona), California Shakespeare Festival (*Much Ado About Nothing, The Winter's Tale* and *Richard II*) and The Acting Company (*Twelfth Night*). She has also directed at the Denver Center, Arena Stage, Berkeley Repertory Theatre, Intiman Theatre, Arizona Theatre Company and Alabama Shakespeare Festival. Her training is from the London Academy of Music and Dramatic Art and the Dallas Theater Center Conservatory. We sat in her office one early summer afternoon.

My training began as an actress attending drama school in England. A great deal of our time was focused on honing our technical skills, but we were constantly being told to pay attention to the text; to let it guide you, by exploring the meaning and listening to its musicality. It speaks to who the character is under every circumstance. You can be wearing pumpkin pants, or slips or leotards. It will always be the grounding element. I know that that training had a lot to do with my love of Shakespeare and loving language.

David Ivers, Artistic Director

Utah Shakespeare Festival
Phone interview 12 February 2015

David Ivers is one of two Artistic Directors at Utah Shakespeare Festival. At USF he has directed *Cyrano de Bergerac*, *The Complete Works of William Shakespeare (Abridged)*, *Romeo and Juliet*, *Twelve Angry Men* and *Twelfth Night*. As an actor he has been in over forty productions, eighteen seasons, including title roles in *Richard II* and *Scapin*, Tony in *Dial M for Murder*, Autolycus in *The Winter's Tale*, Benedick in *Much Ado about Nothing*, Clown #1 in *The 39 Steps*, Jacques in *As You Like It* and Jake in *Stones in His Pockets*. He has also directed *The Cocoanuts* and *The Taming of the Shrew* with the Oregon Shakespeare Festival. He was a resident company member with the Denver Center Theater Company for ten seasons. Other companies include the Alabama and Idaho Shakespeare festivals, Portland Center Stage, Portland Repertory Theatre, ACT and Seattle Repertory Theatre.

I think story, plot, character, clarity has to be front and centre [as well as] language, training, stamina. I also think a pretty deep emotional well. You got to live right on it.

There's no subtext here. You have got to deliver it, especially in our theatres: big theatres that require a kind of size and muscularity. Those things are active. I want to see spit flying.

I'm always looking for, 'Are we classical enough and colloquial enough and clear enough that we're reaching across just in terms of pure meaning? I mean heightened language. Are we honouring Shakespeare's verse? Are we honouring the structure of the language? And yet we're not overly round. We're not overly British. We're not overly polite about it. It's extraordinarily muscular, language that needs to move and have vibrancy.

I think the other fundamental thing in Shakespeare is the notion of creating an ensemble, creating a bunch of people that are cognizant of the opportunity and that were blessed with the opportunity to do it. The kind of work you get out of people when you're generous and kind and you have faith in the process and in them. Big cast plays are going away. So it's such a gift to be able to be in examination of those things all the time.

I'm really interested in muscular, lean, moving productions of Shakespeare's work that get at the central issues that he wrote about.

Kate Buckley, Freelance Director

Oregon Shakespeare Festival
Ashland; 16 June 2008
Revised 24 January 2015

Kate Buckley was a founding member of the Chicago Shakespeare Theater and Artistic Director of The Next Theatre in Evanston, Illinois for four seasons. Her experience directing Shakespeare includes productions of *Much Ado About Nothing* and *The Taming of the Shrew* at the Oregon Shakespeare Festival, *Antony and Cleopatra*, *Timon of Athens*, *Macbeth* and *Cymbeline* at the American Players Theatre, *Julius Caesar*, *The Merry Wives of Windsor*, *Romeo and Juliet* and *Much Ado About Nothing* at the Utah Shakespeare Festival, *Much Ado About Nothing* at Milwaukee Shakespeare Theater,

Marionette Macbeth at Chicago Shakespeare Theater and New Victory Theatre, *Romeo and Juliet* at Chicago Shakespeare Theater and *Macbeth* and *Cardenio* at The Next Theatre. Other theatres where she has directed include the Clarence Brown Theatre, Kansas City Repertory Theatre, Milwaukee Repertory Theater, Madison Repertory Theatre and the Goodman Theatre. I spoke with Ms. Buckley one evening in Ashland, where she was preparing for design conferences on *Much Ado About Nothing* at Oregon Shakespeare Festival.

Working at Chicago Shakespeare Theater was a couple of decades of graduate study. Barbara Gaines and the entire organization gave me an amazing apprenticeship in directing. It was a comprehensive experience that allowed me to develop my personal philosophy about directing and the art of theatre. The practical application of working with this playwright everyday for fifteen years was wonderful.

The actor guidelines of the First Folio has moulded everything about my work with text, whether Shakespeare or contemporary. When directing a Shakespeare play, I start with that text as my foundation, then I look at other editions and dramaturgical research. I started as a folio purist. It's the way that Shakespeare came alive for me as a young actor. 'Oh, there's this system that I can use. I understand it. It works'. I have become less stringent about the technique, but I am more rigorous about what I call service to the playwright. Using the First Folio as my basic manual has been an important tool.

Currently, I am directing *Much Ado About Nothing*. The playwright has set it in Messina, Italy. Why would I take it to Peoria, Illinois when the playwright is very specific about location? He chose that location for a reason. He has written about a certain culture, a code of ethics and codes of honour associated with that society. I am much more dedicated to staying true to what he gave us, riffing inside of that world, than creating a new world. I am not saying that everything I do is period. In fact, we are working on setting this *Much Ado* at the end of World War II.

I am also in preproduction for *Julius Caesar* in which the theatre very specifically has asked me to create a contemporary production. Often directors must adhere to requests from theatres and I am very open to their needs. So we will have contemporary business suits and camouflaged gear. Of course we can create that world, but we aren't placing it in Washington, DC. I am not going to ignore the fact that the word 'Rome' is spoken often in the play. Rome's imagery, tensions and history are of paramount value to the atmosphere of the play. I'm not going to ignore what Shakespeare has written in the play for conceptual ideas.

I also desire actors to trust the playwright more than they trust me, or themselves. He was smarter than we are, ten times over; if we can avoid superimposing our ideas on his work he will make all of us better ten times over as well.

Paul Mullins, Freelance Director

Shakespeare Theatre of New Jersey
Madison, New Jersey; 11 August 2004

Mr Mullins is a company member of the Shakespeare Theatre of New Jersey. His Shakespeare productions include *Measure for Measure*, *Twelfth Night* and *The Merry Wives of Windsor* (Old Globe Theatre), *King John*, *Richard II* and *All's Well That Ends Well* (Shakespeare Theatre of New Jersey), *Much Ado About Nothing*, *The Two Gentlemen of Verona* (American Stage) and *As You Like It* (the Julliard School). Other directing credits include the Chautauqua Theater Company, Connecticut Repertory Theatre, Studio Theatre (DC), Portland Stage and the Yale School of Drama. Mr Mullins also acts frequently, and has credits from The Shakespeare Theatre (Flute, Feste, Leontes, Iago, Richard III) as well as from Indiana Repertory Theatre, Steppenwolf, The Drama Department, Yale Repertory Theatre, American Stage and Shakespeare Theatre of New Jersey.

I'm an actor and made probably half my living in classical theatre. So I've done a lot of Shakespeare. What I bring to it as an actor perhaps, but as director completely, is that we do this to tell a story. How we tell the story the best way is we look at what he wrote on the page. We can put it in a strange place, and we can put people in other kinds of clothing, and we can do all of these things, but we must tell the story by using his words, and making those words plain, and telling the story in a plain way, plain text, matter of fact. I say it to actors all the time: 'These things are matter of fact. In Shakespeare, these people tell you what they think. They aren't hiding a lot of things. If they're bad, they're going to tell you they're bad. If they're good, they're going to tell you they're good. If they can't figure it out, they're going to say they can't figure it out'. So I think that everything starts with those words, and from there, we find what we know about them.

The original practice director

Ralph Alan Cohen, Co-founder and Director of Mission

American Shakespeare Center
Staunton, Virginia; 15 June 2008
Revised with new material 29 January 2015

Ralph Alan Cohen is co-founder and Executive Director for the American Shakespeare Center. Founded in 1988 as the Shenandoah Shakespeare Express, the company toured extensively before opening the Blackfriars Playhouse, a reproduction of the important Elizabethan indoor theatre. Cohen has written extensively, including books, articles and a chapter in the recent volume *Globe Theatre* about original practices Shakespeare. He was a professor at James Madison University where Shenandoah Shakespeare Express originated, and currently teaches graduate Shakespeare studies for Mary Baldwin College. He has directed over twenty productions for his theatre including America's first professional production of Francis Beaumont's *The Knight of the Burning Pestle*. In 2013, he was awarded the Folger Shakespeare Library's prestigious Shakespeare Steward Award. I sat down with Dr. Cohen before seeing my first production at ASC.

Before we started *Richard II* I talked to the company about the splendid. I said to them, 'I don't think it's my job to provide the splendid. I think it's my job to provide the clarity.

It's your job to provide the splendid. I'm not coming in here with some splendid idea, some splendid thing'. I used to feel that I should do that, that I should come in and provide some splendid thing. But the actors make the splendour; if they do the splendour; then we will get twelve times as much splendour as we could get if just one person is doing the splendour.

I am there to make sure we have clarity. To anticipate when an audience is going to be lost. To make sure the actors know what these words meant when they were said. That they know what will be funny. That they know what a particular metrical pattern gives them an opportunity to work with – that's my job. Then my job is to be the decider when we have two paths to go on and somebody has to make a decision about that.

And I am trying to be a director for the audience, for the room. I'm trying to anticipate what they know, how they feel, how the room – visible to actor and audience alike – will feel and be their ombudsman to the actors. Outside the play there is a larger production going on in my view. I have been arguing in print and elsewhere that theatre, in order to survive or thrive, has to do the one thing that movies and TV can never do, which is the simultaneous presence of the actor and audience. How do you embrace that? So all the work we do, when we direct, is to try to recover that feeling of a 'room' where the play is your primary thing, but you are congregating for other things as well. So much of it is about that ambient attention. I want our audiences to have a multitudinous experience. I don't think for a moment, when you see the shows, that the shows have in any way been slighted by that goal. I think you will see, you will remember other things going on, and you will have a sense of having been in the space, been at a party with friend, and seen a good play.

Jim Warren, Co-founder and Artistic Director

American Shakespeare Center
Stanton, Virginia; 1 July 2011
Revised 25 January 2015

Jim Warren is the Artistic Director and co-founder of the American Shakespeare Center. He directed ASC's first show, *Richard III* (in which he also played Buckingham). He has directed over 113 ASC productions, including thirty of Shakespeare's thirty-eight plays. He co-founded the ASC in 1988 as the travelling troupe, Shenandoah Shakespeare Express, with Ralph Alan Cohen. He also conducts auditions across the country, directs several plays each year, hires guest directors and oversees the direction of all the shows in each repertory.

What we're trying to do is pull stuff out of the text. Everybody talks about wanting to do text-based productions, but they don't. The number of productions where somebody's talking about a hat and they're not wearing a hat – there's all kinds of internal staging directions that people ignore. And either they don't see them, or they see them and think, 'Oh, nobody's going to notice that'. What we're trying to do is point the finger at genius-boy-Shakespeare, and point the finger at the ensemble of actors. That doesn't mean I don't have a huge role to play in all of that. I think that my fingerprints on a show [is] about creating a crystal clear story, to include the audience in a way that makes them think they've gone on this journey because they're a part of the story. The actors are connecting with them in a way that allows an audience to feel.

A lot of productions of Shakespeare are stylized – *Henry VI Part 3* in a butcher shop for example – in a way that you notice the form and you notice this great imagery or this great idea, but you don't necessarily feel what those characters feel. You're taking a journey, but it's more like film, a journey where you're outside of the world watching it. To me, Shakespeare's thrust stage and universal lighting means that the audience needs to be inside that story. They need to feel like Hamlet's confidant. They need to feel like they are one of Henry V's army in those scenes. The audience takes on different roles.

As a director, I create this community, story, journey, environment where we feel like we just experienced all of what Prospero did *together*. And hopefully you love Prospero. Hopefully you loved the storm. Hopefully you loved the costume choices. Hopefully you loved all of the things that I orchestrated as a director, but that you're not pointing at me saying, 'Oh, yes, this is Jim Warren's *Tempest*'. I hope that my job as a director is to create more of a community of audience and actor and designer and director. Even when we don't do something exactly the way that we think Shakespeare did it, hopefully we're staying true to the spirit of those staging conditions and creating art that is visceral and exciting for a modern audience because we're playing with these 400-year-old staging conditions.

Stephanie Shine, Artistic Director

Seattle Shakespeare Company
Vancouver, Canada; 13 January 2005

Stephanie Shine led Seattle Shakespeare for thirteen seasons, directing seventeen productions. They include an all male *The Taming of the Shrew, Measure For Measure, Richard II, Hamlet, Henry V, A Midsummer Night's Dream* and *Henry IV Part 1*. She has also directed *The Taming of the Shrew* and *The Comedy of Errors* for Colorado Shakespeare Festival as well as *Romeo and Juliet* for Tennessee Shakespeare Festival where she currently serves as Education Director. A noted actress, she has performed for the Oregon Shakespeare Festival, New Jersey Shakespeare Festival, Seattle Repertory Theatre, ACT, Houston's Alley Theatre, Arizona Theatre Company and NYC's Theater for a New Audience. Some of her Shakespeare roles have included Lady Macbeth, Beatrice, Kate, Juliet, Rosalind, Dionyza, Regan, Feste, Bianca, Hero and Perdita. She is one of twenty-one featured actors in *North American Players of Shakespeare*.

In the past twenty years, my process has evolved into really looking for the story. What story is it that we are telling? And if we make this choice, what story does that tell? I always want to tell what Shakespeare wrote because I figure he knew what he was doing. I don't want to argue with genius because I don't have it. So I look through the play at what he wrote. Then I ask my actors to explore.

I think the plays are kind of perfect. I don't like the idea of problem plays. I think whatever is in there, if we look at it today and go, 'Oh, that play is a problem play, we have to fix it, our dramaturgy will fix it!' I think that that is somewhat arrogant.

I really like to follow the First Folio. I've gotten to be a bit of an addict about it, to direct with it. I like it when the actors are given the responsibility and freedom to realize that they're the most important things that we have.

The physical and visceral director

Ethan McSweeny

Freelance Director
The Shakespeare Theatre (DC)
Washington, DC; 25 June 2011
Revised 28 January 2015; new material 4 February 2015

Ethan McSweeny is a freelance director who has worked at The Goodman Theatre, The Guthrie Theater, Shakespeare Theatre Company, Stratford Festival and Dallas Theater Center. From 2004–12 he was the co-artistic director of the Chautauqua Theater Company. He has directed *A Time to Kill* and *The Best Man* on Broadway. He is a Drama Desk and Outer Critics Circle award winner as well as a Tony Award nominee. His Shakespeare productions include *Romeo and Juliet*, *The Merchant of Venice*, *Much Ado About Nothing*, *A Midsummer Night's Dream* and *The Tempest*. In addition to staging classics by Shakespeare, Aeschylus, Albee, Euripides, Miller, Williams, Chekhov and Pinter, he has collaborated on the development of new works by many leading playwrights in America.

I think my style is for clarity of meaning without explicating the text. Characters don't explicate. They act. I don't have a rule about 'You must take a pause at the end of every verse line' or any other such singular programme. I think all that stuff is great, you can try it on, and take which one works, take which one is interesting. To do any one of them to the exclusion of all others is to miss the point of the variety that Shakespeare offers you. The truth is that a lot of Shakespeare is about rhythm. I can hear the rhythm of the line, and if the rhythm of the line is correct, the sense will come through. I think that's even true of the comedy too. Some of the jokes are rhythm jokes. If you get the rhythm right, the laugh comes.

It's like a language to be learned. I learned it as an apprentice director at an early age from master-speakers and that stayed with me. I don't have to go and score the script to know what the scansion is. It's just there in my head.

I guess for me the production doesn't proceed always from an intellectual idea of what I want to achieve. It emanates from an instinctual and emotional place, and then I go back and bring the intellect to it.

Bruce Sevy, Associate Artistic Director

Alabama Shakespeare Festival
Montgomery; 17 June 2004

Bruce Sevy is currently Associate Artistic Director of the Denver Center Theater as well as Director of New Play Development. He has Shakespeare credits with Alabama Shakespeare Festival (where he was Associate Artistic Director) and the Utah Shakespeare Festival. As a freelance director he has directed at the A Contemporary Theatre, Arizona Theatre Company, Cleveland Play House, Eugene O'Neill Theatre Center, Intiman Theatre, Kansas City Repertory Theatre, Lark Play Development Center, Northlight Theatre, Pioneer Theatre Company, San Jose Repertory Theatre and Seattle Repertory Theatre. His productions at Denver include *Doubt, All My Sons, Master Class, Mrs Warren's Profession, A Christmas Carol, A Cat on a Hot Tin Roof, The Little Foxes, Molly Sweeney, Dinner with Friends* and *The Cripple of Inishmaan*. I interviewed Mr Sevy in one of the foyers of the Alabama Shakespeare Festival before attending his production of *Titus Andronicus*.

When it works for me is when I feel that it is alive. By that I don't mean necessarily that it is loud or jarring or anything, but that the actors are really into it. Sometimes you can feel where the concept is overwhelming the actors and they are subservient to what is happening visually or conceptually. I am not a purist about Shakespeare at all, but I do feel satisfied when everything fits. The world that is being created is honoured all the way through. That doesn't always happen. I think even more than that, I look for the vitality.

I think he is a very vigorous playwright and certainly there is a great beauty and a certain vigour about Shakespeare that I respond to. I like it when actors have been free to go there, and not be a little too static. Sometimes it is just a sense of doing and being in my Shakespeare voice and I'm doing my Shakespeare moves. I sometimes think it gets in the way of simple things like intention, meaning what you say, knowing what you're saying, conviction with which you're playing. I miss that when it's not there. I lose interest.

The times when I really get excited seeing a Shakespeare play are when I felt like it was really happening right there, despite the artificiality of the verse or anything like that. The actors are so committed. It was living.

Stephen Burdman, Artistic Director

New York Classical Theatre
San Francisco; 9 January 2015

Stephen Burdman's directing credits for New York Classical Theatre include *As You Like It*, *The Seagull*, *Malvolio's Revenge* (workshop), *A {15-min!} Christmas Carol*, *Twelfth Night*, *Playing Moliere*, *Henry V* (New York Times Critic's Pick), *The School for Husbands*, *Much Ado About Nothing*, *Hamlet, Prince of Denmark* (Voice Choice), *King Lear* (Voice Choice), *Misalliance*, *The Tragedy of Macbeth*, *Love's Labour's Lost* (BackStage Pick), *The Comedy of Errors* (Voice Choice), *Mary Stuart*, *Scapin*, *The Feigned Courtesans*, *The Winter's Tale*, *The Triumph of Love*, *The Taming of the Shrew*, *King Ubu* and *A Midsummer Night's Dream*. He also has directed *Cymbeline* (NYU-Tisch School of the Arts), *The Tempest* (Pick of the Week,

LA Weekly), *Much Ado About Nothing* (Recommended, *LA Weekly*), *As You Like It*, *Waiting for Godot*, *Hamlet* (Outstanding Production 1994 Season, *Los Angeles Times*) and *Three Sisters*. He is the recipient of awards from the West Side Spirit and the American Theatre Wing for consistent commitment to excellence in theatre.

We do an approach that we call panoramic theatre. It started initially with the idea that, if a show is going be outside, how are we going to hear it if we don't mike it? An issue was: 'how can the speaking actor always stand and face front? And how can they project and use their technique and talent in New York City, which is a loud city? Even in Central Park, which is relatively closed, our initial venue: how can that happen? Panoramic theatre initially developed out of that.

Panoramic theatre is a cross between promenade theatre, environmental theatre, and late nineteenth century staging, plus stuff we've added. So there are crosses and techniques we've created: how to cue, how to walk in. When an actor enters upstage, they can't hear their cue – especially if they're walking any distance, because the person giving the cue line is then facing downstage. We figured out a signalling system, whereby an actor is literally cued who didn't receive their cue line, so they can respond to it.

It's reminiscent of film in that way. But there's motion. When the audience is in motion from space to space, there's a location shift, a time shift. The audience understands that. These shows last two hours maximum because people need to go to the bathroom. There are no bathrooms in many of our park venues. And there's no intermission *because they move*. That's also a wonderful time for the audience to process and talk amongst themselves about what they just saw, what's happening, and where we're going with it.

We start the show at seven, and the sun sets during the course of the performance every night. We use MAG lights. Our interns use them out front. Essentially they have six spotlights, which is a sufficient number of lights to light about twelve actors onstage, which is our average company. The audience starts out very spread out and then they get very tight like a New York subway at rush hour. There can be 500 people a night who are on top of each other and literally running to different venues. It makes it great for kid's attention spans. Children love it, walking with us. (We weren't planning on this at all. I was planning on giving accessible productions in convenient locations.)

The theory of panoramic theatre is: the deeper the audience's involvement, the greater their emotional experience and commitment to the show. Because then they feel deeply committed to everything that's happening.

Timothy Douglas, Freelance Director

New York City; 30 November 2007
Revised with new material 18 March 2015

Timothy Douglas is a New York City based freelance director who spent his formative years with Tina Packer and Kristin Linklater at Shakespeare & Company. While there, he acted in numerous productions including *Richard II*. His Shakespeare directing credits include *Much Ado About Nothing* and *Richard III* at the Folger Theatre and *Love's Labour's Lost* at the Utah Shakespeare Festival. He has also directed at the Guthrie Theater, Mark Taper Forum, Arena Stage, Actors Theatre of Louisville (where he was Associate Artistic Director 2001–4), South Coast Rep, Cincinnati Playhouse, Milwaukee Repertory Theater, the Round House Theater and Berkeley Repertory Theatre. Mr Douglas also directed the world premiere of August Wilson's *Radio Golf* at Yale Repertory Theatre. He has been a guest teaching artists at the Shakespeare Theatre Company (DC) and was nominated for a Helen Hayes Award for his direction of *Insurrection: Holding History* at the Theater Alliance (DC). We discussed his career over tea at his residence in Brooklyn.

Actual communication first happens in the physical and then the spoken word clarifies what's being communicated. Effective use of text is truly amazing. Yet even more amazing is the way authentic communication is first experienced in the body and then realized via the text. My approach has consistently been a physical one, ever since I realized and understood what that meant.

The rage about what is currently going on in the world – no matter what our individual politics might be – requires an actor's profound courage, and willingness to access and be willing to reveal *self*. The brilliance in the design and construction of Shakespeare's plays is that the language is perfectly constructed to provide the actor access to the *self* in communicating infinite heights and depths. What is it in *Richard III*? 'Why should calamity be full of words?' [4.4.126] 'Let them have scope, though what they will impart/ Help nothing else, yet do they ease the heart'. [4.4. 130–1] As actors – and by extension as a people – we have to 'let it out'. In Shakespeare's world and constructions, he gets it all out. Once it's all out, then we are actually free to authentically communicate with each other and really say/express what we mean. When actors are fully aligned with the text and the impact of the given circumstances in a play – and convey those genuine thoughts and feelings – the body doesn't know that it's acting. You are actually having this experience in this moment in time. This Shakespeare text and its given circumstances is triggering something profoundly deep within you.

The difficult feelings are usually the ones that have been identified as painful. Our conditioning has so successfully trained us to believe that uncomfortable feelings are not to be revealed in public. I am adamant that it is the job of the actor to precisely let loose as many uncomfortable feelings as are triggered in the process of creating characters and relationships for the stage! These moments are always the most challenging to reveal. But pain already exists within the actor; it wasn't implanted by the text, but rather the ideas in the text reignite the feeling-presence already dormant in them. I say, 'What possible benefit could there be in holding it back – save for a momentary sense of relief of yet another round of successful repression? Allow it to *release*!' The actor is not revealing his or her own biographical story – though internally to them that's exactly what it may feel like. It is not necessary for them to articulate anything biographical about their personal truths or trauma in that state of intense vulnerability. By using Shakespeare's words – the very words that have triggered such a potent psycho-physical response – the actor unleashes, and viscerally experiences the character's revelation in real time!

It is essential that the process be therapeutic for the actor if it's going to be therapeutic for the audience. The audience is going to have the experience that the actor on stage is having. If the actor is holding back, whether it's consciously or unconsciously, the audience is going to be in a 'held' state. They will literally hold their collective breath when the actor stops breathing. Audiences can intuitively feel what is going on, and can feel when the actor is denying them authentic communication. This is why so many audiences walk away from so many Shakespeare productions feeling ignorant of the material, and are tempted to believe themselves not savvy enough to 'get it'.

Mixing approaches

Kathleen Conlin, Associate Artistic Director

Utah Shakespeare Festival
Cedar City; 1 July 2004
Revised 24 January 2015

Kathleen Conlin, was an Associate Artistic Director and Casting Director at Utah Shakespeare Festival where she had been for twenty-two seasons. She is also the Barnard Hewitt Chair in Directing at the University of Illinois at Urbana-Champaign and a past-dean of the College of Fine Arts. She is a past president of the National Theatre Conference and a former board member of URTA and the Ohio Arts Council. Her Shakespeare directing experience includes *Richard III*, *The Tempest*, *A Midsummer Night's Dream*, *King Lear*, *The Taming of the* Shrew, *Love's Labour's Lost* at Utah Shakespeare Festival and *Hamlet* at the Krannert Center. Other credits include a video, *Performing Shakespeare* and freelance directing work at The Colony Theatre (Los Angeles), Berkeley Shakespeare Festival, the Clarence Brown Theatre,

Michigan Repertory, Peterborough Players and the Illinois and Three Rivers Shakespeare Festivals. She was named a Fellow of the American Theatre in 2005. I spoke with Ms Conlin in a courtyard just outside the Adams Theatre in Cedar City, Utah.

What I admire is work that is physically expressive and where there is a strong sense of the language. It can be manifested in many ways. I don't mean I want to hear one kind of sound or one kind of delivery. I want to be able to detect in the production that someone took the language seriously and *decided* what they were going to do as opposed to a sense of the willy-nilly catch all.

It's a constant struggle of trying to determine what is uniquely *American* in the way we produce the plays. For *me* I think that means having strong speech and a highly physical production because the American culture is more athletic than anything else. We respond to movement, whether it's our own or another's. We love sporting events. Theatre and sporting events are very similar. They have the same kind of impact on audiences. It's just a question of how much is cerebral, how much is pre-planned. If live theatre is in competition with film and video and television, then the way that we carve out even more of what we do is the physical presence and its athleticism.

David Frank, Producing Artistic Director

American Players Theatre
Spring Green, Wisconsin; 8 September 2012
Revised with new material 24 January 2015

David joined APT as Artistic Director in 1990. From 2005 until 2015 he served as Producing Artistic Director. Recent productions directed include *Much Ado About Nothing*, *Twelfth Night*, *Too Many Husbands*, *Blithe Spirit*, *The Cure at Troy*, *Major Barbara* and *The Winter's Tale*. David has spent most of his career heading professional theatre companies, including eleven years as Artistic Director of Studio Arena Theater in New York and eight years as Producing Director of St. Louis Repertory Theater.

When I arrived in America in 1966, I was struck by the differences in the two traditions on either side of the Atlantic. I have been fascinated with the rewards of fusing both approaches ever since.

The particular training I received in England – in the early 1960s, remember – was dominated by a very technical approach; a lot of attention was paid to vocal production, phrasing, colouring and other technical aspects of verse speaking. I got the impression that you could train a voice and a body to be lucid and beautiful, but talent was something that you were either born with or weren't.

Once in America, I was introduced to the works of Viola Spolin and discovered a radically different approach. Here was someone who believed actors could be directed towards the source of their talent. It was through Spolin that I came to understand the vital importance of specificity and spontaneity to the thrilling performances that often resulted. But applied to Shakespeare, it was a bit of a disaster. Seldom was that specificity effectively applied to the details of the language. At worst, the words became vehicles, sounds to be made while getting on with the lusty business of acting.

At APT for the last twenty years, we have based our work on a core company that strives to fuse those two traditions. The results, I think, have been palpable and noteworthy.

Tina Packer, Artistic Director

Shakespeare & Company
Vancouver, British Columbia; 14 January 2005
Revised with new material 28 January 2015

Tina Packer founded Shakespeare & Company in 1978, developed the company and has served as its Artistic Director from 1978 to 2009 where she has directed over fifty productions, including every major Shakespeare play. She is the recipient of the Guggenheim and Bunting Fellowships to write and perform her trilogy, *Women of Will*. It received critical acclaim in a 2013 Off Broadway run. Her company has had considerable influence on Shakespeare companies and training throughout the US. She also served as artistic director of Boston Shakespeare Company. She is the author of two books, *Power Plays: Shakespeare's Lessons in Leadership & Management* (co-author John O. Whitney) and *Tales from Shakespeare, Shakespeare's Stories for Children.* She has lectured and directed at Columbia, Harvard and MIT. Her background includes training at the Royal Academy of Dramatic Art where she received the Ronson Award for Most Outstanding Performer. She worked with the Royal Shakespeare Company as an associate artist and performed in London's West End. I talked to her at a Shakespeare Theatre Association of America conference in 2005 about her goals in founding Shakespeare & Company.

I realized I had to create a theatre company so that we could investigate all the levels Shakespeare himself worked on – political, philosophical, poetical, physical, psychological. Every play I encountered, I realized he knew so much more than I ever could, so it excited me to try and meet him on his terms, (not me thinking up what my concept was of his story). I wanted to develop actors who possessed the skill set of Shakespeare's actors; to work on the human voice and everything it can do (abilities we are losing so rapidly in the modern world), to make the fights so exciting you couldn't bear it, to make the comedy really funny, to really understand the art of rhetoric – the rhythms, the imagery, why this word is against that word, all within the context of seeking to persuade, to debate, to influence. Sometimes it's in the love language – which was a great contribution the English language made to the art of rhetoric, persuading with love and then developing flower imagery by going into a spiritual garden. Shakespeare is the essence of what it means to be human and expressing that through language.

What we've been able to do at Shakespeare & Company is align many disciplines. When I went to drama school we learnt to do a bit of this and a bit of that with little connection between them. We've aligned the voice work with text work, aligned the fight work with voice work, dance with clown and so on. Breathing, freeing the natural voice, expanding the ability to think and reveal, above all studying what it means to be a human, are the demands put upon the actors. We are attempting to rehabilitate ourselves to the openness and energy of the Elizabethan actors. The industrial revolution closed down our bodies, perpetual empire building closed off our voices, and now we are into the digital age, and we disassociate ourselves from ourselves even more. As a director I am focused on the human experience – sets, lights and costumes are support structures – but what humans are saying and doing (and the music and sound effects that interact with them) are the core of the theatrical experience for me.

John Neville-Andrews, Freelance Director

Former Artistic Director, Michigan Shakespeare Festival
Kilgore, Texas; 20 June 2012
Revised 20 January 2015

John Neville-Andrews has been Artistic Producer of The Shakespeare Theatre in Washington, DC and also of the Michigan Shakespeare Festival. He has more than forty years of professional experience as an actor, director and producer. He has taught at the University of Michigan, Yale School of Drama, California Institute of the Arts, Penn State University, the University of Maryland and the University of Rhode Island. His productions of Shakespeare and the classics at the Folger Theatre have received critical acclaim. He has worked across the country at Utah Shakespeare Festival, Yale Repertory Theatre, Williamstown Theatre Festival, The Olney Theatre Center, The Long Wharf Theatre and on and off-Broadway. He received the Smithsonian Institute's Certificate of Excellence and the American Theatre Association Award for 'contribution to Theatre as an Author, Actor and Director'. I interviewed him one afternoon in Kilgore at the Texas Shakespeare Festival where we were both directing.

I used to go and see a lot of Shakespeare because I enjoy it so much, and just by judging what I saw, I got the sense that there was a scholarly approach to the text. That may not be true right across the country, but at various places I did go and see that.

I think that's changed. I think there's a more organic approach to Shakespeare now than there was. There is still a respect for the language, but I don't think theatres or actors and directors are quite so reticent about Shakespeare any more. They've really come to terms with it and they've realized the plays should be seen on the stage. It's pretty much on the page what you have to present, but it can be presented in a very creative and innovate way without thinking, 'Oh my God, I'm violating Shakespeare!' And I think it's good for actors. I think it's a good for directors as well.

In the Elizabethan times the audience used to say, 'I'm going to hear a play'. Nowadays we say we're going to go *see* a play. People have realized that you look at the text, and you see the words, and its so image driven, that what we really need to do is make sure you've got the imagery really bold and vivid. Once you've got that, and there's clarity, you can do pretty much whatever you want with Shakespeare. Very much like I imagine would've happened in Shakespeare's time. I'm sure that company didn't think, 'I've got to stay really true to whatever William Shakespeare wants'. There were a lot of shenanigans going on, I imagine. Shakespeare in this country certainly broadened its approach and broadened its audience's enjoyment for it.

The inclusive director

Timothy Bond, Associate Artistic Director

Oregon Shakespeare Festival
Ashland; 10 June 2004
Revised with new material 7 January 2015

Tim Bond is currently Producing Artistic Director of Syracuse Stage. For eleven seasons he was Associate Artistic Director of the Oregon Shakespeare Festival. His productions there included *Twelfth Night*, *Topdog/Underdog*, *Intimate Apparel*, *Gem of the Ocean*, *Ma Rainey's Black Bottom*, *The Piano Lesson*, *Who's Afraid of Virginia Woolf?* and *Oo-Bla-Dee*. Other directing experiences include thirteen years at the Seattle Group Theatre (where he was Artistic Director for five years) and at Seattle Repertory Theatre, Actors Theatre of Louisville, Arena Stage, Cleveland Play House, Guthrie Theater, Indiana Repertory Theatre and Milwaukee Repertory Theater. He received the Theatre Communications Group/National Endowment for the Arts Directing Fellowship Award as well as Backstage West's Garland Award for Outstanding Direction for *Les Blancs* and for *Blues for an Alabama Sky*. I interviewed Mr Bond in his office in Ashland.

I am a director of colour who has a great interest in illuminating the themes and character journeys of Shakespeare's plays through an inclusive vision and interpretation that is relevant to a contemporary culturally diverse audience. My hope is that Shakespeare productions reflect the diversity of our nation by being cast with a rich mix of talented actors from enough variety of racial, ethnic and cultural backgrounds, that audiences will see themselves included in the world of the play.

These beliefs and approaches have been core to my life as an artist as I have spent many years connecting with artists of colour from many backgrounds, as well as working with diverse communities throughout a number of cities nationally and abroad. One obstacle that I frequently encounter is that the very mention of Shakespeare to audiences and artists who have historically been excluded from Shakespeare makes them feel uncomfortable. They don't feel that it has relevance to their lives. As a young adult, I used to feel the same way because of the nature of many of the productions I had encountered as an audience member. I felt excluded, and like this was a language and a world that I was not welcome to join. But now I see the profound humanity and accessibility of these plays to touch and reflect a much more diverse global society. Shakespeare's works can be inclusive of many different cultures. So I look to cast these plays with actors from any number of different cultural groups, who can embrace and speak that language with their own specific cultural sensibilities and perspectives that truly enrich the work. I believe this deepens the work and opens the door for audience members to make a very human connection with folks from cultures different than their own.

It's not a politically correct agenda. It is simply embracing our diverse culture as Americans, as global citizens. Shakespeare called one of his theatres *The Globe*. As far as we know, he never travelled to all of the different lands he wrote about. He was more than likely writing about people he had met, seen or read about. In other words he used his creative, poetic imagination to explore numerous aspects of the human condition, and to speak in metaphor or slightly out of context about what he saw going on in his current society. At the time he wrote and produced his plays, he didn't have a particularly diverse casting pool, and yet he created an amazing range of characters from all over the spectrum of humanity.

Joanne Zipay, Artistic Director

Judith Shakespeare Company
New York City; 9 August 2004

Joanne Zipay founded the Judith Shakespeare Company in 1995 a company that explores gender-reversed casting. She has produced more than half the canon, including a three-season staging of the entire history cycle of eight plays. In addition to the history plays, Zipay has also directed and produced full productions of *All's Well that Ends Well*, *Macbeth* (OOBR Award), *Julius Caesar*, *The Comedy of Errors* and *The Tempest*. For their 'Unplugged Shakespeare' which is an original approach developed by Zipay, she directed *Cymbeline*, *The Two Gentlemen of Verona*, *Troilus and Cressida*, *King John*, *Pericles*, *Henry VIII*, *Titus Andronicus*, *Richard II*, *Henry IV Part 1*, *Henry IV Part 2*, *Henry V*, *Henry VI Parts 1*, *2* and *3* (in rotating repertory) and *Love's Labours Lost*. Ms. Zipay directed the Off-Broadway premiere production of *Elizabeth Rex* with Nicu's Spoon Theater. She is also on the theatre faculty at Pace University Manhattan and CUNY. After running her company for twenty years, she decided to dissolve it in 2015.

I had learned the dramaturgical approach to the work at The Old Globe as an actor. I started my company. I started giving women opportunities to do things. I morphed into a dramaturg and a director and an actor. Our mission statement is very simple at this point: 'Bringing Shakespeare's language to life with clarity and vitality, while expanding the presence of women in classical theatre'. So while we're thought of as a company offering opportunities for women, the first purpose is actually dramaturgical: language.

The idea of casting women non-traditionally and men non-traditionally, that varies from show to show as to how we do it. Sometimes we do things straight or nearly straight. It just depends on the opportunities for the women involved. It has to start with a good look at the play and an understanding of what's going on in Shakespeare's gender roles. I'm extremely conscious of how gender operates in the plays. So to tweak that without really any reason, or without an awareness of how it operates, can be detrimental, but also just not as interesting as making a choice for a reason. A lot of people go, 'Oh, I thought you were an all women theatre company'. It's an easy quote. Not that there's anything wrong with that, but I'm just much more interested in pushing the boundaries of gender on both sides.

Non-traditional casting has evolved for us. We've experimented with it. One of the reasons I do it is I want to set an example saying, 'Look at all the things you can do!' You don't have to just say, 'All women'. You don't have to just say, 'Gender-reversed'. You don't have to just say, 'Gender-blind'. You don't have to just say, 'Traditional with a few roles changed'. But all of those things can work and all of those things remain part of our season. It has evolved *a lot*. I think we've gone from being very conservative to being much more risky with that kind of work.

Lisa Wolpe, Artistic Director

Los Angeles Woman's Shakespeare Company
Lenox, Massachusetts; 31 January 2009
Revised with new material 4 February 2015

Lisa Wolpe is Artistic Director of the all-female Los Angeles Women's Shakespeare Company, a company she founded in 1993. She has directed twenty Shakespeare productions, and produced and starred in fourteen LAWSC Shakespeare productions, directing twelve of them, including a recent *Hamlet*. She has also directed at the Oregon Shakespeare Festival, Berkeley Repertory Theater, Shakespeare & Company, Boston Center for the Arts, Arizona Theater Company, San Diego Repertory Company, Boston Theater Works, California Shakespeare Festival, Southwest Shakespeare and Sedona Shakespeare. She received an L.A. Stage Alliance Ovation Award as 'Best Actress' for her Shylock in LAWSC's *The Merchant of Venice*, a production that garnered three other Ovation Awards. She claims to have 'probably' played more male leading roles than any woman in history, and has been featured on ABC, CBS, CNN, NBC and PBS. For several years she was an actor, director and master teacher with Shakespeare & Company. She is one of eight directors featured in *Women Direct Shakespeare in America* and was in the first group selected for the Globe Theatre in London's International Fellows Program.

The current climate for women playing Shakespeare is now moving into innovation, evidencing change, offering a more critical look at what Shakespeare was actually doing in his time. I think when all-male companies perform the work, it revealed more dimensions of their understanding of the behaviours and problems of being gendered people, of complex confrontations and contradictions within a greater assumption of what is beautiful and dangerous and good in humanity. Women and men, trans people and any shading or variation of gender – and sexual preference, race and culture (in this more evolved day and age) can play any Shakespearean character onstage, and explore their character's political life, personal life, spiritual connection, their understanding of the Cosmos, with the wonderment and awed respect for the gifts we share as fellow citizens of the planet. As a director, I think that it is very important to speak to the inclusion of all people in our communities, on our stages, and as a result, I call myself both an activist and a director, an advocate for diversity and female empowerment in the Shakespearean theatre tribe. Infrastructures are changing. For me, the most important work is still the excellence of the work, and also, always, to be an advocate for the important shifts allowed by the subtleties revealed in cross-gender casting – and in our new times, this means fostering more all-female productions, gender-flipped productions (men playing women, women playing men), and re-gendered roles (exploring 'what if' a male character is recreated as a female character, or a female character becomes a male character) – and to include actors of all races onstage, not predominately white males who can only tell part of the story of who the Earth's people are. For me, this is a very direct way of changing theatre practice towards a better, more beautifully shared stage for all the people of the world.

Oskar Eustis, Artistic Director

The Public Theater/New York Shakespeare
New York City; 7 September 2007

Oskar Eustis has been artistic director of the Public Theater since 2005. In 1981 he began an association with the Eureka Theater Company (San Francisco) where he was artistic director from 1986–9. While there he commissioned Tony Kushner's *Angels in America*. He became Associate Artistic Director of the Mark Taper Forum (Los Angeles) where he directed the world premiere of *Angels*. In 1994 he began an eleven year stint as artistic director at Trinity Repertory Company (Providence, RI). Throughout his career he has been extensively involved in developing new work. The list of playwrights he has worked with is a who's who of the contemporary American theatre: Rinne Groff, Paula Vogel, David Henry Hwang, Emily Mann, Suzan-Lori Parks, Ellen McLaughlin and Eduardo Machado. He directed *Hamlet* for the New York Shakespeare's Delacorte Theater in 2008 starring Michael Stuhlbarg and was the lead producer on the Tony Award-winning revival of *Hair* and the acclaimed rock musical *Bloody Bloody Andrew Jackson* on Broadway. He has taught at UCLA, Brown University and NYU, and holds honorary doctorates from Brown University and Rhode Island College.

As an historical materialist (which I am) I don't believe we can ever separate ourselves from history. There is no pure truth. We're always contingent. We're always in history. The history of the way the western world has unfolded in the last 400 years has made Shakespeare the most revered author that we have. Our job, then, is to place ourselves in relationship to that reverence. I don't believe that religion is of any use to us in approaching Shakespeare or art.

We [the public] have to go back to the parks in the boroughs. There is something about that initial thing that Joe did with Shakespeare. Because what you are doing is that you're bringing people to Shakespeare who don't need to decide they want to go to Shakespeare, who are just going to the park and there's the show. That's the way you really reach people who are outside of the cultural bylaws.

I think that is a hugely important thing to do because Shakespeare is a part of our cultural language, if people don't speak Shakespeare, if people don't feel like it belongs to them, it is a way of excluding them from the highest levels of discourse in our society. It's a kind of apartheid, which is very real.

You are old enough to remember the flurry of commentary when E. D. Hirsch published *Cultural Literacy*. Actually there was something about all of that. What they were acknowledging is that there is a certain set of references, that if you don't have, you get pigeonholed. You get excluded from a cultural discourse that ultimately is the cultural discourse that runs the country. So part of our mission has to be to bring as many people as possible into that, so that when someone says, 'To be or not to be' at a party, they get the joke. So that there is a familiarity with that work which is necessary because it is part of the language of power.

PART TWO

Preparations for Rehearsal and Production

3

Developing an Approach

Each approach to beginning a new production is different. There are many windows you can open; inspiration comes in a variety of ways – it could be a phrase within the text or a friend's experience or ideas can spring as you're walking down a street. There is always a trigger that inspires me and then the obsession to direct the play begins.

BARBARA GAINES

Developing a production approach is crucial for most directors. As soon as they are hired, they are pressured by producers and the design team to explain how they are going to tackle the play. Where will it be set? What are the chief ideas they have to manifest the production? This is especially pertinent for Shakespeare as they are many possible time frames in which to locate a play. This chapter explores sources for directors' approaches as well as their attitudes about addressing this aspect of the work.

The first discoveries in a script for the director, as well as the actor, are often the given circumstances. 'The specifics of the play need to be the starting point', Esbjornson states. Sifting through them may aid in finding a path forward

90 DIRECTING SHAKESPEARE IN AMERICA

FIGURE 8 Timon of Athens, *directed by Barbara Gaines, Chicago Shakespeare Theater, 2012. Ian McDiarmid as Timon. Photo Credit: Liz Lauren.*

with a production. 'If there is a respect for the text, the play will be a bottomless well of possibilities', he contends. He also believes 'If you ignore the social and political circumstances of [Shakespeare's] original choice, you are denying yourself valuable information'. Esbjornson's production of *Much Ado About Nothing* was set in post World War I Sicily, before Mussolini came to power, in the shadow of Mt. Etna. Esbjornson researched the cultural, political and social aspects of that society and that geography, working through the play scene-by-scene, action by action, to make sure it could contain Shakespeare's play. He discovered useful parallels such as the neo-Futurists and the suffragette movement. 'Suddenly, the parallels between 1600 and the twentieth century came into focus and became the basis for the rest of the production'.[1]

The study of Shakespeare's imagery is a favourite tool for Monte. She examines the text for its archetypes and gripping tales. Then within Shakespeare's incredible poetry, she finds 'layers of rich, complex images. And buried within those complex images are archetypal, iconic symbols that speak to us'. Iconic archetypal symbols often lead her to an approach. For example, in her *Macbeth* the witches became the physical manifestation of the world's growing 'corruption and negativity and evil and darkness':

> Sometimes there was one and sometimes there were thirty. … They were simple, black, but you never saw their faces … this sense that this horrifying darkness is just growing and growing and growing. And in the end, they were just hanging on him. It all came down to one main, beautiful woman ultimately that he just embraced. She was with him until he died.[2]

As Monte explores the text deeper and deeper, she discovers more and more layers, an almost endless number of them.

Thompson and Kulick observe that the plays often confront directors with critical issues and dramaturgical questions implied by the play's action and characters. Why does Hamlet fail to act? Why does Macbeth act so quickly? Who are the witches? What power do they have? What exactly is Prospero's magic? Thompson believes you have to initially solve the major staging issues – such as the grave-digging scene or Caesar's assassination – before you do anything else. Some play issues are 'contextual questions for our culture': how to make Kate's speech at the end of *The Taming of the Shrew* palatable for modern audiences, for example. How do you handle the anti-Semitism in *The Merchant of Venice*? There are also fundamental issues to the play that need attention, such as how to activate Hamlet. Kulick adds, 'Shakespeare sets up a basic question, lures you in, and then refuses to give you an answer, forces you to answer it yourself'. Discovering solutions can be critical in determining an approach.

Other questions of interpretation can be equally important. Esbjornson, warns that how women are portrayed on stage can lead to 'unexamined sexism'. The contemporary director has an 'obligation to contextualize' their responses as well as those of the men around them in such a way as to 'help make the production feel relevant'. He reminds us that the production's choices can lead to unintended points of view.

McAnuff believes ideas 'can come from anywhere' and that '[t]here is no recipe for approaching a theatrical production'. Past experience does not necessarily help the director. McAnuff acknowledges that he needs some time to develop a production idea. 'It is impossible to do too much research or thinking before you start working with actors'. He warns directors to guard against preconceptions as they can blind the director to what is actually before them.

Serban points out the difficulty a director has in finding 'a frame' in which to place a production. Shakespeare's text is extremely pliable and can be manipulated to address contemporary issues. Yet there is a danger in making a frame that is too specific and too focused on present day events; it can become trite. Conversely, one that is too broad and general fails to have any relevance to the present; it can become obtuse. Both approaches can lead to ineffective productions because of a limited point of view.

Frank sees an advantage in having a particular scheme as an approach: it gives the production team 'a coherent starting point'. He adds that the director should also have an answer to 'I want to do this play *because* ...' McSweeny develops his approach by thinking of an audience member 'through whose eyes I then perceive the play'.

Cohen, Warren and Packer report that they subscribe to an Elizabethan model in shaping their approach. Cohen pursues staging that Shakespeare used in terms of his original space and audience. Warren adds that their goal is to 'unlock some power in these plays' through eliminating sets, keeping the lights on throughout the performance and abolishing contemporary technical tools used in many other productions. In addition to following Shakespeare's original staging techniques, Packer focuses on developing actor skill sets that include vocal and physical techniques as well as clowning and combat abilities. Having learned Barton's techniques while at the RSC, she wants a visceral theatre that goes beyond Cohen's and Warren's in that she seeks 'to feel things in my body, have less intellectual discussion, and more embodied experience'.

Some of the directors think of 'approach' as 'a concept'. By 'concept' they mean a ruling idea, a thematic statement, a specific interpretation, a particular setting for the world or a point of view. D. Sullivan sees concept as 'a neat idea that can be summarized attractively'. Conlin states that one of the first things she does, when figuring out her approach, is develop conceptual notes to be used in conversations with designers. These are 'powerful visual statement[s]' that inform the course of the production. Serban argues that the director must have a point of view, 'a reference to now, to us, the art of the present'. Shine thinks of her approach as the 'flavour of a period'. For Peterson, it is a door into the play that is *her* door: '[I]t's our job as directors to discover that single idea that is going to help us create something that feels original'. For *Love's Labour's Lost*, her door became 'These ladies – the princess and her friends – they are camping'. She eventually settled on an American 1930s setting because that was when camping became a popular leisure activity. The goal of establishing a concept is coalescing the production through the concept idea, statement, interpretation, setting or point of view.

A 'concept' can be inadequate or limiting to the production. Eustis remarks that concepts are not 'the same thing as picking a time, period and a place'. He contends there is no concept 'unless it actually reveals something about the story or ... the play'. Cohen observes that actor choices challenge director choices as soon as they are made, a conflict he wishes to avoid. 'It's about their arc and my consultation', he contends. Shine explains that it is only in rehearsal, and usually with great struggle, that she can discover the play: 'what it *is*'. It used to be common for directors to talk with other directors about their concepts, D. Sullivan remembers, but he finds working with a concept to be reductive. His approach is to read the plays repeatedly, 'trying to understand who the characters are before I ever begin to imagine a world for them'.

The introduction suggests that 'context' may be a more useful a term to describe how directors think about these issues today. The last section gives four instances of directors' contextual approaches. Bill Rauch discusses his production of *Measure for Measure*, set in an American inner city in the 1970s in which the actors brought their own ethnic/racial/sexual identities to the table. Barbara Gaines shares approaches to two highly successful productions, a *King Lear* that was developed in response to a friend's dementia experiences and a *Timon of Athens* in which the approach was worked out closely with the lead actor. Finally Stephen Burdman discloses how his production of *Henry V* utilized site-specific locations.

Given circumstances

David Esbjornson: In my experience, highly conceptual productions of Shakespeare often fail if the artists are unwilling or unable to build the work from the inside out. Some productions tend to seize on a singular idea and then attempt to bend the text to fit their concept. The specifics of the play need to be the starting point. Once those are carefully considered a director has the freedom to interpret. If there is a respect for the text, the play will be a bottomless well of possibilities. For instance, where Shakespeare sets his plays is not arbitrary. If you ignore the social and political circumstances of his original choice, you are denying yourself valuable information. You certainly can choose to set a play in another time period but your choice will probably want to be based on the original setting in some important way.

Images

Bonnie Monte: The biggest thing one has to learn is how to create a landscape for the plays – physically, orally, visually – that allows these very episodic stories to move from one location to another in a kind of seamless, graceful way that does not break the audiences' engagement in the story. I developed a personal philosophy pretty quickly and a personal vision for how I wanted this theatre to approach Shakespeare.

What began to interest me more than anything were directors who shared the aesthetic that I had somehow just intuitively felt better about. The stories are so archetypal. Most of them are not perfect stories structurally. But that doesn't matter. They are brilliantly compelling stories. What is most interesting about those stories is, on top of these amazing tales about humanity, overlaying this amazing poetry. [The stories are] told through this amazing poetry. In line with that amazing poetry are hidden in layers of rich, complex images. And buried within those complex images are archetypal, iconic symbols that speak to us. So the deeper you dig, obviously it's like the never-ending onion; it just gets richer and richer and richer. And all of the inspiration that you need to create the visual landscapes for the play – the worlds of the play – are in those images. We here tend to lean toward creating metaphorical kinds of worlds in which these plays can reside. Which are inspired by the imagery in the text.

Critical scenes/central issues

Kent Thompson: In terms of staging it and designing it, you have got to solve the primary problems of the play that the playwright presents to you. *First*. You've got to not leave them for later. My concern, be it a traditional or post-modern director that works for me, is: 'Are they solving the problems of the play?'

Some of them are more contextual for our culture. You've got to solve Kate's speech at the end of *The Taming of the Shrew* because we live in a world where the received view of women is not the received view of women in Shakespeare's time. Even if he's being radical, I think we're in a different culture. You have to grapple with the anti-Semitism in *The Merchant of Venice*. And you have to figure out how you're going to present that.

You've got to deal with the grave-digging scene in *Hamlet*. I find that many of the mistakes that are made in the staging of Shakespeare are because people are not solving those critical scenes. The assassination of Caesar and the tent scene. You've got to have those two scenes work effectively. In *Macbeth*, how do you deal with the witches and the supernatural? And how do you deal with the sensory world of *Macbeth*? How do you make that potent to an audience? I think if you choose to try to *not* do that, then in a way you set yourself up for repeated failure.

Sometimes it's an issue fundamental to the play. How do you make Hamlet's character active? How do you make that character compelling to us for three and a half/four hours? In *The Tempest,* I don't think the storm is the principal thing you have to solve. I actually think the magic is the principal thing you have to solve and the apparitions. I think the storm is part of that. I think you could spend two days in tech on that, and two hours on the apparitions, on the magic, and you've blown it. Because you've really got to answer, who is Ariel? What's this role? Who is Caliban within the universe? And what are Prospero's powers? What does he have to give up at the end?

So I look for the central questions. And I keep dragging myself back to them.

Brian Kulick: So much of Shakespeare's dramaturgy is about a question. Why does Hamlet wait so long? Why do Romeo and Juliet fall in love so quick? Why does Lear divvy up his kingdom the way he does? Shakespeare sets up a basic question, lures you in, and then refuses to give you an answer, forces you to answer it yourself. Shylock is asked in the end of *The Merchant of Venice* why he wants a pound of Antonio's flesh and refuses to explain himself. Iago also seems to revel in going to his grave with the secret of why he was so intent on destroying Othello. We want to know the answer but Shakespeare's characters demur or, like Hamlet, challenge us, as he does with Rosencrantz and Guldenstern, insisting that he cannot be easily sounded like a pipe. In this respect, each production is tasked with coming up with its own answer for these seemingly elliptical actions. Perhaps that is why we keep coming back to these plays, over and over again, to see each director and actor's attempt to answer these fundamental questions. It is Shakespeare's great provocation and we can't resist trying to solve the puzzle.

Questions of interpretation

David Esbjornson: Another important access point for me has always been the interpretation of Shakespeare's female characters. No dramatist of his time created more compelling portraits of women. But their actions (or inactions) are trapped in time. I believe that a contemporary staging has an obligation to contextualize the women's behaviour, or perhaps more importantly, the behaviour of the men around them. If strong and clear choices aren't made, we can be left with unexamined sexism. If a director can present the circumstances that define these women, it can go a long way to making the production feel relevant. Is Gertrude in love with Claudius or does she simply fear him? Was Hamlet's father anything more than a cold unloving husband? Does she pity or despise Ophelia's affection for her son? Does she fall victim to an accident or does she ultimately commit suicide in the duel? Any or all of these individual choices can eventually add up to create and shape a point of view for the production. What is most exciting is when you create a world that feels complete enough to allow for a variety of character impulses, motivations and contradictions to coexist and where you attempt to bring Shakespeare's humanity to life with the complexity that a contemporary audience can understand and appreciate.

Des McAnuff: It is important to accept that ideas can come from anywhere. They can come from a newspaper article, a musical recording, a conversation with a friend, or most mysteriously, from the ether itself. There is no recipe for approaching a theatrical production. Ideally, the company is going to invent fresh techniques every time they enter the arena.

Relying on craft that served you yesterday can be foolhardy in that it won't serve you on the scene you are working on currently. There can be endless reasons for wanting to put on a particular play. Perhaps you are working out something that is deeply personal or perhaps you are responding to some outrage of the time. Feeling passionate about the work is what's essential. Relying on your preconceived notions about a play can be a great trap. I like to treat all plays as if they're brand new, even if they are hundreds of years old. If you've seen a play produced several times, it is vital to develop amnesia about your experiences so that you are not dragging some dusty old prejudice along with your fresh ideas into the rehearsal room.

Once you have a good reason for doing a play, you need to hit the books. It is impossible to do too much research or thinking before you start working with actors. At the same time, you don't want to serve the wrong masters. Filmmakers sometimes storyboard in advance of shooting them. You never want to shoot your storyboards. You want to shoot the scene. You want to capture the performances of the living actors, not the sketches that you've dragged onto the set.

Andrei Serban: Sometimes we make Shakespeare cheaper and poorer than what he is for the sake of trying to make him more available. In the more successful of our attempts, we are searching for a kind of energy that is the highest in us, to become more alert, trying to find ourselves through Shakespeare. What interests me is to find my own development and grow into the largeness of the play, which is already larger than my own personal experience or my own understanding.

Shakespeare, more than any other playwright in the history of theatre, is generously open for us to experiment in the theatre, to improvise wildly in all kinds of directions. He allows us to express our whims and fantasies, but at the end of the day, we should examine going back again and yet again to the text, how much of our action corresponds to the deep meaning of the play. It is a question of levels. There seem to be seven levels of understanding in a line, like Jacques's 'seven ages of man'. Improvisation, yes, but also analysis, the creative imagination brings rigour and free instinct together.

What is the right approach? The question remains open each day we go into rehearsal. There is no ready-made answer. If one does, let's say, one of the history plays, where we deal with political power and political ambition, invasions, violence, we decide, for instance, to make allusions to Iraq or Bush or Obama, it's okay. One can do that. The play will stand on its feet because the play is too strong to fall apart in any interpretation. But unfortunately we reduce it. We impose a horizontal direction, while eliminating the philosophical, the metaphysical side that each play subtly contains. In other words, we avoid the invisible vertical connection. We reduce it to an event that is happening at the moment, but in doing so, it kills the larger perspective. It makes it too accidental and takes away its universality. Now if one does the opposite, which is: 'I'm not going to make it about middle east, Bush or Obama or last night's hot news. I'm going to make it only about the big questions of mankind – something more generalized and abstracted, avoid putting people in jeans, keep it traditional, respectful and solemn'. No good either. It becomes sterile, flat, boring. Why? Because the story still *has to relate to us*. It has to become *our* story. We should be touched and say, 'This is about us'. At the same time it is not only about 'the little us', but it opens a perspective of what we may become. A reminder of man's struggles here on this planet, but also of his potential, of his place in the larger venue, the cosmic connection.

So one has to have a point of view. One has to have a reference to now, to us, the art of the present. At the same time, not reduce it, not manipulate it for a political or social cause, because one risks making it so obsessive and small and petty that one can better read an article in the *New York Times* rather than do Shakespeare. Why cripple Shakespeare like that?

Point of view

David Frank: Sometimes you have a point of view from the very beginning, an idea that led you to choose the play in the first place. You need to be able to tell yourself, 'I want to do this play *because* ...' In the course of rehearsal, that 'because' gets enriched, and occasionally it is substantially changed. These plays ... you keep learning from them. But you, your designers, everyone on the team need a coherent starting point.

Ethan McSweeny: When I direct a play, I think I rehearse with an idea of a prospective audience member watching over my shoulder, although I don't always know whose eyes I am borrowing until the work is done. For instance, on *Romeo and Juli*et at the Guthrie I was aware that the theatre has an extensive high-school programme in which something like 50 per cent of the eligible students in Minnesota were going to see the play. In early previews, I realized that the audience member looking over my shoulder was indeed one of those teenagers, and that the direction was evolving to tell the story in a manner that would be exciting and relatable to them.

In a similar vein, I've just directed *The Tempest* for the Shakespeare Theatre Company in Washington, DC and I was aware at the outset that, by virtue of its placement in the calendar, this would be the 'holiday' play. Now I don't think that anyone would necessarily consider *The Tempest* a Christmas classic like *Nutcracker*, but it did mean that the theatre was programming to a very multi-generational, family audience and I think that caused me to emphasize certain elements in the story, to devote resources to the clowns and a flying Ariel and a Masque performed by large-scale puppets, for example. And perhaps it even extended thematically to an emphasis on the ending where, while still filled with ambiguity, the predominant mode is one of forgiveness.

It was very much *The Tempest* I wanted to make, but one does not create in a vacuum. I don't believe any approach is really devoid of context.

Following an Elizabethan model

Ralph Alan Cohen: We didn't start with these great principles of 'original practices' – we only cared about a thrust stage, a visible audience, and two hours traffic. What happened is that we began to discover that every time we tried an original practice approach people said, 'Oh wow! That's actually better than what you were doing'. So what we have actually done is get more serious about it. We started to trust the stage directions. For example, kings enter first in Shakespeare's stage directions, and because they're frequently talking when they enter, then they are talking with their backs to the people who follow. At first that seemed wrong, then we realized it showed status.

We are interested in Shakespeare's staging, not because we are interested in museum theatre, but for the exact opposite reason. We are interested in trying to get the most modern, the most avant-garde, the most 'edge' theatre we can get out of those processes.

So, for example, when you see the intervals and there's music in the intervals and you see the kind of interaction between audiences – all of which happened at the first Blackfriars – think about environmental theatre. Think about the way those actors in those shows have to perform. Jim [Warren] and I had been aware from the very start that we cannot be confused with Renaissance Fair sort of things or any of these re-enactments. But what it is, is trying to find the dynamic that produces great stuff. How do we find that dynamic? The best way, I think, is to ask what the playwright might have had in his head – the space, the audience – when he crafted the play, then let's produce it in a way that makes it fresh and new by using its first dynamics.

Tina Packer: I first did Shakespeare as a player. Shortly after leaving RADA, I went to the RSC where I played the Princess of France in John Barton's *Loves Labours Lost,* Luciana in Clifford William's *The Comedy of Errors,* Phrynia in John Schlesinger's *Timon of Athens* and understudied Ophelia in Peter Hall's *Hamlet.* Being at the RSC was of course astounding – and John Barton's approach to the structure of the verse was a revelation to me. We had learnt nothing of it in drama school. But I found, as time went on, I wanted to get even more deeply into the language, feel things in my body, have less intellectual discussion, and more embodied experience. This was the start of a long journey for me to try and define what I thought was important for actors, in the playing of Shakespeare. I became a director so that I had the power to follow through on my intuitions, that I could spend time experimenting with voice, clown, fight, dance, and of course structure and the art of rhetoric. And as a director, I followed the Elizabethan model of staging plays, developing an open actor/audience relationship, combining music with the production in a symbiotic way, ran the scenes straight on from each other, very little scenery, made the fights as breath-stopping as possible, allowed the clowns to improvise and so on. I want actors who can do all these things.

Jim Warren: What were Shakespeare's staging conditions? From the beginning, our mission has been recreating those stage conditions. It not only produces great entertainment, but there are things written into these plays that get covered up if you play in a different kind of arena. I think that by returning to the staging conditions of 400 years ago, we actually unlock some power in these plays that were written for that, that you cannot do with great sets, great lights, and great kinds of technical things. You can create great theatre. I don't mean to say that if you use sets and lights, you're not going to have a good show. But it's different.

I think there's something special about leaving the lights on, not having a big set other than your theatre scaenae frons, and keeping the action moving. When you don't have set changes and light changes, then you're able to start one scene at the end of another scene. They're able to go seamlessly. And to me, that represents a huge departure from the way a lot of us approach theatre today.

Concepts

Kathleen Conlin: I like to be able to think through visually, in a very loose way, what could be a powerful visual statement before I even start talking to a designer. I just begin to improvise and free-associate around images generated by the text. Then at a certain point, I sit down and actually write conceptual notes about what I'm interested in pursuing in that production without dictating what it's going to look like, but outlining the direction of the world of the play in this production. From that point, it becomes the collaborative process with the designers.

Stephanie Shine: I start to think about where the play feels like it lives. Every once in a while something will happen. 'This play should live here'. I may put it there. Lots of times I just want a flavour of a period. I don't have to research this, like at Colorado or Utah, a sort of cartooned fully envisioned idea of what our thoughts about New Orleans might be like in 1810. Not realistic. This is infinitely more fun than trying to be doing something historically accurate. Who cares about that? It's much more fun to go, 'Hmmm, I bet it might look like this'. I don't need to research Shakespeare. So I just think about the flavour of it. 'This feels like it is post World War II somehow. What would that say if I put it there?'

Lisa Peterson: In the past, I have always tried to define an American world for a Shakespeare play. Usually, I try to find an American context. And I don't mean just picking a period, because sometimes I think that can be limiting, but thinking about the play's issues through a contemporary, American lens. Because that's the world I'm living in as I work on that play, and I think it's essential that we use Shakespeare's plays to reflect on our lives now.

When we did *King Lear*, I had had this idea: I was interested in the economics of the play. Sometimes a concept grows out of a particular speech. For me the key speech in [*King*] *Lear* is his prayer in the rain to 'The unhoused poor'. You know, 'I have taken too little care of this'. As far as I'm concerned, that is the turning point in the play. That meant that I wanted the play to take place in a world that an American audience could look at and see the economic parable. So I chose to set it in the dying moments of the robber barons, imagining Lear as a kind of Carnegie, surrounded by an abandoned steel mill. It was a world in which you also have bread lines. When I first met with Jeffrey DeMunn, who played Lear, he was sceptical. He thought, 'Oh, why can't we just wear simple robes?' And I said, 'Well, all I can say is that this is what stuck in my head. This is the door that I found when I was reading the play'. That's what I was thinking originally. It turned out to be much more abstract than that.

Ultimately, I don't believe the trick of the setting provides the primary experience of the play. Yes, you have to decide what people are going to wear. But when all is said and done, it doesn't really matter what they're wearing. That's just a way in. It doesn't really matter whether the characters are wearing doublets or wearing suits. What matters is what those characters say and feel and *do*. But still it's our job as directors to discover that single idea that is going to help us create something that feels original. I don't think about that when working on a new play because it *is* original. I don't have to work hard to interpret it for myself. With Shakespeare, I do feel a responsibility to myself to find a way into it that's uniquely mine.

Challenges and limitations of concept

Oskar Eustis: I hate productions that think having a concept is the same thing as picking a time, period and a place that you set Shakespeare in, and that somehow that's a concept. There are different names for it. I sometimes think of them as costume conceptualizations. Well, it's not a concept unless it actually reveals something about the story or reveals something about the play. It's just a period with costumes. It's boring.

Ralph Alan Cohen: We get people so smart that nobody does idiotic things. What happens is they make choices and I go, 'Wow!' It's just not concept theatre. It can't be, because the director's concept is going to be at risk the minute an actor makes a choice. If I've got a concept going and she's got a concept going, then it's going to be at risk. It's about their arc and my consultation. It's about making sure that these things work nicely together.

Stephanie Shine: I am just amazed when I hear that people are so sure about what a play is *about*. I never know. I couldn't begin to explain to you about a play or a particular production until I am in the rehearsal with the actors I've cast and I see what we all bring. Then the play will unfold itself to you. That is why we do these plays over and over again, because they are always different in different heads with different embodiments. There are some truths that will always be existent. If something new arises specifically, I will speak to it with a particular audience with particular actors in a particular setting. There's nothing else like it. But you don't know until you are in the room. And sometimes you don't ever know, ever, but it is what it is. I love that, because I think, 'What it is, *that's* the play'. But you've got to search for it.

Daniel Sullivan: I always get nervous when someone asks me what my 'concept' is. It always sounds like I'm being asked to come up with a Hollywood pitch or like I'm being asked to sum up a complicated idea in two sentences. I find that reductive. It reduces the play to the confines of some neat idea that can be summarized attractively. I find that extremely limiting. Certainly you have to create a visual world for the play but too many 'concepts' cram the plays into unyielding single-minded ideas that don't allow the rich behavioural life of the plays to emerge.

I read the plays many times trying to understand who the characters are before I ever begin to imagine a world for them. I'm a slow reader to begin with, so you can imagine how long that takes. Weeks, really, before a suitable world begins to emerge.

Examples of context approaches

Context: Societal, Cultural, Political

Bill Rauch: I'm often, often, often interested in cultural context in terms of a production. I feel like societal context, cultural context is hugely significant in our lives. Certainly in interpreting a Shakespeare play.

In 2011, I directed *Measure for Measure*, Shakespeare's social justice play. We set it in a 1970s American inner city, and broke major ground for our company in our approach. It was a break-through work for me personally as well.

All of OSF's Shakespeare [productions have] been cast multi-racially for years, but usually 'colour blind' – race and ethnicity were not an explicit factor in storytelling. This approach of course has the advantage of creating an ideal world in which race and ethnicity don't matter, but it can have the unfortunate effect of making the play feel less like the world we live in, in which race and ethnicity too often do matter a great deal. At its most extreme negative expression, as the great playwright August Wilson once famously complained, actors of colour in such Shakespeare productions can be seen to essentially be playing white people.

In our *Measure for Measure*, each actor brought as a given starting point for the character his or her own ethnic/racial identity. Isabella was a young Latina novice from a low-income neighbourhood, and her brother on death row was of course also Latino. The Duke was an older white politician, Escalus an older African American woman, and the Duke's appointed deputy Angelo was a rising political star from the same Latino neighbourhood as Isabella and Claudio but aggressively out of touch with his barrio roots. Marianne was a white woman residing in a mental hospital after her multiple suicide attempts over her treatment by Angelo. Mistress Overdone was a male-to-female transgender character played by a tall Asian-American actor (the transgender choice was the only one that made sense to us in a modern setting in terms of explaining why Claudio and Mistress Overdone are in the same prison since contemporary prisons are gender-segregated; Mistress Overdone's being stripped by guards of her female clothing to reveal a male body underneath was extraordinarily painful).

The production's world was aggressively multi-racial but the heartbeat of the production was Latino. A trio of female mariachi musicians transformed themselves from custodial workers in City Hall to a strip mall sex club house band to court officials in jail, always playing instruments and singing in Spanish throughout. Claudio's pregnant girlfriend Julieta was a monolingual Spanish speaker, accompanied by a social worker that translated between her and the monolingual English-speaking characters, especially the Duke.

The set was a simple multi-purpose room with a linoleum floor, fluorescent lighting, and a large conference table. A huge venetian-blind-covered window of real glass on the back wall revealed projections behind that immediately transformed from neighbourhood exteriors to interior hallways, effortlessly shifting the room from scene to scene. Of course social justice (and especially its absence) play out in such dingy and non-descript rooms throughout our country.

Context: Language, imagery and text

Barbara Gaines: An example of developing an approach happened this season (2014) with my third production of *King Lear* within twenty-one years. The first two were in the context of an ancient place and time. Then five years ago a very dear friend of mine developed dementia – and I watched one of the most brilliant minds I'd ever known disintegrate. He would repeat himself again and again within a half hour and that behaviour reminded me of Lear in the beginning of the play. He repeats himself: 'Will someone tell me who I am' and similar questions regarding his identity. In the first two productions, those questions were acted rhetorically but after experiencing my friend's devolution, I realized that Lear may well have been in the early stages of dementia – so those questions could be delivered as real questions: 'Will someone tell me who I am?' I'd never recognized the possibility of those questions NOT being rhetorical, because I hadn't experienced the disease personally. Anyone who retires, let alone gives up a kingdom and expects to keep his or her power over others, could not possibly be in their right mind. So the premise of dementia began with a personal tragedy.

Then, simultaneously, I heard a little known Sinatra song on the radio. It began 'Where do you go / When it starts to rain? / Where do you sleep / When the night time comes?' In my imagination, these lyrics were Lear on the heath and the context of the show grew into a contemporary one, with a tyrant who happens to love Sinatra's music and was in early stage dementia.

So developing an approach to Shakespeare or other projects comes from inspiration from every moment I live. I never know where or when an idea will be born.

Context: Historical placement

Barbara Gaines: It was my friend, Ian McDiarmid who suggested *Timon of Athens*. We'd wanted to work together for a number of years and when he suggested the show I was thrilled because I knew he'd be singular in that role. It was also the perfect time in history to present *Timon* since it was only four years after the 2008 financial crash.

The theme of the play revolves around the issue of money – having it and losing it – versus friendship, both true and false. Are we our money? Who are our real friends and how do we know? What happened to Timon that made him feel that he had to buy love and friendship? Was he merely unwise, guileless or more manipulative in his need to give? Certainly his own feeling of self worth was severely reduced or else he wouldn't have snapped. But there is little evidence in the text that answers these questions.

Both of us were committed to doing it in a contemporary world, considering the theme of wealth, within and without. Great wealth attracts lots of people, but true friendship in anyone's life is rare. Timon's successful life seemed believable in Chicago, which has a very active national and international financial market. Professionally he lived within the world of hedge funds, where someone can gain and lose hundreds of millions within seconds. And Ian suggested that he keep his

British accent that would emphasize him being an outsider within a rarefied world.

A year before the show began rehearsals I interviewed eight major financial leaders and learned a tremendous amount about the personal side of finance. Since I have no understanding of economics, I concentrated on the emotional side of their lives and their friends' lives. We discussed the agony of the crash, the horrific results of greed, including the complete lack of conscience that led to the crippling of our economy. Those discussions were passionate, instructive to the process, and helped give me a context that went directly into the show.

It was fairly simple to figure out how to physically transplant the production into today's world. The first scene took place in Timon's marble office building. There were eight large screen TV monitors with the financial numbers of the day changing – making and breaking lives, within a world of great skill, luck and tremendous anxiety. The show stayed in that city and wealthy environment until Timon's dramatic exit from his home, when he went to a rocky, mist filled waterfront, where the sound of the waves was deafening. The sound of the surf's unrelenting ebb and flow seemed to heighten Timon's bitter, confused and lonely life. The last part of the show's landscape was similar to Brecht with all its empty hopelessness.

One of the key moments in the play is the first banquet scene in Timon's home. Since Ian is a man of gentility and class, we needed to find the right gesture for the first scene, when Timon has 'Amazonian' women come to entertain his guests. Since he loves ballet, I decided that his Timon would hire ballet dancers. The women and men came into the room dressed as swans from Tchaikovsky's *Swan Lake*. They were classy, beautiful and full of grace and the choreography was classical until, at a certain point in the music, a bass saxophone took over the melody. Suddenly the girls were stripped of their long organza gowns and began a more erotic blues version of the dance on top of a long table.

Regarding the musical landscape, the blues with all its wit and pain made a dramatic impact within the show. As the plot heats up, we brought in lyrics about our homes being full of rats looking for cheese and taking over your life. Through the emotion of the blues you felt that the rats were abandoning Timon's sinking ship. This theme ran through the show – and all of our financiers and traders were in the aisles of the theatre as the show ended, smoking cigars and looking at the faces of the audiences, as if to say 'We're coming to your house next'.

Ian and I edited the text, getting rid of all extraneous characters, scenes and then condensing a few together. He was a phenomenal partner in that adaptation and I learned much from his brilliant instincts for theatricality and character. With plays like *Timon* and *Henry VIII*, a director should feel free to condense characters and scenes to clarify the plot for the good of the whole.

Context: Location, setting, environment

Stephen Burdman: I was taken with Norman Mailer's *The Naked and the Dead*. The first section of his book he talks about the voyage on the boat and what it's like to be a sailor going into Southeast Asia for World War II, and how frightened these young men were about going to war. Today crossing the English Channel you can drive, you can take the train. There are a lot of ways to go. But it was a treacherous journey at that time. It wasn't a long journey then. I think it took a day and half or two days to sail it, but the conditions of the waters are still terrible. It's a bumpy ride. So I was very interested in that and then I noticed of course, right across – a ten minute sail away is Governor's Island from our Battery Park venue. So I said, 'Okay, we have to go. So we're going to start with England in Battery Park. Then we're going to load everybody on a boat and go to France. So we loaded 500 people each night on a boat. And we sailed across New York Harbor, which became The English Channel, to France.

They disembarked. The soldiers got down and prayed, as they would before battle. And then we marched onto Harfleur. En masse. So that's 500 people plus fifty cast and crew marching on Harfleur. Somehow early on we started doing a rhythmic march. And the audience picked up on it. We were the only people on Governor's Island. So you heard marching. Nightly. And then the people who played the French had already been on the island for two hours (because of the way the ferries worked). So we marched up to Harfleur and then the French came out. And we had our first huge battle at Harfleur. All of a sudden it was, 'Oh my God, where did these people come from?'

We did, as we always do, an adaptation. In that case specifically, *Henry V*. There are a lot of characters that you don't know who they are. One of my concerns has always been, 'How much history do you need to know for a history play?' And *Henry V* is unfortunately one of those plays you have to know a lot of English history. So I adapted it in such a way that there were two camps. Henry had the Archbishop and two others – I cobbled together roles. Henry had three people around him. The King of France had the Dauphin and two other nobles with him. They became the centre. And then we actually cast a group of about twelve young guys. We called them 'actor-combatants' and they alternated between English and French.

Because of the audience's movement, with panoramic theatre that allows us to change between stage-left and stage-right. The audience never knows where the cast is coming from. In traditional theatre, France is stage right. England is stage left. And it's always consistent. We totally mixed it up. The audience is always on edge and never knows. That gives a huge freshness to it.

And then, of course, you get to walk into Fort Jay. And it is a period castle. Our audience is game. They're in shorts and T-shirts and sneakers and they just plop on the ground and they don't care. We actually had a terrible storm blow in during one production one night, one performance. I knew because I had Doppler radar on my iPhone that it was going to come in really strong and then literally thirty minutes later be gone and then it would be 100 degrees again. So I didn't stop it. We all got on the boat, which happened to be covered. We were soaked to the bone. Halfway to Governor's Island, the rain stopped and this magnificent rainbow appeared. Off the back of the boat, the audience was saying, 'Oh my – you know, it's a gift from God'.

In the same way, we came back from Governor's Island each night, it was dark already, and we got to see the beautiful sky lit Manhattan. I would joke with the audience. 'Oh, I had 'em turn on the lights for you'. And they all loved that. They were going to places they had never been.

4

Research and Analysis

One of the great challenges of repertoire is that it is impossible to be original. It's a misquote, but Liviu Ciulei said something along the lines of, 'If you think you're doing something original in the theatre, then it just proves you haven't done enough research'. I comfort myself and challenge myself with that over and over gain. You want to be original and you want to be authentic, but you must remember that other talented individuals of all kinds have encountered this exact same series of challenges and come up with solutions that are often going to be similar.

ETHAN MCSWEENY

Most directors use research to prepare for production. Over the past decade extensive resources have appeared 'at our fingertips' with computers and the Internet – a development Frank informs us, that has changed the entire research process. Sometimes discovering a play's production history can intimidate a director who relishes a direct connection with the text that is not influenced by a third party. Zimmerman admits this was a concern when she first started directing.

FIGURE 9 Hamlet, *directed by Darko Tresnjak, Hartford Stage, Floyd King as First Gravedigger. Photograph by T. Charles Erickson.*

To begin their study, Woronicz and McSweeny read introductions to the plays in such editions as the Arden Shakespeare and the New Cambridge Shakespeare. Woronicz, like Douglas, does not do extensive production research. He leans on his designers to do the majority of it. McSweeny confides that in avoiding production research on *The Merchant of Venice*, he 'stumbled' upon facts that 'supported my initial inspiration'. His purpose was not finding a unique approach – which he admits is near impossible with Shakespeare – but rather to discover 'something that breathed life into the play'. Conversely, Rauch does extensive research in three areas: academic and historical investigations, production history, and discussions with actors playing the major roles. Monte's research leads her to compile 'copious notes' to be shared with the actors 'lists of things I think they should look at'. Once in rehearsal she shares pertinent visual and scholarly books with her actors. She also seeks parallels in the work of painters and other visual resources, as does Zimmerman.

Before he arrives at an approach, D. Sullivan must first analyze and research the play. It is less about examining 'various interpretations' and more about discovering the play's original context. He warns that due to the enormous amount of material available, one can 'become lost in a kind of academic swamp'. On the other hand, Kulick devours 'thousands of pages of Shakespeare scholarship' as part of his preparation. Mullins, like D. Sullivan, wants to know 'why it was important for Shakespeare to write that play'. Shine avoids visual stimuli, preferring to utter Shakespeare's words out loud. She seeks aural sources to analyze. Ivers draws upon his acting experience to 'figure out what thematically speaks' to him. Tresnjak and D. Sullivan talk to directors and theatres that have staged the play for advice on what to prepare and what are problems. They both commit the play to memory as part of their preparation.

Most of the directors disclose that their analysis starts with reading the play repeatedly. Some speak the text as they read. When Kahn reads aloud, it forces him to 'internally connect' with each line. Douglas relishes 'the vibrations of the text moving through my body'. Lamos reads the text as if it were a novel. Buckley interrogates the script as if it were a new play. Woronicz, Lamos, Douglas and Ivers explore the text as an actor might. Not surprisingly, all four have actor backgrounds.

Directors exploit other analytical methods. Analyzing Shakespeare's word choices – asking why Shakespeare used a certain word in a specific placement – is important for Kahn and Frank. Buckley must enter 'the text into my computer, the First Folio, spelling, punctuation, all of it' which she finds is an essential 'cellular, physical exercise'. Thompson assays what 'the meaning of the story will be for myself and the audiences'. Conlin pursues 'thematic and character progression'. Sevy looks for current resonances and 'What's happening now?' Frank focuses on 'What happens next?' and

'Why did [Shakespeare] pick those words?' McSweeny asks, 'Why does this character do that? Why do the next thing?' He records ideas for activity, actions and business that come to him. He also divides the play into French scenes, formulating a title for each one that reveals the play's spine and structure. Kulick examines 'word patterns and image clusters'. Ivers discovers 'the thematic journey that speaks to me in the play'. Serban sees directors as sculptors trying to reveal 'the human element ... to realize that all characters in Shakespeare hide and reveal a deep and complex humanity'.

Research

David Frank: You isolate yourself somewhere where no one can get you. These days, actually, all you really need is your laptop. It used to be you'd have to have Schmidt [*Shakespeare Lexicon*] and Onions [*A Shakespeare Glossary*] and twenty-six volumes of the *Oxford English Dictionary*, along with access to a good library for the special demands of each production. Now you just need the *OED*, Google and several of the great editions that are readily available; New Cambridge, Oxford and Arden come to mind. You've got those three, the *OED*, Google and you're pretty much set.

Mary Zimmerman: When I started doing Shakespeare I was quite intimidated by the production history. I avoided any research into that at all. I wasn't confident enough. I thought it would either influence me or I'd begin to think my ideas were stupid or I was going to discover it's all been done this way many times before. I didn't want to know that. I wanted my primary relationship to be with the actual text in an unfiltered way. In my work in adaptation of old texts, some classic, some obscure, I've often been the only adaptor I'm aware of, and my practice has always been to lean into the most intimate possible relationship with the source text without regard to secondary criticism. I'm less that way now. For *Pericles* I was very curious how other people had done it. I looked up pictures on the Internet and so forth.

Henry Woronicz: When I start working on a play, it's mainly about reading it. I will do some background work if I am not familiar with past productions. Or if I am not as familiar with the play, I will get some background work in terms of how this play has been interpreted. I've always liked reading the Arden introductions. Most of the introductions in many of the plays will give you some jumping off points, whether it's the Pelican or the Penguin. I don't do an exorbitant amount of outside research. Depending on what the period might be, etc. I totally rely on the designers in that regard.

Ethan McSweeny: I didn't want to do too much research because I was afraid of it getting in my head while I was trying to create the show. But then as I created the show, I kept stumbling across more evidence that supported my initial inspiration. Then I thought I better know a little more about the production history of it. Within the introductions of most editions of the Shakespeare plays now, there will be a limited production history, often sort of Anglo focused, but I'm glad to say increasingly, as New Cambridge and Arden learn that they have a big market in America, increasingly including American work. It gives you a background on it. Then when you do *The Merchant of Venice,* you quickly realize that probably every conceivable period has been tried, (except, I believe, the one I did, set in the 1920s on the Lower East Side of New York). The obligation was not to find a new direction; the obligation was to find something that breathed life into the play in a way that I wanted to tell the story. In the case of *Merchant*, I was interested in a time when multiple immigrant groups, Italians and Jews, were struggling with one another for enfranchisement in a world dominated by the old money represented by Portia and the estate at Belmont.

Bill Rauch: I'm very interested in essays that have been written about the play, and academic research, and historical research about the context. I'm equally interested in production history. I *love* watching other people's productions of the play I'm directing! I know some people, their imaginations shut down, but it always inspires me. I can't get enough of it. I want to see the past productions that have happened here at OSF in archival videos. If there are BBC recordings of British productions, whatever is out there, I'm hungry for it because it just inspires me! I may want to steal a choice. A choice may piss me off or leave me cold. But all of it fires up my imagination about what it is I care about most in the play.

I also love to engage in dialogue with the people who have been cast. Dan Donohue who played Hamlet was in many ways co-author of the production. We conferred together on all casting and design choices. We spent over sixty hours working through every line of the multiple folio and quarto versions in order to handcraft the text for our production. That attention to detail, right down to whether we wanted to use the comma, dash or exclamation point that were presented as options by various versions, led to a depth of engagement that served us well by the time we reached the rehearsal room.

Bonnie Monte: I won't go into rehearsal without certain things done. I have two books that I keep for every show that I do. There's my little notebook, and then there is the script with all the blocking. In my little notebook I write copious notes about what I want to say to my actors on the very first day at the very first minute – how I want them to start pursuing this particular project from the very beginning. I will go in with a list of things I think they should look at, things that I am really inspired by throughout the pre-production process. I will put very carefully point A, point B, point C about a really strongly supported choice that I have made about a particular thing – whether it's a character choice or a conceptual choice. So that notebook gets pretty filled up prior to even going into rehearsal.

I will bring in scores of books so that they have a quick easy reference for things. Not just books of scholarship but also painting. Most often other visual artists will inspire particular ideas for me. There were Serov portraits and paintings all over the room during *The Cherry Orchard* because that was a frame of reference. It was the people that were peopling our world around us.

Daniel Sullivan: For me research and analysis come before I would attempt an 'approach'. Research includes close reading of the best critical thinking on the play that's been written over the past 400 years. And there's a never-ending supply. So you have to edit that to minds that you have come to trust. If you don't, you will become lost in a kind of academic swamp.

I read as much as I possibly can, not about various interpretations of the play, but about what was going on in Shakespeare's own world at the time he wrote it. Even Shakespeare's historical plays are peppered with the details of Elizabethan life and very often you can't understand a passage unless you know those details. I find that after a month or so of study, I've basically memorized the play.

Brian Kulick: Before I do a Shakespeare production nowadays, I try to read every critical gloss I can on the piece. I'll read thousands of pages of Shakespeare scholarship. Invariably every scholar will be right about one thing, but they won't necessary be right about the totality. Sometimes what you realize is that a small handful of scholars, together, can help guide you. It's too big of a universe, a dramatic universe, for a singular person to understand. It's very rare that I read a piece of commentary and say to myself, 'Nailed it'. That's the beauty of Shakespeare. It's what makes those plays so incredibly rich; they are open to so many potential interpretations.

Paul Mullins: By the time I know it's a play about Richard II, I will read about Richard II. I don't know everything in the world about Richard II at this time. You always find there comes a point where Shakespeare creates his own Richard II. It only has so much to do with the man who ruled England. I want to know about this aspect because I want to know why it was important to Shakespeare to write that play. What about that man's life interested him? The people of England, why was he important to them and what was it about it? And I want to read what other people think about him. I want to get as much information in me, so that when we sit down with the designers, or when we sit back down at the table, we can talk about 'why'. But we also can say, 'Isn't that great? Let's throw that behind us and look at what it says'.

David Ivers: I, fortunately have benefited by having been an actor for so long now and been in so many of his plays, that I often find that if it's a Shakespeare play I've done before, that I have some entrance to it based on hearing it as an actor. And that's valuable because it's not just that you're inside of a storyline as a character, but performance – especially where I've been working as an actor over four or five months of a performance hearing the play that many times for eight times a week or whatever – is really valuable in terms of starting to figure out what thematically speaks to you. And I think that's the next step for me. So reading.

Darko Tresnjak: Something strange about directing today is that it moves, far too often, from picking a play to moving to a concept, leaping over the text. When I know I'm going to direct a Shakespeare play, especially a Shakespeare play, I try to grab as many editions as I can. I do as much research, not just into the text, but also into the production history of the plays. So I download anything I can find about every production done. I talk to all of the major theatres in the country that have done it in the past few years. Then each night I memorize a different part of the play. In general, if I'm not completely off-book by the time I begin, I'm pretty close. I like to have it all in my head.

As a habit, I want to be over-prepared. I like to do it well ahead of time. Then I don't do it for a couple of months before I begin. What sticks in my brain has resonance. What doesn't stick, while probably interesting, just probably will not have a bearing on the production. I find that in directing a Shakespeare play, I'm not writing a thesis paper. You do the research. I always tell my students, as you do your research, you figure out what sticks, what is visceral, what is important. Then you must ignore a whole bunch of things with confidence. Otherwise there's no taking everything in. But sometimes there's a kernel, a jewel that illuminates a certain text, sometimes the whole play. That's most helpful.

Analysis

Timothy Douglas: I read the script aloud to myself many times. I thrive on, and am inspired by the vibrations of the text moving though my body. I do look up the truly obtuse and specifically Elizabethan and historical references I don't readily understand, but just enough to frame my references.

Michael Kahn: I read the play for the story, even if I know it, just to get the story to hit me that first time. Then I read it again. Eventually I start going scene-by-scene to make sure that I understand. I start reading it out loud to myself, which is always very revealing. All of a sudden I have to internally connect with a line in some way. When I don't, I go back and think, 'Wait a minute. I don't know what the heck they're talking about here'. Then when I figure it out, I begin to think I may be getting in contact with Shakespeare. I don't think he ever put a word in lazily. If he did, I don't know about it. He was a great poet and therefore, whether he wrote hastily or not, I don't think he just tried to fill up pentameter. He actually made choices as to why those things are there, why those particular adjectives are there, why those particular words are there. I don't try to figure out how it must be said. I just try to figure out why they're there.

Mark Lamos: I spend a few months working on and thinking about the text. I don't listen to recordings or watch films of the play, if in fact they exist. I need to get as close as possible to what Shakespeare wrote. Just the words. I want a personal experience – just the writer and me, alone together. As one would read a novel. I look for various themes as they are delineated or reappear, repeated words. I speak most of the play aloud to myself, all the roles. This is an enormous help, because I can go back to thinking like an actor instead of a director.

Kate Buckley: When starting work on a text, I approach it as a new script, as if Shakespeare had just dropped it off on my desk. That's true of any play. The very first part of my process is to type the text into my computer, the First Folio, spelling, punctuation, all of it. I need the cellular, physical exercise of getting the text into my body. I will sit for days, and as I type it, I say each part aloud. That happens as soon as I am hired, which could be between six months to a year in advance of the first rehearsal. Then I'll go back into the text, taking a closer look at punctuation and spelling, changing the 'f's' to 's's' to make it readable for the design team. I can teach it to actors, but design teams do not like deciphering a text very much: 'So what is *this*?' [*laughs*] Then I re-work it for basic grammar, punctuation and cuts if the theatre has requested a specific running time.

Next I read it and read it and read it and read it and read it. This helps me to formulate ideas for production – emotional, conceptual and visual. Once the design is set and casting complete, I leave the script alone until the first day of rehearsal. I want all of it to be fresh – working from an uncluttered space in my brain. I hope to respond to actor ideas without demanding a certain kind of performance from them. I wish to stay open to their ideas.

Kent Thompson: I start on the text a good six months before. I try to read it as much as I can. I try to look at lots of different editions. I look at the First Folio. I think I am driven by two ideas. One is that I keep trying to figure out what the meaning of this story was (as if I could ever figure it out) to this playwright Shakespeare. Then I try and figure out what the meaning of the story will be for myself, and the audiences that I will bring to it. Hopefully there's some congruence in there. The challenge for me is less about, 'Okay, let's pick the period that we run the play through', which I think I did for a while, than it is 'What is the experience that I want this audience to have in this world of this play?'

Kathleen Conlin: I really like to do my own close text analysis. I do it on the basis of, not just cognitive things in terms of what words mean and what sentences mean, but I also like to do the analysis on the basis of thematic and character progression.

Bruce Sevy: I go into the play and see how it is resonating for me on whatever level, but also an investigation of the text itself. I try to go into it with as few preconceptions as I can. 'What are they saying?' 'What's happening now?' I get very detailed. I read the play a lot. I read a lot of information about it. There is also that subjective part of where the play resonates for me. Or how I feel like it resonates now – things that leap out at me in the play. And that they're always, particularly in Shakespeare's case, relevant.

David Frank: My most basic responsibility for any production came clear to me when reading E. M. Forster's *Aspects of the Novel*: he suggested that the highest common factor (and it's not very high) of all effective novels, is the ability to make the reader ask, 'What happens next?' And if it is important for the novel, it is even more essential for the production of a play.

For me, one of the most important quests is trying to identify the special character of a given playwright's voice. What's special for Shakespeare is that you have to spend time with almost every word – and those words will incite relationships, story, character and tension. You have to sniff out every detail and ask yourself, 'Why did he pick those words? What did those words mean to him? What was he after?'

Sometimes you conclude, in retrospect, that your starting point was wrong-headed. Or you alter course in mid-rehearsal and risk ending up with an indecisive muddle. But if you honour those words in a way that communicates to an audience and tells a good story, you won't go too far wrong.

Ethan McSweeny: My work is moment to moment. I start with a question. I say, 'Well, why does this character do that? Why do the next thing? And why do they do the next thing?' As we answer those questions, we accumulate story. I don't have a formal system of beating the lines out. I think that work happens in repeated readings, parking the script in the back of your head and allowing it to gestate there.

If I have a thought, I write it down ... about an action or an activity or something that could be going on. I like my Shakespeare to have activity and actions and business. I don't love it when people just come out, stand there and talk. I feel like Shakespeare actually wrote things for actors to be doing. Sometimes it's almost like theatre archaeology. You can actually uncover a bit of business that really illuminates the story. I like to look for those. To find those, you have to put yourself in settings where there is something to do. Then you can decide how does that person, that character, fold the laundry in this scene. Does that perhaps express an inner anger they might be covering? Is it with excitement about what is going to happen on those sheets later? No matter what the action, there are a million ways it can inform the line and I do like to look for things *to do* so that it's not just 'words, words, words'.

One thing I always do is fairly detailed scene breakdowns of French scenes, of entrances and exits, giving every one a title. I find if I don't do this for myself, I haven't taught myself the spine of the play as I see it. As I do my breakdown, I am forced to confront the play's structure and what it means. What titles I'm giving the scenes, usually tell me something about what I think it's about – not that it isn't going to change, but it tells me something about my initial impulse.

Brian Kulick: I'm fascinated by word patterns and image clusters in Shakespeare. Take, for example, the word 'bear' in *The Winter's Tale*. The first time we encounter this word it is in a line of Leonte's, he tells a servant to, 'Bear the boy away'. 'Bear', in this sense, is about a weight that must be literally carried, a bit later there is the famous stage direction, 'Exit pursued by a Bear', now our 'bear' moves from verb to noun and becomes a ferocious animal. Then 'bear' is used in terms of the guilt Leontes feels, it is an existential weight and finally, miraculously, there is 'bear' in the generative sense, as in bearing fruit or a child, of fecundity. You can track the tonal shifts of this play by how the word 'bear' is used.

The same is true of image clusters in a play like *The Tempest* where we follow the image pattern of men trapped by wood. First there are those sailors in a tempest tossed wooden boat which has become their coffin, then there is the image of Caliban who was imprisoned in a tree, than there is Ferdinand's labours (carrying log after log) and finally, in the end, there is Prospero who reminds us that he is encased in this 'wooden O' of a theatre, The Globe itself, and asks us for his release by the clapping of our hands. His last words are 'set me free'. Isn't this, ultimately, what the entire play is about? The breadcrumbs of meaning can be found in this image cluster of men trying to escape their wooden/casket like imprisonment.

David Ivers: I really try to find the thematic journey that speaks to me in the play. For instance, I directed *Romeo and Juliet* right after my first son was born, and I could not get away from that story being told from the parents' perspective in a way that I hadn't necessarily thought of before. What if it's the parents' story? What if it's the story of this is our family that fucked this up? And we are the ones who have to live with it everyday after the final tomb scene? And that really started to inform the play in a different way I hadn't thought of. I very rarely go at a play saying, 'Oh, I want to do it this way'. It's usually in response to the relationships that are revealing themselves in the play as I continue studying.

Andrei Serban: The question for me is: 'How can one come back to the rigours of the text, and then illuminate what's in the text and make the performance richer?' I'm always confronted with Shakespeare material the way a sculptor is in front of stone, before starting to shape it. A play is like very hard granite. That's the resistance, the granite. It's difficult to mould, to shape, to reveal the stuff that's in the granite pigment. It's an attack against the stone and at the same time it's a revelation. At times I think directing is like sculpting. The human element must always be the reason of sculpting: to realize that all characters in Shakespeare hide and reveal a deep and complex humanity. How to be human, not only 30 per cent, but 100 per cent? This is the ultimate purpose of doing theatre at that level.

5

Preparing the Production Text

With many of Shakespeare's plays, it is necessary to select and edit the text. In the case of a play like Hamlet *it will define the production. In most of my productions I have shaped the play by adding characters, blending scenes together, reversing their order or as in* Measure For Measure *reminding the audience of Isabella and the Dukes' connection by using an earlier segment of the play in the final act. Shakespeare's plays were constructed by a company of artists, all of who contributed in some way to the writing. Much of that information has been lost to time so it is often up to the director to imagine a re-construction of that process.*

DAVID ESBJORNSON

Soon after being engaged to direct a production, a major question the director must answer is: What text are we going to use? There are several sources one can consult. They can contain considerable differences. For instance, there are

FIGURE 10 Henry V, *directed by Bonnie J. Monte, The Shakespeare Theatre of New Jersey, 2007. Jack Wetherall as the Chorus. Photograph by Gerry Goodstein.*

three original source *Hamlet* texts: two quarto versions – a supposedly bad one and a good one, as well as the 1623 folio rendition.[1] Lamos and Eustis defend the efficacy of choices they made in their respective productions concerning the 'How all occasions do inform against me' soliloquy which appears in a quarto version, but not the folio. Lamos chose to cut it while Eustis left it in. Both recognize that the *Hamlet* text should be abridged for production. This leads us to a second question: What material gets eliminated?

Editors examine source texts and other evidence to compile a version that comes closest to what they believe Shakespeare's original intentions were. Like archaeologists digging through layers of earth to uncover the past, current wordsmiths look beneath the surface of the source material in order to get past those who stand between the modern reader and Shakespeare:

actors who might have influenced or changed the text, theatre managers who may have cut it because the performance was running long, quarto/folio editors and compositors who may have misinterpreted the sources or changed the words and punctuation, and of course the censors who eliminated objectionable material. Thus there are many possible hands that could have altered the text before publication. Unless the director chooses to follow one edition completely, they, too, must act like editors and archaeologists in shaping their production text.

Many directors manipulate the punctuation. MacLean uses the folio as his primary source. His decisions are based on 'how a moment might play' and the 'intentions that will [best] enliven a scene'. He also looks at how a choice might support 'the music and imagery' of the piece. McSweeny is drawn to the New Cambridge edition because of its punctuation choices. He believes 'punctuation equals thought' and therefore the play's text constitutes a critical decision in determining the character's cogitation. Appel discusses how she held meetings with the dramaturg and voice and text staff. Over the course of a week, they would argue the pluses and minuses of each punctuation and word choice.

Tresnjak reminds us that Shakespeare's texts need to be moulded and cut. Reasons for cutting the text are many. Warren argues, '[H]e wrote far more material than the actors ever performed'. Ivers seeks a 'clear vision driven cutting … that enhances clarity'. Woronicz and Frank cut if the word or phrase is incomprehensible to the audience or calls attention to itself. Unnecessary repetition is a factor for Warren and MacLean. Gaines recognizes taking care of her audience's time commitment is a reason for making the plays shorter.

Zimmerman has discovered that when she has cut seemingly superfluous text, she finds it is there because of a staging reason, such as to cover a costume change. Lamos warns that another danger with making cuts is potentially interfering with the rhythm of the scene. This can cause the scene to feel longer or not as satisfying as it might otherwise be without excising the text.

Directors employ several principles in making cuts. Tresnjak mentions structural issues with Act IV as motivating cuts for his *Antony and Cleopatra*. MacLean and Warren work to honour the verse line. Warren adds that at American Shakespeare Center, rather than making large cuts, they snip small chunks throughout. D. Sullivan, MacLean and Peterson wait until they are in rehearsals to make cuts because the actors influence how the text will play. Eustis, Gaines and Metropulos provide examples of how they employed major cuts in their productions and their justifications for doing so.

Just as Lamos counsels that cuts can make a scene seem longer to an audience, similarly Kulick warns that the play's reception can be affected if you transpose a scene. On the other hand, McSweeny reports that he took considerable liberties in transposing scenes in his *The Merchant of Venice* in order to present one storyline more effectively on stage. D. Sullivan cuts scenes because the 'emotional narrative impedes the scene'.

Frank reminds us: 'making Shakespeare's words accessible and potent for a modern audience is at the heart of our mission'. Although he often emends the text when a word sounds familiar, but means something entirely different, he argues that achieving a clear context can make the audience understand a word. Lamos adds that frequently a word can be understood 'if the actor a) knows what he's saying, and b) shapes the line with stresses and end stops'. Gaines, McSweeny, Metropulos and Kulick believe that since the plays are living breathing entities, they were meant to be 'reworked' and 'manhandled'. Kulick cautions directors to trace the ramifications of any change through the entire play to assure it does not 'come back and haunt you'.

Burdman alters the text, sometimes substantially, for his site-specific productions, finding ways to adapt it to the specific locations where it will be performed. He also adds 'insert scenes' implied by the text to enhance the use of a given site. 'It's about fitting the play to the space and the audience', he says.

Consulting different editions

Darko Tresnjak: The way that I approach things, it's a rigorous yet messy process, going from the Folio to the Arden. I love the Arden editions. And then I just grab as many different editions as I can, and pore over them, and then start putting together a kind of overview script for the actors.

Punctuation

Calvin MacLean: The Folio is often the best guide, but I am not doctrinaire about this. I often take several months to prepare a text, comparing and adopting one or another editor's solution. I want it to be punctuated in a way that I have a pretty clear idea of what Shakespeare is trying to say and how a contemporary actor will speak it. I'm attentive to the meter, attentive to what I may learn about Shakespeare's intentions and strategies with the language. This part of the research is a lot of fun for me.

I'm also very conscious of how a moment might play, what seems to me to be the most interesting set of intentions that will enliven a scene, and how that is created by the text. How a phrase moves to its operative word. How the music and imagery of the language might affect an actor.

Ethan McSweeny: I often start with the New Cambridge because I just like the font and find it very legible. That was a preference I developed a long time ago and I've remained relatively loyal to it. More than just the surface, I usually respond to the punctuation in the New Cambridge. Really, all of our punctuation is received and a matter of editorial argument. I find New Cambridge uncluttered and meaningful. But to be fair, that is a matter of style and those styles shift when new editors take on the text and make a case for their commas, semi-colons and periods.

A big part of my work is a conviction that punctuation equals thought. Where there's a punctuation mark, there's a thought change for a character. This is even truer in contemporary work where they don't have the advantage of the verse line to also indicate thought change. Another way of viewing 'moment-to-moment' work is 'thought-to-thought' and to that end it helps to break the thoughts down into their smallest integers.

Libby Appel: Here, in late August, I will have a week in which I will sit with Barry Kraft (the dramaturg on *Richard III*) and Scott Kaiser (the voice/text person). The three of us examine the text word by word. And Barry always comes with comparatives, other printed versions of the text (folio or quarto). We do not work from anyone's edition. *Ever*. We work from the Ur texts. Barry brings in, side by side, quartos if there are multiple quartos and the folio. Sometimes there is only a folio version. We go back to the original text as best we can, as obviously Shakespeare didn't oversee the printing of them. And then we decide on punctuation and word choice. It's *phenomenal*. And we do at least a week of that kind of text work, intense text work, every day.

Cutting

Darko Tresnjak: You don't necessarily honour a play by doing every single line. I think the text needs shaping for actors, for productions. It's a different set of criteria, depending on the situation.

Jim Warren: I think he wrote far more material than the actors ever performed. Once he wrote it and gave it to the company, he didn't own it. I think he knew the actors would pick and choose what stuff they wanted to perform. He was there and he could tell them, 'I had this in mind or that in mind'.

Andrew Gurr, the first head of scholarship with Sam Wanamaker at the Globe, writes in his preface to the New Cambridge First Quarto Edition of *Henry V* that there was a maximal text, and then there was a performance text. When it came time to print the texts, we don't know what actual text went to the printing house, whether it was a quarto form or folio form. The one they were actually using for performance was too valuable to go to the printing house. So what version did the printing house get? And what did they get with Heminges and Condell who put together the First Folio versus some of these other quartos? We have no clue what Shakespeare performed, what he preferred. Yet our company is also based on the idea that the texts matter. I think it was a much more fluid thing than what we have today.

David Ivers: I have a different attention span in a way, than I think our audiences do for Shakespeare. So going along with the core belief about clarity comes a core belief about a responsible and clear vision driven cutting of text. That's not to say that I have one belief about cutting extensively or not cutting extensively. I just have a belief that the scripts mostly benefit by some trimming, and by trimming that enhances clarity.

Henry Woronicz: I will get pretty quickly into a cutting, editing things that either take me out of the play or that I don't feel can serve the production.

David Frank: You try to keep as much as possible but there are passages that whatever you do – short of grossly indicating the meaning – they are going to be unintelligible; insisting on their inclusion whatever the result strikes me as mere hubris.

Calvin MacLean: I won't cut anything until I fully understand it, even if I think it will interfere with an audience's patience with difficult language. When I do cut, I tend to cut repetitions and superfluous action. I'm cautious, however. I try not to cut a lot of the play until I am exploring it with actors. I try to consider an audience watching the play. Of the entire play, what is really crucial to hear? What is thrilling and interesting to hear? And what is less interesting or more difficult for a contemporary audience's patience?

Barbara Gaines: There's another motive behind the cutting of a play in Chicago – one more practical than literary. Most of our audiences come to the theatre after a long day of work and many take trains or buses home at night. As we all know, some of Shakespeare's texts can take up to four hours if left uncut. If I were directing at a Festival, a destination for Shakespeare lovers, I think I'd be inclined to edit less than I do, because if you're on vacation you can sleep longer in the mornings. Our blessed audiences go home late and get up early. I believe it's our responsibility to tell a great story and help them make their trains too.

Jim Warren: Most of the plays he wrote were either for 'The Theater' or 'The Globe'. They were both outdoor theatres and that audience moved around a lot. I don't think they were staying there for the whole show. I think he built repetition into the plays because he knew that that audience needed to hear something three times to get it. That's a place that we go to trim things.

Mary Zimmerman: There are times when you're simply reading a text and you say, 'Well, this can go'. But the moment you're in rehearsal, you figure out why it's there, and it's usually for a very practical reason. For instance in *Henry VIII*, there's a huge crowd scene, and then there's a silly-seeming thing where lords exchange barbs about the French and jokes about the French and how the French dress and so on. You really think, 'Well, this can go'. But the moment you're in rehearsal you realize what the little scene is for: it's for everyone who just exited to get to the other side of the stage and re-enter into the next gigantic pageantry scene.

It hasn't changed in 400 years. Contemporary scholars often proceed in reverse order: reading the play before seeing it – something unheard of in the time of its origin – and doing so, they may tend to attribute all kinds of thematic resonance to those odd moments, which may or may not be there. If you find it there, then in a way it is there, it 'becomes' there. But the primary motive may well have been the practical contingencies of the stage, of moving the thing across the stage.

Mark Lamos: I've never transposed scenes, but I've become bolder about cutting and editing. *A Two Gentlemen of Verona* I staged recently at the Old Globe ran ninety minutes, and it was fleetly spoken and acted. Nothing important was lost, and there were still moments of rumination as well as time for Crab the Dog to work his sublime stage magic. And my last *Hamlet* at Delaware Rep ran just a bit more than two hours. We decided to dispense with the glorious and, yes, necessary 'How all occasions do inform against me' – as is often done. Though it's become my favourite soliloquy, the rising movement towards the end of the play proved more important to me.

You have to be careful, of course. Occasionally the wrong edit can actually make a scene feel longer, because if the bridges between big moments are gone, you don't understand how the characters arrive where they do. And they generally arrive at the most extraordinary places. The closet scene in *Hamlet* is a case in point. It's almost impossible to edit because the sweep and flow, the tumultuous peaks and sudden dips are so carefully wrought by the playwright. Once you track its music through with the actors, it's exhilarating for them; if the wrong bits are left out, they tend to struggle to make any sense of all the wild and whirling words.

Darko Tresnjak: I think *Antony and Cleopatra* is such a gorgeous play. I think structurally there are problems in the fourth act. When I talked to all of the different companies that have done it around the country in the past few years, everybody goes, 'Oh boy! That fourth act! We wish we had tackled more of it. We wish we had struggled with it more'. That in particular is a warning [about the] fourth act with those fifteen scenes. It needs taming. It needs shaping. So that was a concern, figuring the structure of the fourth act. I did some cutting in that act.

I realized fairly early that the intermission had to go after Act III, Scene 6. It almost comes to a boil, but not quite. And then right after intermission we start with the build-up to the first battle. Then there's a second one and then there's a third one. And so I structured it in terms of the events between the three battles that take place in the second half of the play. I find that the second half of *Antony and Cleopatra* can get very loose and disjointed. Focusing the performance, especially in the second half, shaping it, was really important.

Cal MacLean: I try to maintain the poetry at all costs – the rhythm and music of the language.

Jim Warren: We try to do liposuction, rather than amputation. We try to do a little here, and a little here, rather than: 'We're going to cut Fortinbras all the way out of *Hamlet*; we're going to make *Hamlet* a domestic tragedy rather than a political tragedy. We try to take the text that's given and keep all of the characters, try to keep all of the scenes. That doesn't always happen. There might be a messenger that goes here or a small character that goes there. Where is repetition happening in a way that we can lose something and still keep the general thrust? When it's a character like Polonius or Claudius, where part of the character is their wordiness, it gets a little tricky.

When we're cutting in places that have verse, we try to cut whole verse lines when we can, or this half-line adds up to this other half-line to create a whole line. We're not slavish to that, because, especially in his later plays, he's writing in such a complicated way that we can't always do that. We can lose this bit of three and a half lines, but it's going to leave us a half-line some place. We can live with that.

Daniel Sullivan: I make gross decisions fairly early on: like what to cut, where the intermission comes, the clothes, etc. Well you have to, don't you? Unless you have a year to rehearse. But a lot of it I leave until rehearsals. Because I still don't know how the play really works yet. That takes actors. I've always believed that what makes these plays great is that Shakespeare was writing for actors in his company. He had a human being in mind. So all the preparation means very little until the actors arrive. That's when the real discoveries are made. I try to approach the plays as if they had never been done before and I love when actors have the same spirit of adventure and discovery.

Lisa Peterson: I do line through cuts so that the actors can see what's gone. And then I bracket cuts that we should consider. That way, an actor can easily look at the cut line and say, 'I want to say that'. They will anyway, but it's less work than if they go to their own Arden or whatever and they look it up. I think it's good. I like having the choices exposed, right there in the rehearsal draft.

For me the cutting remains very open and fluid in rehearsals. I will court arguments. I like arguments. If an actor has a good strong argument for keeping something, I'll say, 'Well, okay, let's try it for a while and see' unless I feel very strongly about it. In that case I'll say, 'Listen, I have studied this for months. I really think we have got to cut it. We are never going to keep the audience with us in the giant outdoor theatre. We have to come down in three hours'.

Oskar Eustis: We cut it. I'm not a fan of the contention that the [*Hamlet*] quarto and the folio have to be viewed completely autonomous and self-contained works, that each of them has their own intention or that the folio is a rewrite of the quarto. Maybe that's genealogically true, although I don't really believe it, but leaving out 'How all occasions do inform against me' does not help a production of *Hamlet*. I know Jameson thinks it does. I don't think it does. I think it makes it worse. I think you need that to understand the humiliation of Hamlet towards the end. Of course it's in the quarto, not the folio. And you have that stuff that's in the quarto that really shouldn't be. So I am not a textual purist by any means. You need to make the text for the production that you are making, secure in the knowledge that the text will be there after you are done with it.

Barbara Gaines: Orson Wells said: 'We all betray Shakespeare'. I begin there with an apology to William. Since the text is a living organism and Shakespeare was an actor, a man of the theatre, I freely adapt the script, if there's a good reason to do it – for theatre is an interpretive art. Since each play's needs are different I try and figure out what the impulses are that I'm receiving from the text and how I can make them clearer.

In our recent *King Lear*, I wanted the script to be totally focused on Lear's journey – so the back-stories about Oswald and Kent didn't make the final cut. We were left with a laser like focus on his descent. And although I'm well acquainted with the entire text, I didn't miss the language that I cut.

Penny Metropulos: I will admit that I have done some radical cutting. I think the most radical was the time I cut almost the entire fifth act of *Timon of Athens* because I felt like this was a story about Timon. He dies, and we have another twenty-five minutes of a play? With people we haven't even seen in ages? That was not a story that was interesting to me at the time, particularly on the [OSF Elizabethan] outdoor stage. You don't do something like that carelessly, but you have to follow your artistic impulses sometimes to make something come alive.

Transposing scenes

Brian Kulick: One of the things that I have learned is that this sort of cavalier treatment of the text is much more tricky then I first thought, and that when it comes to large structural issues, Shakespeare is usually right. When I was doing *Twelfth Night,* there was this period of time where we swapped the order of the opening two scenes. I tried starting the play with Viola coming in and then followed that by the proper opening scene where we discover Orsino in the throes of melancholy .We had this huge twenty-foot sweep of blue raked stage and people would literally slide in. The first moment of our production became Viola's entrance. You'd hear her screaming and she'd fall twenty feet, sliding downward, followed by all the sailors and luggage. It was a great way to start a show. We thought, 'That'll start the show off with a real BANG!' During previews we went back and forth, trying out both of these openings: our version and Shakespeare's proper opening. Invariably we found that the applause at the end of the evening would be greater if we did the opening the way William Shakespeare wrote it. There's something about setting up a world of longing and melancholy, and then having the energy of a young woman, unsure of herself, fall into the space, screaming all the way, that was ultimately the right sequencing.

Ethan McSweeny: *The Merchant of Venice* is three worlds: it's Venice, it's the Jewish quarter, and it's Belmont. It's very easy for productions to prioritize one over the other. It's very important that they actually all exist in some level of equality. Increasingly, I am finding the 'three world' structure very prevalent in all of Shakespeare – it was true when I did *A Midsummer Night's Dream* and *The Tempest*. And in all of those plays, the real challenge to the director is to be able to direct those different worlds and their genres, equally well. Often a concept will favour one over the other and I am always on the lookout for the one that will allow each to flourish proportionally.

I also had this real feeling that after you reveal the three worlds, Scenes 1, 2, 3, the order almost doesn't matter again until you get to the casket-choosing scene of Bassanio. So I re-cut a bunch of stuff so that we would stay in Venice longer and come back to Belmont. Venice, Belmont. The play can very quickly go boom-boom-boom-boom-boom back and forth between the two, and that's fine, but I didn't want to necessarily have that many of those kinds of transitions. I was trying to see if I couldn't follow one story longer. I did some gentle editing to make that happen.

For me it doesn't proceed always from an intellectual idea of what I want to achieve. It emanates from an instinctual and emotional place, and then I go back and bring the intellect to it. *Merchant* is an important play, but I felt relatively free with the text. The folios and quartos that we have are all matters of argument and differences. You have to remember that this stuff is breathing. It's alive. It's porous. You can work it. It wants to be worked. It doesn't want to be reverenced.

Replacing, emending and adapting

David Frank: I'll change a word. I don't often want to change a word that an audience knows it doesn't understand, because they will figure out the meaning from the context. I'm more likely to advocate changing a word when its contemporary meaning is familiar, but was very different 400 years ago. In those circumstances, anyone can be misled and lose a pivotal sentence. And sometimes, something tiny – changing a conjunction, for example – can clarify an entire speech. And, occasionally, depending on the circumstances, you have to do more. But you need to be terribly careful and keep reminding yourself that making Shakespeare's words accessible and potent for a modern audience is at the heart of our mission.

Mark Lamos: I'm often asked if I re-arrange or re-organize a text, or re-write lines. The answer of course is, 'of course'! The text is over 400 years old, so it will occasionally need some slight updating for a modern audience to understand what is meant. On the other hand, many arcane words that have disappeared from modern usage can be completely understood by a modern audience if the actor knows a) what he's saying, and b) how to shape the line with stresses and end stops. These strange and beautiful words give another gloss to the reality of the play's situations and characters.

Brian Kulick: I don't think the text is sacrosanct. I believe, when you look at the various quartos and the folio, that these plays were constantly revised for different occasions. When you look at the work that a lot of scholars have done with *Othello* and *Lear*, you can see that Shakespeare kept revising these plays, kept adding and subtracting, based on his opportunities of experiencing the text with an audience. I've always felt that the initial performances of these plays probably used less text than what we might find in the quarto or folio. I have this somewhat elaborate imaginary scenario in my mind where Shakespeare gets into these endless arguments with Burbage about cuts and paraphrases, I can see him screaming, 'I can't take this! You put, "To be, or not to be" *where?*' And in this imaginary scenario of mine, Richard Burbage responds, 'Bill, you can't do that. It's too much, it's endless! Save it for the book. *This* is what we're going to do'. In this respect I am not a purist, I don't think these plays were meant to be treated that way. They were meant to be manhandled; it is part of their textual DNA.

So yes, cut, change, with the caveat that Shakespeare usually knows what he's doing. Change at your own peril. If you change, you change the organism and it has a ripple effect because everything in Shakespeare has a pattern. It has a life. So if you change something, you're not just changing it in that scene. It's going to come back and haunt you. So you have to work. If you're going to eradicate something from the text, it's not usually in just one place. It's going to come back in four or five other places. Each time you're going to have to deal with it. Don't be naïve. If you cut the senators in *Timon* because there's too many of them and because you don't have the budget for them, there's going to be a moment, usually in previews, when you realize, 'Oh, that's why he needed all those senators'.

Stephen Burdman: Before I coined the term 'panoramic', we started adapting the show to the venue. Shakespeare might have said it's an 'elm tree', but we knew it was actually an oak tree the actors were referring to, so we did the word substitution and it became an oak tree. The whole notion of panoramic theatre is that the whole script is adapted to the venue and sometimes changes are made to it. For example, we do something called, 'insert scenes'. Scenes that Shakespeare talks about happening offstage, we actually stage and they happen during the audience's movement. For example in *Henry V*, we staged Bardolph's execution. And we actually staged it. There was a bell that happened to be there as part of an art installation. So the audience was there. We saw him being led off in chains. I remember he had stolen something from the church and we didn't hear the execution, but we heard the bell toll. At a distance. So it was symbolic. With insert scenes not everybody gets everything, but it's that experience of knowing what's happening.

An audience moves roughly seven to ten times during a show. The audience actually picks up and moves and follows the actors to another area of the park. The notion of panoramic is about the adaptation ultimately. It's about fitting the play to the space and the audience. In panoramic theatre, the audience is at the centre of the action. The audience feels the action is happening around them all of the time. So Richard III would enter the back of the audience with swords. Then people would go, 'Oh my God', and they'd have to move out of the way so he can walk through with his whole retinue. *King Lear* had a real heath. We had a three and a half acre lake. We did *Seagull* and Trigorin got to fish in the real three-acre lake. And the audience watched him fish. So he comes in saying, 'I was just fishing'. Well, yes he was, because he was right across the lake fishing. Of course, he didn't catch anything. We didn't bait the hook. So this adaptation with the movement results in an audience's involvement.

6

Working with Designers

> *There is an actor and a director named Dakin Matthews, who did the adaptation of* Henry IV *that Jack O'Brien directed at Lincoln Center. I've known Dakin for many years. I haven't seen him in years, but I worked with him for a while. He used to talk in this regard, he said, 'You know, you can have terrific ideas, wonderful new ideas about a Shakespeare play. They just better be as good as his, or they're not going to hold up'.*
>
> HENRY WORONICZ

Usually design discussions happen well before rehearsals begin – in some instances as much as a year ahead of time. The process has changed considerably over the past couple of decades. Budgets have gotten smaller and the number of projects designers must take in order to survive has increased. It is now common for them to work on multiple projects in theatres geographically remote from each other.[1] This dictates the need for frequent one-on-one conversations, as well as the ability to readily access a designer's visual research and designs in online sharing sites. It has also increased the likelihood that the first time the team is physically together is at the first technical rehearsal.

FIGURE 11 Cymbeline, *directed by Mark Lamos, Lincoln Center, 2007. John Cullum as Cymbeline, Michael Cerveris as Posthumus and Martha Plimpton as Imogen. Photograph by Paul Kolnik.*

Most directors expect to discuss the play with their designers, brainstorm solutions to design problems and staging issues and participate in creatively imagining and conceptualizing solutions. Some directors like to converse, others to share notes with the team. In this chapter, directors discuss what they do to prepare for working with designers and design meetings, how they like to talk with designers and their attitudes about this process.

Gaines, when reading and studying the text, notes images that occur to her; she experiences these visualizations 'as if [they] were a film'. She then shares them with her designers who she hopes take them and transform them into 'electrifying' solutions. Ultimately she seeks a 'synergy' in their partnership. Eustis also conceptualizes ideas before he works with his designers. Buckley, in her pre-design homework, seeks 'visual inspirations for the emotional connection to the play'. She prepares detailed image books as well as scene, character, location and time breakdowns that she shares with the production designers and staff. Like Gaines, she hopes her designers improve on her ideas. Zimmerman believes her role is to determine 'how to frame or set the play'. There are many possible approaches to consider. Will it be a period production? A contemporary one? A hybrid mixture? Then one has to decide 'the degree of design'. Will it be representational or presentational? And although open stages are in vogue for Shakespeare settings, 'there is no neutral on stage'. Every choice signifies. MacLean writes a 'critical reading of the play' for his designers. In it he records what he thinks are the play's 'most exciting ideas', what he hopes to convey to an audience and 'why it matters to them and me'. He avoids descriptions of what he sees and hears to prevent dictating design solutions. Metropulos views the process as 'mysterious' and admits she does not have a singular method that she uses to prepare.

Next, the director moves into communicating with the designers. Lamos loves discussing the play and what it 'might mean to audiences now'. McAnuff prefers to have all of the designers meeting together in the same room because 'I have found that the most profound advances happen when the creatives are gathered together. Thompson wants everyone involved to freely express their ideas. Similar to MacLean, Conlin starts the design conversation with 'written notes as a way to get things launched'. Metropulos brings an image or a thought to the first meeting with her team. She believes 'questions are the key' to successful conferences. 'You hold on to that image or thought that seemingly came out of nowhere as the *central* question. You ask that about every moment in the play. If it holds, then it will work'. Douglas wants to share his feelings about the play: 'What the play is saying ... how it resonates with what is going on ... in our world today'. He also avoids dictating while encouraging the team to freely talk and affect each other in the emerging designs.

D. Sullivan selects designers 'like I'd cast an actor; someone whose aesthetic sense fits with the play'. Eustis points out that designers do not all work the same way or are 'right' for a given project. Frank and Kahn prefer to work with designers with whom they have had a prior relationship. D. Sullivan also believes set designers need to have 'a sculptural sense of space and how the human figure will move in it' which they communicate in a model. Serban prefers a design that is 'unfinished business'; he wants a flexible solution that can be 'reshaped simultaneously with the evolution of the ideas in rehearsal with the actors'. He finds unyielding concepts lead to 'boring predictability'. Rauch pursues societal and cultural contexts as expressed in the clothing and the world of the play. Woronicz believes the rational for choosing a period is because 'these elements of that period reflect these elements of the play'. He warns against designers' and directors' great production ideas as they often mean 'the script and the language then suffers'. McSweeny likes to sketch his initial ideas and bring those to the designer – not to be recreated, but to open a discussion. He also believes that how the production responds to the theatre space should be a fundamental concern: 'Every theatre presents you with a problem set ... the problem of the integration of this play in that space'.

Tresnjak and Rauch describe two opposite viewpoints on creating the play's visual world. Tresnjak finds contemporary clothing productions at odds with the language in Shakespeare's texts, while Rauch is primarily interested in contemporary cultural/societal contexts. Both represent current schools of thought on the subject – Tresnjak's more language based, Rauch's more visually interpreted.

Finally, Lamos offers an observation about ground plans. They must be 'fluid' in a way that Shakespeare's spaces were. He also likes to work with a 'centre obstacle' so that the characters 'circle and sweep' in their movement through the space.

Preparing for design meetings

Barbara Gaines: Once I begin working on a play, studying it's many meanings, images begin to appear in my mind – I see the play as if it were a film. Many of those images make it to the stage. I share my visual ideas with my designers and they usually take good ideas and make them brilliant ones. Working with so many creative people is the oxygen within my world. I find that as I describe a scene or moment, ideas keep coming, spurred on by their questions and comments. The synergy of our collaboration takes literature and makes it visual, dynamic and theatrical. I depend on them to solve the unsolvable and to make the impossible possible and electrifying. These meetings are treasured and their work priceless.

Oskar Eustis: Designers start to get involved after I start to have initial thoughts about what it is. I don't know exactly what it is until I started to visualize what it was. Not even visualize what it was. Conceptualize.

Kate Buckley: We trade visual ideas. Inspirational photos – from the library, from books, from the Internet – images that turn me on. For example, with *The Taming of the Shrew* last year here, I knew I wanted shutters. So Todd Rosenthal [the scenic designer] and I shared photos of scores of Italian shutters. I had just been working in Milan, which gave me a footing in the physical world of Italy. I also share visual images with the lighting designer and of course costume designers. I share music with the sound designer. All of this communication is about having the same basic language as we create a world. I was playing with the idea of seeing a restaurant, a piazza and a fountain square. So then it became a matter of saying, 'These images have inspired me to dream a bit. Look at these images, the colour, the textures'. So, we share visual inspirations for the emotional connection to the play.

Often summer festivals assign resident designers to a project, which can be of great assistance to me when trying to understand the procedures of a theatre. Sometimes I am able to bring designers into a theatre, but it is becoming a rare event. There are probably five set designers, five costume designers, three or four sound designers that I enjoy working with because we have developed a creative shorthand. They understand my artistic tastes and I understand theirs. Although I share this imagery with designers and say, 'riff on this', I expect them to create in order to make my initial ideas better. There's a lot of back and forth communication, e-mail and talk before we actually sit in a production meeting.

That's where I am right now on *Much Ado*. I've done all my research. My script is ready. I've chosen a period, atmosphere and a location for design. The next step is to get deeper into the text.

I divide the play into French scenes, rather than Act I, Scene 2, etc. I keep the Folio on hand and other editions for reference. I also have done in pre-production a scene/actor-character/location and time breakdown for the production. This is valuable for the costume designer for changes, the lighting designer for time of day and the stage manager for creating rehearsal calls. In this way, the entire team has an excellent idea of our progress. You see [shows me her breakdown] day seven. So there is never any question about who is in what scene or where we are during the week. It is preliminary and can change during rehearsals but it is helpful to all of us. I also do a preliminary set and prop list, double check it with the set designer, hand it over to the stage manager and say to myself, 'Okay, now I am going to concentrate on the actor'.

I have five research books – play analysis, criticism, text analysis, character analysis and inspiration images. These research books live in the rehearsal hall. Anybody who would like to learn where the ideas for production came from can study them.

Mary Zimmerman: Design is such an interesting challenge with Shakespeare – how to frame or set the play. Sometimes its short notice and it all goes extremely fast. Sometimes you have a year and you're thinking about it in the back of your mind. The designers have their due dates that are a couple of months out from actual rehearsal. But they have various markers of those dates along the way. So you start thinking immediately. Even when you're reading a play, if you're imagining doing it, you have to be thinking about that because design is so incredibly vocal in the meaning of the play. It generates meaning.

With Shakespeare, you have your choice of a thousand different approaches. His plays, with few exceptions, are set in the past (I mean the past even to him) or in Illyria, places that never existed, places we certainly have never been. So you research those actual places. Italy, Verona and so forth, while at the same time wondering about how Shakespeare might have imagined those places differently than we imagine or know them now. You research Renaissance Elizabethan England. Or you decide you're going to be more contemporary. Or you're going to make up a period. And you think about the degree of design. Is it just pictorial with actual representation of various places? Or is it a more open feel, a presentational approach?

I think most people nowadays approach it by framing the action in a more open way. The plays were written for a stage that did not have much scenery on it. They move so swiftly and the scenery is created through the speech so much that it's best to not think, 'We'll bring this enormous piece in for France. And we'll bring this other colossal piece in for the battle'. Sometimes those scenes, especially battle scenes, have four lines and then you're in a different place. It's great to rush onto the stage and make the place by naming it. Only by naming it.

On the other hand there is no neutral on stage. You have to make a choice about the character and quality of the setting and what that does for you in staging, and do for the play in the creation of meaning. There are a thousand choices to be made. Our *Pericles* ends up being set in a room. This has nothing directly to do with the story, but it's based on a Shaker meeting hall. We didn't intend to imply, 'This is a bunch of Shakers come to a play. They come on with bonnets'. Not at all. But there's something about the purity of those lines and the simplicity, the openness and the faithfulness, in fact. *Pericles* takes place so much outdoors, but also there are interior scenes. So we painted it all, every inch of that room, monochromatically a pale greyish blue so it could be like the sky or an open seascape. But it is, nonetheless, a room that provides entrances and some shape and some dynamic energy for those actions to butt up against. It can be indoors or outdoors rather easily. We decked it as though it were the deck of a ship. Those Shaker rooms have planked floors as well. I love design. Design guides so much of what the audience sees and understands.

Mara Blumenfeld has done my costumes for years and years. We have a joke: The very first thing that sponsors of the show or just casual people want to know about your Shakespeare play is, 'What period is it in?' We have decided to make a decision about that. We say we've done the Gorgeous period, the Charming period. I think *Pericles* was in the Delightful period. We're serious about that. But Mara and I like to do hybrid things. I was determined to use the Elizabethan collars – the air filter collars – in *Pericles,* but to joke a little with them. So the women wear them, but with them they wear sleeveless dresses, sort of strapless dresses, which is a combination that has never existed in the actual history of clothing. Nevertheless it kind of read as 'traditional'. If you put women in gowns whose hems touch the floor, that have a certain sort of silhouette, it reads as 'period' although there never was such a period. I like that for plays like *Pericles* and the plays that happen in a never-never land.

Calvin MacLean: I know that I begin by writing what amounts to an essay on my critical reading of the play. This essay tries to address three things: to express what I think are the most exciting ideas in the play, what I want to communicate to an audience, and why it matters to them and me. In this essay I also describe the particular set of actions I will emphasize. The essay also describes the *things* I will need to tell this particular story. It amounts to a lot of lists and descriptions of particular staging or staging imagery that I'm imagining. I try to avoid describing what something might actually look like or sound like, leaving that for the designers to contribute. Rather, I throw out initial impressions – partly because I want designers to respond to that, to have a collaborative discussion that might venture into unexpected territory. I like to put it down on paper because writing disciplines and clarifies my thinking. When I get it down on paper and I'm going over it and editing it for the third or the fourth time, I'm figuring out much of the production.

I think this process evolved because I was often dissatisfied with conversations with designers in which I was getting lost by my own undisciplined language or thinking. Working often with designers who were not onsite, or had a limited amount of time, it became important to get some things down that designers could read and think about when it was most convenient for them. It becomes for me something to refer to later on in the process to remind me of my original intentions ... helpful even if I have abandoned them for newer ones.

Penny Metropulos: I think that design is the most mysterious process. There is no set process for it as far as I am concerned. You read the play. You carry it around all the time in your head. You are constantly thinking, looking at things. I do a lot of visual work, looking through a lot of books. I look through a lot of paintings. I look through a lot of timelines of history to see if anything catches my eye. I read poems, writers from the period, or the period that I am thinking about and I listen to music. Images are just coming at me. If you are dry, you just pick something out of the blue that might inspire you. And sometimes it goes down a dead end, and sometimes it makes you go, 'Well that made me think of blah, blah, blah'.

What is invisible in this play that I want made visible? For me, that will always lead to something mysterious, dramatic and human.

Talking with designers

Mark Lamos: Dramaturgical work begins when I meet with the set and costume designers. Very often they are the very first people with whom you talk about the play months in advance of the production. Their intelligence and their acuity infect the process right from the beginning because they are thinking about the text too, but in a different way. I occasionally have an idea about how the production should look before we meet, but more often than not, we have a conversation about what the play might mean or say to modern audiences now, just at this moment. Or what we 'see'. Sometimes a designer might say, 'You know, when I first read the text, I thought that we should put the whole thing on a pile of sand'.

'Really? Why?'

Bingo, you have a dialogue about the play going. This initial meeting launches the entire production, and when I return to the text, visual ideas come into play as well as really fresh new insights into the words.

Des McAnuff: The one thing I try to do on every production, whether it is Shakespeare, a contemporary play or a gargantuan musical, is to try and get people sitting in a room at the same time. I have found that the most profound advances happen when the creatives are gathered together. This is particularly true with the designers. There is a tendency to have a whole slew of meetings one-on-one. While this can feel terrific and stoke the directorial ego, it is much better when you create a vast cross section of ideas and opinions so that everyone is talking to everyone else, and even more importantly, listening. One of the reasons the former Soviet Union collapsed is that the government was very stingy about sharing information. They did not want the scientists, for example, to have access to the big picture. They made everyone specialize. This ultimately prevented Soviet scientists from the kind of intuitive leaps you can only make when all of the information is available to you. While democracy can be quite messy when you're directing people, it is ultimately better when you get everyone in the group thinking.

Kent Thompson: I really encourage people, anybody in the theatre, to bring in ideas to the process of working on a play. Those ideas come from everybody. I certainly will say if I have a particular period [in mind], but I'm really going back to the things that appeal to me about the play, the things that start to get me going about the play. And that's what I want to hear from them at the first design [meeting]. Some people show up with research. Some people show up with a set. Some people show up with varying things, and then we'll take it from there. We'll probably go through generations of changes to try and to figure out how we stage the play. The scene designer and I will try to stage the entire play, scene-by-scene-by-scene.

Kathleen Conlin: We start with my written notes as a way to get things launched, and then do phone calls where we start talking back and forth about 'what ifs'. 'What if we actually settled on this period as opposed to that period?' Keep in mind that in terms of costumes, if we decided that the period is 1830, we're going to have a certain kind of silhouette. 'Is this what you want? Do you want to go in that direction? Well show me the historical stuff on it'. We then, over time, blend historical influences with contemporary thought. Then I try to think simultaneously, not just what the visual image is, but also what's possible with our resources and our stock. It's already starting to focus itself for the particular theatre.

Penny Metropulos: When I walk into the first meeting, I need to have an idea. I can't spend that twelve or fifteen hours of initial time, wasting their time by saying, 'Well, I don't know. What do you think about it?' I go in, and try to offer them what my singular point of view on the play is, the things that may have inspired that point of view. I may have paintings or drawings or music or poetry or philosophical thoughts or my wild journal that I have kept – something that will feed into that first meeting. I ask them what their initial impressions of the play are. I ask them questions and throw out, on the table, all the questions that I have been asking myself. 'How does this work? What do you think about this?' Good questions are the key.

When I was preparing *A Midsummer Night's Dream*, I was looking up at the clouds one day, and thinking about dreams. I thought, 'Well, of course. The entire thing is a dream! Shakespeare's living in a dream'. Well, when you put that on the table for a designer and say, what is a dream? Bill Bloodgood will say, 'What is the image of a dream?' And people say, ' A pillow!' 'A Bed!' 'A Cloud!' 'Well, what is unusual? It is not just a bed. It's a bed that's floating'. And then we had a floating bed! And suddenly it has a crescent moon on top of it and the moon is going to be lit from the inside. And I say, 'Oh, wait, ever since I did *Timon of Athens*, I've had this glass box in my head. I can't get it out' And everyone chimes in. 'Oberon could put all the fairies into the box and lock the box'. 'The box holds dreams!' 'The entire play is a dream'. 'From the minute the audience walks in, we are in a dream, and it's going to go all the way to the end'. It just goes on and on like that ... *because you have asked the question,* 'how do you make the invisible, visible'.

What begins to happen, then, is that you hold on to that image or thought that seemingly came out of nowhere as the *central* question. You ask that about every moment in the play. If it holds, then it will work.

Timothy Douglas: Somehow, throughout time, every Shakespeare play reflects the present. With designers, I talk about my feelings about the play, what I think the play is saying, and how it resonates with what is currently happening in the world. I prefer not to dictate the physical design of the production unless I have an indelible image that shows up in my head, which is rare. I particularly enjoy bringing the entire design team together at the beginning of the design process and conduct a kind of roundtable approach from the very first conversation. I prefer to have all of us influencing each other's individual processes from the very start. In so many important ways, the approach to the staging and tone of my productions are heavily influenced by the designers' collective and ongoing input.

Attitudes about working with designers

Daniel Sullivan: I work with many designers. I choose a designer like I'd cast an actor: someone whose aesthetic sense fits with the play. Most designers have a broad range, but when I look at the essence of the play, someone will occur to me who seems visually at the centre of the play, or at least how I see the play. Some designers are careful and exacting, some are messy and improvisatory, some love simplicity, for others the more ornate the better. I suppose the one common denominator in good design is a sculptural sense of space and how the human figure will move in it. Without that you just have a picture. A lot of designers don't work from sketches, but work first from models to get that sense of space. There are also designers that don't come to the table with the design already in their head. They develop an idea out of a discussion about the play. This is particularly necessary with Shakespeare. How can a designer intuit how I would approach the play? There are an infinite amount of approaches possible. I'd be appalled if a designer brought a design to a first meeting. I've sometimes had several meetings with a designer before an actual design emerges. Usually I find we will talk about a scene (usually the 'problem' scene) and how you each see that. 'How do you do this?' Very often that 'how' will suggest a space and we will go from there.

Oskar Eustis: Because the designers I work with are very different people. Some are right for some projects and some are right for others. The designer I work with most is Eugene Lee. As a designer he doesn't have an intellectual bone in his body. You say some things; he says some things; you say a few more things; he'll draw it for you and he'll come up with some wild idea and you either say 'Yes' to it or you'll say, 'No, no no'. So the pictures are actually part of the dialogue with Eugene. But designers are different. You'll never see this from John Conklin: totally meticulous as a designer, a very detailed process of sketches and thoughts. Eugene does everything on the back of napkins.

David Frank: It is always exciting working with a new designer, but it is hard to beat a relationship you have built up over decades. I've worked with Bob Morgan since Jack O'Brien introduced us my first year in Buffalo. That's thirty-two years we've been working together. We don't talk about how the clothes look in any detail. We talk about the play as a whole, and then, what the clothes do for the play and what part of the story he can undertake as costume designer. Over the years, I think we have both developed a strong desire to simplify as much as we can; we've also gained a deeper understanding of how difficult that is to achieve.

I love working on the set. It's always been fun for me, but the process varies enormously. With some designers, some productions, you just talk about the play and the ideas start to flow – envelope ideas, back-of-napkin ideas.

Realistic interiors on our big outdoor thrust stage always pose fascinating problems for us. A play like *Major Barbara*, written with multiple realistic settings in mind, requires a unified conceptual approach that can embrace each of the locales. What is the minimum physical set required to tell the story? Often it is surprisingly little. What else do you want the set to do? How does it serve the staging? Can you reduce it to one powerful gesture? Sometimes all I crave is an eloquent platform, a tension in space focused on the relationship between actor and audience. Developing this kind of understanding with a designer can take many years, and then every now and again, it is so simple and easy, you wonder what all the fuss has been about in the past.

Michael Kahn: I best work with designers I've worked with before because we understand each other. I now don't think of design in the way I used to. I used to think of design a lot, and currently I don't think about it as much. I think that may be a failing of mine now. I don't say that with assurance. Designers have a very different style from when I was beginning. There are a lot of new ideas about design, which I am enthusiastic about. Sometimes I'll be intrigued by a designer's idea. Then if things go well, I'll be glad I did that. Sometimes once I get into rehearsal I wonder exactly why I actually did this. I'm best working with people I've worked with before. We talk to each other in a particular way.

Andrei Serban: The ideal design is unfinished business, a kind of work in progress that can be flexible enough to change and get reshaped simultaneously with the evolution of the ideas in rehearsal with the actors. Of course, when I work in the world of opera, at the Met, Paris, or Covent Garden, the set is a much too early 'finished business'. The model of the set has to be delivered eight months in advance. Everything will be thoroughly designed long before the rehearsals. It happened often that eight months later we discovered working with the actors-singers a totally new way to do the piece, a new visual possibility, but the frustration was big when we were ordered to stick to the already built set, to find that nothing can be changed, nor adapted to the new ideas. Therefore a concept that seemed good before became rigid and suffocating now.

That's why I prefer to work in theatre, in an atmosphere more open and fluid, where things are easier to shift. I work best when I don't have to force and not arrive at conclusions too early. An ideal design for a Shakespeare is to have elements in an open space that can be transformable – fragmented elements that are flexible and playful, rather than constructed sets. That would allow the imagination to run free. Because the danger is that too much scenery kills the imagination. Imagination has muscles as well. The audience needs to work its muscles too. Theatre is a gym for the imagination, also a provocation for the actors to work harder, to create with their bodies a space, at times more invisible, where spirits and fairies can feel at home.

Ideally I would like to have a designer with me who understands this rather than settling too early into, 'Let's decide to do it in that period with such and such historical reference for sets and costumes'. That stiff concept is a prelude to boring predictability. Let it appear, gradually, even if we don't know what it is. Not knowing for as long as we can, as nerve wracking as it is, before the play reveals to us its real face, rather than what we imagine the play to be. We have to discover what the play is really about, which all of us at the start honestly do not know. Search and discovery, these are the most valuable words when I work, especially with Shakespeare.

Henry Woronicz: The design process becomes about figuring out what world to best set this play into. And first the director has an idea about that. 'I want to put *Hamlet* into the 1812 period, because these elements of that period reflect these elements of the play'. There is an effort that has to be made (because it can be so wide open) of not overwhelming the production. A lot of modern productions of Shakespeare get too interested in the director's idea and the designer's ideas. The script and the language then suffer. There is a fine line you have to tread. You give just enough support for your Shakespeare production without overwhelming the language.

Ethan McSweeny: I'm not a particularly good drawer, but whatever my initial impulses are, I sketch them down involving the scenery. I'm fortunate enough to work with designers who are willing to look at my sketches and know not to do exactly that but to use them as departure points. The closeness between my initial sketch impulse and what Andrew [Lieberman] did on *Merchant* is fascinating, considering how extraordinary the design is and how it's nothing like I ever imagined *per se*. But he did tease out the essence of where my imagination was heading. Just now on *The Tempest* with Lee Savage, I kept drawing this bow of a boat and a mast submerged in the ground, and he was able to interpret that beautifully.

A lot of what I imagine has to do with where the performance will occur: it is the place, the theatre itself. Every theatre presents you with a problem set. How you solve that problem with your design, where you solve the problem of the integration of this play in that space, is very important to me. So some of my responses are not even about the play; they're just responses to space.

Harman Hall is very large. It has this finished detail that goes all the way around the stage house. You can try to not encounter that feature or you can go ahead and embrace it. I've done it both ways. *Merchant* chose to embrace the idiosyncrasies of the room. I've found that downstage right and downstage left are often neglected spaces in this theatre and yet they can be very powerful. This design really lets us play into those spots. That's something I expressed to Andrew early on, that I wanted to preserve that. Then he came up with essentially taking the grid of the Harman, putting it all onto the stage. Then he actually covered the whole stage in columns and then cut away some. That's how we got that shape. He had the windows. They were milk plexi on the doors and he invented them being a little more transparent. I responded by inventing the shades and out of that came the design. I look for collaboration and conversation.

Jennifer Moeller, on *Merchant*, had a number of great costume ideas. Part of that was also propelling us into the

1920s. She could show us what those choices would mean. Would it work for Portia to dress up like a man? Could we come up with a believable version of that?

I regard the designers as a sort of brain trust. I encourage them to talk to one another. I encourage them to cross over in discipline. If I feel entitled to give notes to everybody, then they can be entitled to give them back. I'll decide. I'll edit.

Two contrasting views on design approach

Darko Tresnjak: There's often a tendency to update things, to do things contemporary. But I find it really tricky, especially with Shakespeare, because it's the clothing. The contemporary clothing doesn't eliminate the language and there's this enormous discrepancy. You don't end up even here; you end up on the moon. It's just becomes this odd sort of art artefact.

Bill Rauch: Cultural context is really important to me and societal context – that really matters – as expressed especially in what the actors are wearing, the world that they live in. Always creating the world, inventing the world, even if we're trying to be slavish to period detail or to a contemporary setting – a particular contemporary milieu – it was still creating an inventive world with a palette that's colour coordinated. It's an invented world, but I need to understand the context before I can move forward. The design process leads to so much for me.

Ground plans

Mark Lamos: In a Shakespeare production, 'the ground plan's the thing'. I spend a lot of time with the set designer to make sure we have a set as fluid as the Globe's was. Multiple entrances, and on a thrust stage I often ask for a centre 'obstacle' around which the characters must circle and sweep in order to get where they're going. During text study I've been careful to note which scenes were written to be played on the Globe's 'inner above' and 'inner below' – as far as scholarship can inform us. This helps inform the design process, even though it's often unlikely to include such places.

7

Casting

To hear the play come alive after months of study is one of the most exhilarating moments in the whole process. It's also very useful for my understanding of the text to watch and listen to vastly different actors read the same speech or scene, one after the other, for two or three days at a time. I begin to understand the resilience of the text, how it gives itself to so many different interpretations, many of which make great sense and are occasionally very different from my own personal conception. The audition process forces me back to text work, as I think about the actors I've seen. It's truly transformative.

MARK LAMOS

Gaines reminds us of the disproportional importance of casting to the success of the production and the many questions that must be resolved. How large should the cast be? Do we double or triple cast roles? How important are the minor characters to the production? Because of the size and complexity of producing these plays, additional skills are required of the actor. How experienced is the potential

FIGURE 12 A Midsummer Night's Dream, *directed by Daniel Sullivan, Free Shakespeare in the Park, Public Theater, 2007. Keith Randolph Smith, Tim Blake Nelson, Jay O. Sanders, Jesse Tyler Ferguson, Ken Cheeseman, Jason Antoon. Photograph by Michal Daniel.*

cast member with Shakespeare? What are their abilities when it comes to speaking the language and handling the verse? Can an actor make it sound natural? Can they physically express the character while speaking the text? What is their background in stage combat and dance? Do they share the director's ideas about how Shakespeare should be performed?

Still other casting issues surface. How do we assess actors' abilities in auditions? Should the director interview them? Read with them? Ask for an additional piece? Give them an adjustment? Should the director avoid choosing the most polished and finished auditioner? What is the value system by which the director judges the actor?

Esbjornson applauds 'a more contemporary approach' to Shakespeare that has produced 'an informed, highly skilled American actor who can achieve precision with the speech without losing a deeper emotional connection'. Rauch wants 'fearlessness' in his actors who, with their choices, will risk emotional vulnerability. Zimmerman finds 'mental acuity' in an actor to be a key trait as well as someone who can speak the language 'naturally and with as much variety as we speak every day'. She also needs an actor who can access their emotions. Appel looks for intelligence and craft. D. Sullivan requires technical language skills along with the 'ability to improvise rhythmically within those demands'. Buckley seeks an actor who possesses strong vocal skills and is smart. She finds honesty to be the most important trait. Douglas reads with potential actors, believing his 'ability to connect' with each actor he casts will lead to an ensemble in which everyone connects with each other. Cohen demands that actors demonstrate an affinity for Shakespeare's language and 'make specific verbal choices in their heads', but also be able to connect directly with the audience as well.

How do we handle race, gender and perceived sexual orientation in the selection of the company? Eustis states that all white productions (except for the servants) communicate 'America is basically a white country'. Plays in other countries such as Japan or Africa cast all the roles, servants and rulers alike, with native actors from that country. Should we not make the cast look like America? How do we avoid unintended political statements? For Douglas, colour blind casting does not exist, only non-traditional casting: 'I have to think very carefully about *who* I am putting *where* – in terms of gender, in terms of race and in terms of perceived sexual orientation'. Bond refers to this as 'inclusive casting' instead of 'colour blind casting'. He rejects traditional casting, which he says is essentially 'exclusive'. The director should 'think of how their choices will be perceived on the diverse populations in your audience'. Like Douglas, he believes the director must consider how you can achieve a sense of hierarchical balance. You can cast a person of colour as a villain if you also cast a person of colour as a hero/good guy.

How should women be cast in the plays today? Conlin struggles with the notion of casting women in what have traditionally been the male character roles. Tresnjak also dislikes cross-gender casting unless it's an all male or all female production. On the other hand, Zimmerman sees her mission as casting more women. She does this by casting them in exposition scenes, where the characters discuss what has happened offstage. She also finds other roles that can be cross-gendered, such as the necromancer in *Pericles*. Zipay's company has, over time, developed an approach that is now centred in non-traditional casting for both women and men. 'You don't have to say, "Gender-reversed". You don't have to say, "Gender-biased". You don't have to say, "Traditional with a few roles changed". But all of those things can work'. Wolpe, is a director/activist who has been an 'advocate for diversity and female empowerment in the Shakespearean theatre tribe'. As mentioned in Chapter 2, she directed and produced all female productions of Shakespeare for many years. She believes '[w]omen and men, trans people and any shading or variation of gender – and sexual preference, race and culture ... can play any Shakespearean character onstage'.

Desirable qualities for Shakespeare

Barbara Gaines: When I was a young actress in New York, I saw a sign in a famous casting director's office. It said: 90 per cent of directing is casting. And that's the truth.

Bill Rauch: First of all, what I value in an actor approaching Shakespeare is fearlessness. I feel like what Shakespeare demands of the performer is that you have to be connected emotionally. You have got to be willing to take risks, emotional risks, interpretive risks. I don't think you can make safe or neutral choices within Shakespeare and have it be successful. Fearlessness. Passion.

Mary Zimmerman: What you really need in an actor for Shakespeare is a smart person. You need people who have an easy relationship with the printed text and understand it's only the recording of speech spoken as naturally and with as much variety as we speak every day – as much variety in pace, in pitch and in volume. That's how we express ourselves in life. We do not express ourselves by elongating our vowels. We do not express ourselves by putting a melody on top of what we say. We change pitch, pace, rhythm, volume and stress with lightning speed as we are speaking. It takes a certain mental acuity and a certain speed and a good ear.

Above all, it's an intimate, natural relationship to text. I want someone who understands speech as thought, and print as simply the record of thought or speech – not as some fancy, difficult thing that you have to tip toe up to and caress in some ridiculous way or telegraph to the audience that you're really working. It should be the opposite. It should seem like you're not 'speaking Shakespeare'.

Then of course a good actor is a good actor is a good actor. Someone with all the depth of feeling and empathy that these plays ask for. You want someone who is funny in life, charming, easy to work with. That's incredibly important to me. Someone you like being in the room with, because the audience by extension will like being in the room with them. I don't want big ego heads. Some of these plays do have big starring roles, but they are also always ensemble plays. Your bench needs to be deep. Some of those tiny characters are really important and have beautiful things to say in really great scenes. The talent needs to go deep in the cast. That stuff is more important to me than physical proximity to the character. It's just mental ease with the text.

You're working on a play and you're reading it and reading it. Then you do auditions. The moment you're in auditions, it opens up. You say, 'Oh I see! The scene I thought was impossible is not impossible at all!' Once it's spoken by someone who understands it, it's not difficult. It starts becoming real. It's embodied. Shakespeare's such a good read on the page that unfortunately those plays are treated as if they're literary words rather than what they are to me, the fossil remains of a live event. They are not what they are until they are embodied. The little inexplicable scenes suddenly become completely explicable once you put them on their feet.

You always want in your cast some old farts who've been around and have done a lot of it. They are so beautiful. It affirms that if you were good in the first place, you get better as you get older in this profession. The oldest person is often the best person in the cast because they've loved it enough to do it this long, and they know a lot, and they have reached a state of relaxation with it that can't be simulated. I don't mean to make a hard 'there are no exceptions' statement about this. Sometimes it will be the youngest child who is really good. But the old people have nothing to prove. All they want to do is say the text really clearly and give that story and that thought out in the way it is best served. They tend to, if they're good personalities, in the gentlest and least snotty way, mentor their colleagues. They'll very gently say, 'Now why do you think you're saying that to me? Is it because ____ ?' Just very, very gently. I don't mean those quarrelsome snobs. I mean really open hearted people. It's like having a very brilliant assistant director embedded in the cast. They do some of the heavy lifting for you with the other cast members. Undercover.

Libby Appel: Intelligence. Skill. Craft. I'm huge on craft. They have to get their tongue around these words. They have to have their breath to support to the end of the sentence. Not just the intention to get to the end of the line, but really the breath to get to the end of the line. Well, of course we all look for truth and imagination. We look for somebody who's going to bring something to the party.

Daniel Sullivan: The first thing I look for is facility with the language. Certainly an understanding of the technical demands of the language, but also an ability to improvise rhythmically within those demands. Imagine a good jazz drummer who can improvise around an insistent beat.

Kate Buckley: The bottom line in casting is to hire for talent and not a quality. Voice with Shakespeare is the most important skill for an actor. Then I'm interested in what I call 'thinking' actors – intelligent people wise about their craft, their function as a character, and have mastery of their instrument.

What I look for in an actor is honesty. Most actors I talk to say, 'Oh, you are so text specific. I'm going to have to work hard on the text'. I say, 'The text we can deal with. I want a real person on the stage who is not speaking Shakespeare. I don't want to hear Shakespeare. I want to hear a real person who chooses to speak in poetry.

David Esbjornson: Shakespeare belongs to all of us. One of the best things about our American Shakespeare productions is the diversity of our actors. The range of performers capable of performing classical work has increased dramatically in recent times. Historically, an approach to Shakespearean verse focused primarily on vocal technique and traditional approaches to the verse. While there is no question that technique is critical, over-emphasized speech can run the risk of creating an unintentional formality. Thanks to a number of great training programmes, a more contemporary approach has helped to create an informed, highly skilled American actor who can achieve precision with the speech without losing a deeper emotional connection. This makes our actors strong players on the world's stage. The passion and uniqueness of American classical actors have inspired British actors and directors in turn, and the notion that only the English can do Shakespeare's plays well has finally begun to fade away.

Timothy Douglas: I don't use a reader. I read with every single actor that comes to audition for me. So I can make the connection then. I don't need an actor to bring in the performance. I rarely hire the most polished actor who comes to audition for me, because usually they have so completely done it that there is no room for me to collaborate. That shows up in the audition process. So it's nothing to do with their talent or the greatness of who they are, but I am not interested in spending four or five weeks with trying to get you to agree to be a participant. So my theory about that is (and I learned this from Stephen Wadsworth), if I can make a connection to everyone that I cast, perhaps everyone will have a similar kind of connection to each other. Even though they're not the same at all. But the ability to connect, I don't need them to be the same, but are they willing to be open? I gain several days of rehearsal with this way of casting. I don't have to talk about how we are going to approach the work.

Ralph Alan Cohen: We get people who can believe in what we are doing. We *have* to have actors who are extremely aware of language. So in auditions we're very careful about looking for the people who make specific verbal choices in their heads, not just specific movements. We see a good actor a lot of times who is not interested in the language. The people we sign are people who are interested in the language.

When we audition, we bring people into the space in groups of twelve. And they see each other work. We tell them immediately, 'Look at us. Don't look away. When you talk to us, you talk to us. Use each other when appropriate'. So we try to see what it is that they can do in an atmosphere like that with the people around them. How do they create the room? How do they behave with the audience? Right from the audition, we are looking for people who are comfortable with this connection to the audience. A big difference between what we do and most theatres is that the audience is a part of it.

These twelve people get about an hour. We'll have as many as twenty groups of twelve people coming in. We see them do their monologue; we see them do sides together; we hear them sing. It's a very musical company. It does its own music. The process starts there with text and with your audience all around you, and everything about the process after that is text based and audience based.

Racial diversity in casting

Oskar Eustis: Most serious major Shakespeare theatre companies or Shakespeare productions at regional theatres would be embarrassed to be entirely white ... When they do Chekhov in Japan, they don't cast white servants. They cast Japanese servants. When they do Chekhov in Africa they don't cast European actors, they cast African actors. When you do Chekhov or Shakespeare in America, if you assume that you should be casting all white actors, you're not making a statement about Russia or about England. You're making a statement about America. You're saying that America is basically a white country. Because always and everywhere the casts of shows are made to look like the country of the show that is making the production, not where the play was originally written. And there still is that underlying assumption by far too many people that this is a white country that does outreach to other peoples. It isn't a white country. If we do our staging with all white actors, then we are lying about the country.

Timothy Douglas: At the moment in America, there is no such thing as functioning colour blind casting. I am a passionate proponent of non-traditional casting, however, which continues to reveal wonderful and unexpected truths as a result of the practice. But I am required to think very carefully about *whom* I am putting *where* – in terms of gender, in terms of race and in terms of perceived sexual orientation. That becomes very important when preparing to construct a story for American audiences and is a fun part of the process for me.

Being a director of colour allows me to get away with taking more risks with casting. I perceive the world through a male, African-American lens. Issues that surround race and diversity remain a constant and involuntary conversation for me everywhere I work – even when the play at hand has nothing inherently to do with race. Within the American regional theatres where I mainly work, I am almost always the only black person in a leadership position in the building when directing a production. Most of the time I am directing ethnic-specific plays or I am pushing for re-imagined productions of Shakespeare and other plays that are not traditionally mixed-race. The practice of non-traditional casting always elevates the conversations about race and diversity and perception by making the audience more sensitive to their inherent realities. I've had so many conversations with so many kinds of people that I can usually convince anyone who questions my casting choices. My confidence in my ability to effectively address (mis)understandings about race and culture, however, in no way diminishes my passion and requirement for collaboration.

Timothy Bond: As directors, we should seek a more diverse group of actors involved in telling these stories. I believe deeply that it enriches the work. It enriches the dialogue and discoveries in rehearsal. It enriches the characterizations because there are perspectives and a variety of experiences around the table. I think it becomes even more relevant because we see what our nation looks like collectively reflecting on our stage. It's what the great experiment of America is about: E Pluribus Unum – from many, one.

When I see productions of Shakespeare cast with an all white cast or with people of colour only in subservient roles, I don't see this as a 'traditional casting'. I see it as exclusive. I experience these productions as political statements that one race of people (even though I believe that race is a social construct) is more human than another. As a person of colour, I feel when I see these productions that a statement is being made that I am not as human as someone with white skin, because I am not included in the people in this world. When cultural specificity is not chief among the concerns of the story or plot or themes of a play, I believe that exploring an approach to peopling the play with a diverse cast, and putting together a diverse design team to explore the work, can open that play up to a wider, richer possibility.

I am saying, 'How can you balance what that appears to weight the play towards, in terms of the hierarchy, somewhere else?' I am quite overtly interested in giving more opportunities to artists of colour when possible. It actually opens up more roles, rather than cutting them down.

Sometimes people begin to get a taste of being more conscious about those issues and rather than being 'colour blind', they will then *not* put someone in a role they should have because they are not willing to go all the way through the whole exercise. In *King Lear,* for instance, I *can* have Edmund played by a person of colour, even though he is a villain, by having the Duke of France be a person of colour and he is a good guy. Now we have a nice balance and there is no hierarchal statement being made. There are no issues about, 'How come he had a family and the bastard is black?' Or 'the bastard is Latino'. 'Am I making a statement about bastards, about those people in those cultures being a certain way? Well no, because I did it over here and it didn't work that same way. So now I've balanced it out'. That's just being conscious.

A Raisin in the Sun, in my opinion, is a culturally specific play and a brilliant one. Lorraine Hansberry is specifically exploring a lower class black family in Chicago in 1959 that is experiencing racism within a white dominated culture. To not cast that play in the culturally/racially specific way Ms Hansberry has thematically drawn, would be to break the back of the world of the play. For me, the plays of Chekhov don't inherently discuss themes that are specific to race, but deal with human comedies about work and leisure, complex relations between men and women, improving social conditions, justice and fairness, desires for a new life. Chekhov plays, as well as others, are also quite nicely open to a wider audience, and artistically enriched with multicultural or inclusive casting opportunities.

I don't use the term 'colour blind casting' when it comes to approaching Shakespeare. I am not blind and I don't think audiences are either. The theatre is an image box. I have been a big proponent of approaching these projects with and commitment to inclusive casting or multicultural casting. Inclusive casting also includes gender, ability and sexual orientation. I still find myself consciously aware of the political, social and hierarchical contexts of each particular play, as well as its echo and resonance for a contemporary audience, and not so much its historical context. I am seeking unique perspectives and illuminations of themes through a diverse lens that connects these plays to contemporary audience experiences.

Cross-gender casting

Kathleen Conlin: I can't bring myself to put women in the traditional male roles, unless I was doing a very specific, conceptual production. I look at the number of male actors and the number of female actors I have to hire, and it just galls me that women are not getting the work. So, in our discussions, we try to balance it with the other shows that we choose. We try to balance it even with the Shakespeare that we choose, to see if there are enough significant female roles. I'm always inching up the number of female equity. Reactions will be, 'Well, we can get by with a non-equity woman in this particular role'. And I'll say, 'No, I think you've got enough guys here. We need to make sure that the women are cast appropriately too'. That to me is the biggest struggle.

Darko Tresnjak: In general I don't like doing it unless I'm going to do it full out all male or all female. I'm pretty conservative about that. The few times that I've had to do it, like at the Public with the ten-person *The Two Noble Kinsmen*, of the queens in the big scene at the beginning, two of them were played by men because of the cast size, because of economic limitations. The actors were great. I just didn't like doing it. So unless I was to evolve an all male or an all female production, I don't do it and I don't like seeing it without knowing why. Sometimes there's an extraordinary, extraordinary woman who wants to tackle *Hamlet*, like Diane Venora, who did it at the Public. I just haven't gotten there yet because I haven't found a good enough reason to do it.

Mary Zimmerman: I try and put more women in the plays than may be called for by Shakespeare. If there's a scene between two gentlemen, it very often can play perfectly with two gentlewomen. They're often little gossip scenes: 'What's with the king?' 'Well, I've heard it's because his son is an ass'. There is no reason for that not to be two women in the court we never see again instead of two men. In *Pericles* I made the necromancer a woman. I try and get more women in the cast. Women are great. They don't get as many parts in Shakespeare. It can be twenty-three men and three women. I try and find parts.

Joanne Zipay: The idea of casting women non-traditionally and men non-traditionally varies from show to show as to how we do it. Sometimes we do things straight or nearly straight. It just depends on the opportunities for the women involved. But that has to come from somewhere. It has to start with a good look at the play, and an understanding of what's going on in Shakespeare's gender roles. I'm extremely conscious of how gender operates in the plays, so to tweak that without really no reason, or without an awareness of how it operates, it can be detrimental, but also just not as interesting as making a choice for a reason. It's much more fun. And a lot of people go, 'Oh, I thought you were an all women theatre company'. Even our recent press for *Richard III* said it was an all woman *Richard III*, even though none of our press releases said that. Not that there's anything wrong with that. But I'm just much more interested in pushing the boundaries of gender on both sides.

With *Richard III*, for the first time, non-traditional casting has evolved for us. We've experimented with it. One of the reasons I do it is I want to set an example saying, 'Look at all the things!' You don't have to say, 'All women'. You don't have to say, 'Gender-reversed'. You don't have to say, 'Gender-blind'. You don't have to say, 'Traditional with a few roles changed'. But all of those things can work and all of things remain part of our season. I think we've gone from being very conservative to being much more risky with that kind of work. *Richard III* was the first production – full production – that was gender-blind with text and design, with a commitment to women, women in the title roles, and all the contenders for the crown as well – anybody who could possibly become a contender. We stuck with those as much as we could with *Richard III*.

But I had a Clarence walk in the door. It was a guy. And I said, 'This is my Clarence right here!' I wanted a man to play Margaret. I couldn't find that. You start with an idea, but then it's got to be the most practical for the role. Which takes it full circle to what we started with in the beginning: 'Look, women can play these parts. They're not given the opportunity to do them'. So we had a female Richard, a male Lady Anne. King Edward was played by a woman. Clarence was played by a man. Margaret and Elizabeth and the Duchess were played by women. The prince was played by a woman playing a boy. It was all mixed up. Some of the actors switched back and forth between various genders. It was set in the rock and roll world where gender bending is part of the scene. So it was a lot of fun and worked rather well.

I did start out very, very conservatively in the beginning – thinking the plays have to be, for the most part, cast very traditionally, and then seeing if I could find a way to give women more opportunities to bring it up to a 50/50 mark.

PART THREE

Rehearsing the Production

8

Beginning Rehearsals

Although there should always be great joy in rehearsal, great laughter and hilarity, I think the overall process, the movement of directing anything is a sort of sad one for the director. In the beginning you are so necessary. You have this physical proximity to the actors; you're right next to them at the table. Then they're up in front of you on their feet. So then you're sometimes up there and sometimes sitting down. Then suddenly you're the one sitting down all the time and they're over there. Then you're in the theatre and you're in the house and they're on the stage, further away. Eventually you're not even in the theatre. It's a process of leave-taking and loss for yourself and of creating your own obsolescence. And that's how it should be. You become unnecessary. At first you're necessary every second and then you're not necessary at all. That's what it is and how it should be.

MARY ZIMMERMAN

FIGURE 13 Avery Glymph, *Rachel Mewbron, Sean Fri, Dan Jones and Matthew Pauli in the Shakespeare Theatre Company's 2014 production of* The Tempest, *directed by Ethan McSweeny. Photograph by Scott Suchman.*

In the first part of this chapter, we see different strategies for handling the first day of rehearsal. Buckley does not like to 'lecture' the cast about her approach and ideas. Rather, this day is about 'adding the most important element: the actor onstage'. Before the first read-through, Frank instructs his cast to 'Do what you're ready to do!' He knows there is likely to be an actor who is petrified that they will make a fool of themselves. Cohen points out that instead of a first read through, the American Shakespeare Center asks the cast to rehearse together without the director for eight hours. They then perform a run-through for the director. This scheme means 'the play is already the actors' to some extent, no matter what the director then decides to do' with it.

Rauch considers collaboration to be the primary principle operating in his rehearsals. He sees his role as editor of actors' ideas and choices. He also urges his cast to be vulnerable and take risks and push their choices as far as they can. Gaines, Kahn and Buckley also mention that they collaborate closely with actors. Gaines believes rehearsals must feel safe so 'imaginations can soar'. She sees herself as a guide, but respects her actors' input because they must make the choices play throughout the run. Kahn feels he 'participate[s] viscerally and intellectually' in the actors' work. He hopes, by opening, they know their roles better than he ever did. Buckley does not like to discuss problems in rehearsal. Instead she asks her actors to 'Show me what you mean'. She regularly wants her actors to tell her where there are problems. Then, together they brainstorm solutions.

Other directors perceive their role as exerting more influence on the actors. Shine, while operating as the actors' partner, pushes them to explore beyond the first two choices that they have discovered. The production will be 'richer' for it. Serban sees the process as both subjective and objective: he first works intimately onstage with the actors. Then he removes himself and observes their work from a distance. This induces an antipodean tension within himself and the company concerning the emerging performance. He also uses antithetical methods when rehearsing: he investigates the text closely and critically, and then ignores it while freely improvising. Douglas works to 'access the actor immediately in a way that doesn't put them further in their head'. He induces actors to commit to their initial impulses. When they encounter problems, he trains them how 'to shift the focus' from themselves to something else, which frees them to reveal the moment. Ultimately, he believes his job is to 'teach them how to think'. Packer's objective is to 'work as the Elizabethans did', directing actors to fully embrace Shakespeare's words 'on the deepest level – understanding the philosophy and psychology' of the text. She analyzes where the energy needs a jolt and where the pacing must slow so the audience can genuinely hear what is being said. Most importantly, like many directors, she wants the text to speak to us today. Monte argues, 'Every single moment of the production must be specific'. This leads to generating character behaviour frequently missing in Shakespeare productions. Mullins does not like for his actors to stop or slow down the action: 'It just needs to go'. Zimmerman points out distinctions among types of actors who require different responses from her. She sees herself as the conductor who leads the cast, but does not teach them how to perform.

Some directors set specific rehearsal goals for themselves and for the company. Buckley likes to work on ten pages of text each day. Lamos wants his cast to learn the lines as soon as possible. Douglas confides that in every Shakespeare production, there is one scene the actors hate. His solution is to rehearse it a little every day. It always becomes everyone's favourite scene, he says.

Some directors establish a specific rehearsal atmosphere. McSweeny refers to rehearsals as 'a committee meeting that lasts for nine hours'. Zimmerman states that she has an 'open door' policy for her rehearsals and that there should be a lively yet disciplined atmosphere in the room. For McAnuff, 'what is truly important is to make people feel really safe – safe to make mistakes, to make fools of themselves, to be wrong, to be exposed – without ever feeling that there is a danger they will be taken advantage of or persecuted'.

Finally, Kulick shares an observation on the nature of rehearsing Shakespeare. You can study the play for months and go into rehearsals thinking you know the piece. But 'it really will not reveal its true self – what it really is – until about three weeks into rehearsal'. He argues that this is because the language contains a specific energy that, once released in the rehearsal room, reveals 'a very different play than the one you thought you were working'.

First day

Kate Buckley: Before the first day of rehearsal, the pre-production design work should be finished. There should be no surprises for me in this regard. Then the first day of rehearsal is about adding the most important element: the actor onstage.

On the first day of rehearsal, I don't talk much. I'm not a lecturer: 'The play, as I see it, means such and such'. The very first day of rehearsal, before we start, I shake everybody's hand, a one-on-one welcome. 'I'm glad to be working with you', sort of thing. After a business meeting takes place, the designers show the results of their process. I often find my designers to be more articulate about the play than I am. Once show-and-tell is over, we read the play. Everyone goes home and I think about the actors, 'Okay, how do I perceive this actor in this role, how will he or she handle this character's strengths and weaknesses? Do I have to make adjustments there or don't I?'

David Frank: We do the read-through that everybody does. Everyone has their own individual approach to it. One director insists, 'NO ACTING!' Another urges, 'Come on, we're all friends, embarrass yourselves, give it a go!' And I, ever the compromiser, advise 'Do whatever you're ready to do!' Because I know there's some poor actor new to the company terrified that they are going to embarrass themselves. And nothing is gained by pretending you are ready when you are not. So, 'Do what you're ready for. And do remember, this may be the last time for some weeks you hear what's said about you in the scenes that you're not in'.

Ralph Alan Cohen: Our actors arrive off book on the play and the first thing they do is what we call a 'Ren Run' – Renaissance Run because it's patterned after early modern rehearsals – in which they get eight hours *without the* director to put on the play for the director to see. (Tiffany Stern's book on rehearsal was a breakthrough work for us, another example of trusting that early moderns knew their stagecraft.)[1] What that means, obviously, is that the play is already the actors' to some extent, no matter what the director then decides to do. Usually 90 per cent of their choices are fine with me, so it feels to them like the play is coming out of their heads – and of course it is. Sure, if you have a director that says, 'I don't like any of it', it's not as much theirs, but even then, they have more ownership. And every year during the three months of our Actors' Renaissance Season, they do five plays without a director at all – the whole thing is a 'Ren Run' – and all the plays gain. It all comes back to the actors.

Working with actors

Bill Rauch: In the rehearsal hall, I pride myself on trying to create a rehearsal room that is really inclusive, where the best idea wins, where there's safety for people to speak up and share their ideas. Very rarely, but occasionally, it can become chaos because there are too many cooks, too many opinions. Then you have to pull it back. God forbid that it was just up to me and my ideas and my imagination. That would be awful! It's a collaborative art form. The actors are the ones who are living with these characters and living with the language coming out of their mouths, so I strongly believe in trusting their instincts. They may have multiple instincts. Part of my job is helping to edit which of those instincts they follow, how to take an instinct and an impulse, and go deeper with it and take it further, and take it to its extreme. Exploration is just keen in me. I absolutely do not have the gift as a director of coming in with prepared blocking and telling people where to move. I know that there are crafts people who may also be wonderful artists, but they are also crafts people where they can see it all and just put it out there and do it pretty quickly. That is not one of my gifts.

Barbara Gaines: Once trust has been born, there's no limit to the creativity that takes place in the rehearsal room … and hopefully there's always room for laughter throughout that process. But it's always my goal to create a safe place so their imaginations can soar. There are no bad ideas, because something that doesn't work can always lead to something fantastic that does. Having been an actor for nearly twenty years, I approach the text in rehearsal with each character's intent in mind.

The biggest lesson I've learned is that directors are merely guides; we inspire other's creativity and then we try and shape those performances. If you have an idea that an actor doesn't like, find another one. They're performing eight shows a week and they must be connected to every moment they perform. There are always other ideas.

Michael Kahn: I go into rehearsal. I'm very interested in what the actor finds out because I think it is collaboration. At the beginning I think I know the play better than anybody in the room. By opening night I hope the actors know their characters better than I ever will.

When I direct, I find that I can live through all the characters on stage in some way. I can't quite explain it. But I know that it's less about my ideas than it is about what's going on and how it all fits together. I think, in some form or another, I've tabled my ego in the rehearsal to participate viscerally and intellectually in what's happening with the actors.

Also, I like actors to rehearse pretty full out all the time now. I don't mean over-act and I don't mean push. I don't believe in this mumbling 'saving yourself', even if you're carrying the script. 'Make a choice! Do something! Let the other actors respond to you!' It's amazing how actors can do that if you allow them ... to say it's what you'd like.

Kate Buckley: I tend to work fairly fast. I do not spend time talking in rehearsal. If there is a problem, an issue, a disagreement, I will ask the actor to execute the idea. 'Show me what you mean. Get on your feet and do it'. Out of that comes my riffing on it or them riffing on it a little bit more, or us coming to a meeting of the minds about a moment, and then we proceed from there. It's about working on your feet all of the time.

The most wonderful thing about this process is that actors get into a rehearsal groove. When it's not right, they can see it, feel it. 'I've got an idea!' 'Okay, great, next time we do it, try it'. After every rehearsal I ask, 'What are you feeling uncomfortable about? Anything wonky? Anything odd? Anything not speaking to you? Anything you don't think you know how to work on? Let's talk about it now, before we move on'. And that seems to do the trick.

Stephanie Shine: I am trying to change the way that people rehearse. In my years of being an actor, I became aware that normally, as actors, we choose the first choice, maybe the second choice, and then we spend the remaining two and a half weeks refining and perfecting that initial choice, instead of working exploratively. I'll say to some of my actors, 'That was a great choice. Instead of that first one, you should do something else. What happens if you do that? What does each one feel like? Look at his nose. Think of all the circumstances. What else could happen? Even if we go back to the original choice, the exploration will help refine that and it will be much richer for it'.

Andrei Serban: Part of the rehearsal is listening to one's hunch, as Brook used to say. Listen to one's intuition. Work from intuition. Then, be totally heated up into whatever our subconscious imagination is allowed to bring and the facets of the subconscious imagination is allowed to open. The next day I like to look at it with distance, a total cool look. The director has to step out and look from a distance to what the actors are doing. The role of the director is to help, to be a friend in need. Mainly the director is most useful when they can step out and observe: be involved totally with the actors, improvise with them, laugh and cry together, even act with them. Then there is the moment when they need to step out and look and try to see from the point of view of the audience, from the point of view of a distant third eye. The audience also should be able to be involved in the experience and be able to watch, become observers. Uniting two opposite methods, Stanislavsky and Brecht: identification and distancing. Shakespeare invites both attitudes. We may really feel uplifted by his challenge for a new vision.

We start by reading the play. And then we forget the play. This means half the day we just read and discuss in great detail every image, sometimes every word, the connection between sound and syllables that compose a word … one can spend years on that fascinating analysis and discovery of what made Shakespeare select one pattern of words, why this and not another? And the other half we do improvisations, exercises that are totally free and apparently unrelated. Next day I ask, 'What is your impression of the play? Your impression of your character?' This is done at a very early stage in which we know little: through improvisations, playfulness, through the exercises, not yet concerned to fix or to stage anything, but to come up with all kinds of compositions and try-outs for possible development later. Then go back to the text. We read the text deeper. Then the words become active, the bodies and the words start making a connection, like the sensation of falling in love for the first time, that fresh memory from youth awakens … we become more sensitive, that is what matters most.

Timothy Douglas: If I am working with someone who is a stand and poser, not a revealer, I'll keep picking at them. 'Okay, try this. When you do that, this is what I am feeling'. 'I am feeling that too'. 'Well, but that is not really what is coming across with what you are doing'. They get frustrated. They think that they are doing it, and something else completely is happening. Although the source of it is exactly what I am asking for, yet it comes out differently. Remember the old Rocky and Bullwinkle. 'Hey, watch me pull a rabbit out of my hat'. And he pulls a lion out of his hat. That's what's going on. And they say, 'But I am so frustrated. I don't know how'. And

I say, 'Okay, so speak the text from that place of frustration'. It doesn't matter what they are feeling, as long as I can keep the actor working from what's actually happening with them.

By teaching all those years I absorbed how to access the actor immediately in a way that doesn't further put them in their head about whatever it is that they are working on, whatever it is they're trying to 'make better'. But as Einstein said, 'You cannot focus on the problem at the level of the problem. You have to elevate. You have to get to another vantage point to see the whole thing'. If we are stuck, my job is to shift the focus. Then, once we have connected, we look back with fresh eyes. It's the classic 'Let me sleep on it'. You get away from it for a moment. The voice work is purely technical theories and exercises that elicit much. But our primary job is to teach them how to think.

Tina Packer: I work as the Elizabethans did: in love with poetry, physical prowess and the mysteries of the universe. Actually what is being said, in this present moment, is where I spend most of my *time*. An actor needs not just to say the words Shakespeare wrote, but own them on the deepest level – understanding the philosophy and psychology. For example 'There's nothing good or bad but thinking makes it so' is an extraordinary statement. If an audience member can ponder that for a moment, it can change her life. How do I make sure that gets said in the right place on stage, what needs to happen around it, how do I reinforce that idea with the tech elements and so on? When does the energy on stage need a boost? A jig? A murder? A joke? Has Shakespeare written it in, or do I need to provide it? When do we need to slow down, reflect a little? At which moment will we be silent? The overall oral/aural story must be framed, but rarely subsumed in visual effects, bent to the director's concept. Shakespeare was proposing so many new ideas (many of which are still new today) that its important we let him speak.

Bonnie Monte: Every single moment of the production must be *specific*. It must be massively specific from an emotional point of view, from a physical point of view, from a director point of view, from a behavioural point of view.

And that leads to the second thing, which is *behaviour*. It is mostly ignored, particularly in Shakespeare. What makes Shakespeare brilliantly come alive is allowing the actor, or encouraging the actor [to behave], because in a lot of cases they don't think they have to do anything except say the words. It's like, 'I'm sorry you're a human, you must behave'. And then finding the specificity of what that means behaviourally. Everybody makes fun of me. They are like, 'Bonnie, Bonnie, Bonnie, specificity, specificity, specificity!' And I am like, 'Yeah. That's why you guys are such good actors because you got trained here with specific things!' They are like, 'We know, we know, we know! We're just making fun of you!' I will sit with a young director or a young actor and say, 'Do it again, do it again, do it again. It wasn't specific'.

Paul Mullins: In a Shakespeare play what matters to me is that the play keeps moving. 'You're stopped. Go'. You know Shakespeare's actors didn't stop. They didn't do anything to stop. Not that I don't stop. There are places in my plays where it stops, but I think for the most part the idea is that it keeps moving, that it flows. It just needs to go.

Mary Zimmerman: With some actors you say, 'So when you come into the scene, what do you think you're feeling towards her? Why do you pause there?' Then you talk about that for fifteen minutes. Then you turn to another actor, and you say, 'Act II, Scene 1, line 30, the one about thus and so? Faster. Pick it up'. And that's all that actor wants or needs. You're trying to learn their vocabulary and how they work and how they need to process what you are doing. I don't force or require anything. Some people like to warm up. Some people, their warm up is having a cigarette and reading the paper. That's exactly what they should be doing, if that's what they want to do. You respect the individual processes of your actors and their capabilities and what they need.

I'm not real good at handholding. I feel like I'm casting professionals. We'll work on the scenes. I don't want to have long phone calls at night about ____. It's their problem. I think of it like an orchestra. The conductor is not teaching the musicians how to play. They know how to play. He's shaping the way in which we're all going to play this together. The pace, pitch, volume, rhythm, emphasis we're going to use to get the effect we think we should have, to tell the story we think is there.

Goals, atmosphere, energy

Kate Buckley: My goal is ten pages a day. I don't always accomplish that length. Sometimes it's seven, eight. If I can work at a ten page a day pace, and we can run earlier, the actors get very confident.

Mark Lamos: I encourage the actors to learn the lines as quickly as they can. Until the lines are firmly inside the memory, really deep, insightful work can't begin. Sometimes during the first few days of staging I'll give a couple hours of rehearsal time to the stage managers and assistants to run lines with the actors – even on scenes we may not yet have staged – so that they are more fluid when we work. Actors who arrive completely prepared, with most of their lines learned, are already way ahead of everyone else and are exhilarating to work with. Ditto people who might have played the same role in a previous production. Even if we disagree with each other, we both know what we're talking about. They know the play in a way I don't – they've already lived in it. I can learn from their experience.

Timothy Douglas: Every play I direct, particularly Shakespeare, there is one scene where the actors are like, Uhhhhh!' In *Pericles* it's the fisherman scene. And because they're like that, it is harder for me to get them excited. And I'm like, 'Uhh!' So what I learned was, you come to that scene and you rehearse it a little bit everyday. Twenty minutes everyday. And every time they say the language, it's like 'Uuuuuuhhhhhh'. But then we go through it, and then it happens every time. For those actors, it becomes their favourite scene. The fisherman scene in *Pericles* is one of the most beautiful, poignant [scenes]. More gets communicated about life's philosophy in that scene than in the rest of that play. The rest of that journey for Pericles hinges on what he learns from those fishermen.

Ethan McSweeny: I was trying to describe rehearsal to someone who was not in the theatre, a friend who did not understand why I had not called or emailed him back for a couple days and I said, 'Rehearsal is like a committee meeting that lasts for nine hours. And you take a break every hour and twenty minutes, and someone not on the committee comes to ask you a question. At the end of the nine hours, you set the agenda for the next day's committee meeting. It's a very public, full event. You're not alone. You're not in private very much with it. And you do it six days a week. It's very, very busy.

Mary Zimmerman: I have a very open door in rehearsals. I always say, 'The rehearsal process is sacred but it's not fragile. Anyone can come and walk in. I welcome donors. I welcome anyone to come from the staff. Visitors, people have friends from out of town. Fine. Anyone can come in at any time. It's strong enough. We're not going to crumble. In fact, we better not crumble because it's meant for other people'.

We laugh all the time. Even if you're doing the bleakest play on earth, it's not called a play for nothing. We are playing and we should be laughing. But I don't sit there and tell personal stories. I don't go into long anecdotes. We work hard. Some people think that because in my normal process of adaptation I write the script (alone, in my bed, in the early hours of the morning) during the same time frame as rehearsals, that there must be a kind of airy-fairy, loosey-goosey vibe about the whole thing and that's how we'd be with Shakespeare as well. Absolutely not so in either case. I don't have time for that. It's really disciplined actually. We start and we go. On break we might chat about the movie we saw last night, but it's all Shakespeare all the time.

Des McAnuff: I was sitting at the worktable in a technical rehearsal. It suddenly occurred to me that everyone in the room hated me, 'every actor on this stage at this moment really hates me'. I remember thinking, 'That can't be good. You know, that just can't be good'. I was so very demanding when I was young. They used to call me things like the Tasmanian devil and refer to my rehearsals as Mr Toad's Wild Ride [*laughter*]. There is a moment when putting on a large show like a musical, where you really do have to push people beyond their own limits and take them places that they themselves don't know they could go. I had that happen on shows like *Tommy*, where it's just monstrously fast and intense, and even at times quite dangerous. You have to make sure that everyone is alert and taking care of themselves. I accept that and my role can be at times unpleasant for me and perhaps unpleasant for others, but I think that what is truly important is to make people feel really safe – safe to make mistakes, to make fools of themselves, to be wrong, to be exposed – without ever feeling that there is a danger they will be taken advantage of or persecuted. If you lose it once, they know it can happen again. So you have to resist ever being unreasonable even when you feel it is justified. I hope I have changed a lot since I was young. I hope I am more confident. I hope I am more collaborative.

With young actors, sometimes I remind them that everyone in the room is talented. What distinguishes us from others who have talent is our craft, knowledge and dedication.

Brian Kulick: You can read a lot of scholarly work about a Shakespeare text in advance. You can do a lot of thinking about a Shakespeare text in advance, but it really will not reveal its true self – what it really is – until about three weeks into rehearsal. You can have a good educated guess going in as to what it might really be, but you really don't know. Shakespeare's language traps a certain kind of energy. Once the actors become versed in the particular use of that language – once they grow into it and are able to control it, own it – the energy is released, the genie is let out of the bottle and the energy of these words can manifest a very different play than the one you thought you were working; it becomes a play of action, a play of energy, of primordial forces at war with one another. But the actor and director need to arrive at a certain level of competency to get to that place, to be able to release this energy. Then suddenly there's a different beast in the room. If you think of a Shakespearean text as a forest, you may go hunting for deer and what you discover in the middle of Shakespeare's forest is a bear.

9

Table Work

I've had the experience of working on a Shakespeare play where we didn't talk about the play around the table. Then we're three weeks into rehearsal, and all of a sudden rehearsal breaks down into an enormous discussion of what something means. Which then has ramifications for everything we have done, and it shifts everything. If you have a number of those, it can derail your whole production.

JOANNE ZIPAY

Traditionally, table work occurs at the beginning of the rehearsal phase, with a few directors returning to the table periodically. Length of time devoted to this stage can vary significantly. Some directors sit at table for only a day or two or three, others for a full week. Still others will do this work for a week to ten days, and some employ it for up to two weeks. Longer table work sessions were more common a decade ago. For many, the pressure of shorter and shorter rehearsal periods has meant there is less time for this work. Additionally, most companies can no longer afford for actors to come to rehearsal without having done some pre-rehearsal text work – perhaps even being off book on day one.[1]

FIGURE 14 Romeo and Juliet, *directed by David Ivers, Utah Shakespeare Festival, 2011. Christian Barillas as Romeo and Magan Wiles as Juliet. Photograph by Karl Hugh.*

All but two directors I interviewed did some form of table work. Typically, the play is read at the first rehearsal by the full cast. Often the next step is for the director and cast to sit and discuss the play. This usually includes studying and scrutinizing the text for various characteristics. The actual textual analysis and table discussions can contain several activities.

Buckley, Zimmerman, Frank and Monte read the play through once or twice, but then begin to get up from the table. They read and table work a scene, and then start working it with the actors on their feet as they work through the play scene-by-scene. This approach appears to be more and more prevalent in recent years. Lamos and Shine, however, differ considerably from the norm. Lamos avoids a read through until all of the table work has been completed. Shine, on the other hand, likes her actors to get up on their feet right away without a read-through or any table work. She will sit to examine language characteristics and clarify meanings later in the process, after the actors have spent some time physicalizing the text.

There are several possible purposes for table work. Thompson, Kulick, Cohen, McSweeny and Packer use it to clarify textual meanings. Thompson and Kulick question what the words and speeches specifically mean. Cohen has a methodical approach of paraphrasing for his company: 'change all the nouns, verbs, adjectives and adverbs ... keep the proper nouns the same as well as the prepositions'. McSweeny asks key questions: 'What does this mean? What is the action? How does it play? What does it do to the other character that makes them do something to you?' Packer describes her process of 'dropping-in', which she says is 'almost the opposite of table work' as the actors sit close, facing one another. Her goal is to get the actor to embody the words on a deep level 'in relationship to the person' with whom they are rehearsing the scene.

Tresnjak warns that actors download various editions from the Internet with varied punctuation choices. Some of this is useful, but some of it must be discarded. Analyzing the scansion and punctuation is important to Gaines who, like many American directors, uses the First Folio as her basis.[2] Kulick is also 'obsessed' with punctuation, criticizing edited texts that he feels are over punctuated. Shakespeare's texts were sparsely punctuated, he argues, and meant 'for the ear, rather than the eye'. He considers what each mark means in terms of 'weights and measures', pauses, breaths, eye blinks, acceleration and deceleration. Cohen examines the text for figures of speech, irregularities and a change from formal to informal word choices. Lamos not only loves analyzing punctuation, but he also relishes examining the sound characteristics of the language, including rhyme, alliteration and assonance.

Some directors use table work to determine the specific story that the production will tell. For Douglas, there must be agreement about the narrative and the given circumstances – which includes how the actors feel about a circumstance.

McSweeny has discovered that 'if you want people thinking about stories, you've got to get them telling stories'. His next step is to focus on the actors' comprehension of that story.

Directors use different criteria in getting the company on the same page. Peterson wants unity on the play's central issues. Metropulos seeks group consensus on text, story, relationships and character. J. R. Sullivan is after cohesion 'with the main idea' and the 'conceptual approach'. Woronicz seeks agreement on what the major moments are. Lamos looks to 'get a sense of the sound and meaning of each scene and character'. Determining the event of each scene is vital for Eustis. Ivers believes the structure is primary and uses punctuation and the timeline to help construct it. For Tresnjak, the company needs to understand the energy shifts, while Kulick considers how 'language leads to action, action leads to energy and that energy becomes a kind of rhythm'.

Warren, Neville-Andrews and Kahn describe how they develop different stratums as they are at table. For Warren, it is a five-layer process, with repeated passes through the play. Neville-Andrews is interested in using table work to 'get to know the actors, their chemistry' and what kind of research they have done. Kahn breaks the play into scenes, starts working through scene-by-scene. In the first week, he asks the actors 'What are you talking about? What did you say? What did you just hear?' By the end of week one, actors are ready to move as he starts the next phase: exploring their impulses.

Rauch and Thompson share how they return to table work even well after that phase of the rehearsal has finished. This is when they will discuss stakes, phrasing and operatives.

At the end of this chapter, I have included an extended discussion by Des McAnuff and his dramaturg, Robert Blacker on a technique they use when table working a Shakespearean text: 'image chains'. When compared with what other directors do in their table work session, I find their approach to be unique.

Everyone at table versus scene-by-scene

Lisa Peterson: I like to do at least four days of table work. Every group is different of course. Some casts are great at table work. It's revelatory and interesting. They're interested. Some casts are not. Maybe it will be three days, if it's a cast that just is antsy and wants to get up.

Penny Metropulos: Basically it takes about a week and a half. In a normal theatre, that would be one whole week of rehearsal, thirty–forty hours of rehearsal, spent on table work.

Daniel Sullivan: I spend at least a week or more with the actors at the table just reading through the play and I generally don't start staging until I feel the actors wanting to move. It's always kind of a sad time for me. I love sitting and talking about it.

Darko Tresnjak: I cannot neglect the table work, especially working in the rep. It takes as long as it takes. I have no preconception how long it's going to take. If it takes two or three days, fine. If it takes a week and a half, if it takes ten days, it takes as long as it takes, until we get on the same page with the text.

Kate Buckley: When I first started out, it was 'Table work, table work, table work! We must be at the table for at least a week'. Because of the financial demands placed upon the theatres now, the schedules are very tight, so I start the staging as soon as possible. This process is: read a scene, table work the scene, read it again, talk about it a little bit more, get it up on its feet for very basic blocking and move on to the next scene. I do that until I get to the end of the act – part one – then run it, then tweak it.

Mary Zimmerman: My first two or three plays, I did that standard thing where the entire cast sits around the table, reads the play. First they have a regular read-through. Then they do another read through. Then you go scene-by-scene. I felt the pressure of the boredom of people who aren't in that half of the play or that scene – it was working on me to make me rush. I realized we weren't really doing the work. I would say, 'Well, generally it's that ...'. I could feel the pressure. I'm very conscious of other people's time.

About two productions ago, I started to do it this way: We read the play a couple of times together, chatting about it in an informal way, and then I say, 'Thank you very much'. My tendency is to get on our feet instantaneously – partly, I suppose, because that is how I work when I am working on my own scripts. But I force myself to continue that intense table work with Shakespeare, but I'll do it only with the people in that scene, and only scene-by-scene. That way we can indulge ourselves ruminating and clarifying all we want. Then, when the other actors start to see the play, when we are doing longer runs of scenes and of acts, it completely tells them what play they are in. It does the work so much more efficiently. I don't feel the pressure. They are intensely interested.

I had this experience so many times of being scanty on that table work with the whole group because I felt the pressure – like the whole room weighing down on me. Those arguments can go on for five minutes on a single line! That's fine for us who are interested, but I just feel the tedium of that for other people who are just interested in the results. They're not in the scene. So I was sometimes really skirty on that stuff. But you have to watch out, because skirting on that with Shakespeare will get you three weeks later when you're having the most difficult time on a scene. 'Why is this actor not understanding my note? Why is he playing it like that?' Finally you say flat out, 'What do you think that means?' You find out he or she thinks it means something entirely different than what it does mean or you assume it meant. And that is why the whole scene is playing so oddly and not functioning and not working. It's because someone is in a different scene than other people on the stage.

David Frank: I do like to do a lot of table work, but not multiple read-throughs of the entire play. I can't keep all that in my head. I like to work on it scene-by-scene, taking whatever time is needed to develop a common understanding of the language and of our first draft of the dynamics of the scene. What is the essential story? Where are the conflicts? Where are the critical 'pivot' moments in the scene, the moment that sends the scene shooting off in another direction? And what do we learn about the characters. If you have done that work thoroughly with experienced actors, a lot of the staging will look after itself.

Bonnie Monte: I will say to them, 'We will not spend a lot of time on table work like most directors do'. I will do two days on general table work for the whole gang together. Then we will immediately get up and do rough, rough, rough blocking, so that you have a physical, tangible framework for the world that you're inhabiting. We do incredible intricate table work on each scene right before we go to block it. So the blocking process takes me a little longer. I will table work for a couple of hours a scene or two or three in the morning that we are going to block that day. Then all the information is fresh. So it keeps all the intellectual discussion in concert with the progression of the physical world. Some people table work, but then they stop talking about it all for the rest of the process.

Mark Lamos: For two or three days the entire cast along with the stage managers, the dramaturg, perhaps the costume designer, the voice coach and anyone else who might be of use, sits down after introductions have been made, and then we begin to slowly work through the text. I don't do read-throughs, they put actors on the spot too much, I feel. Having been an actor myself, I want everyone in the room to feel a sense of relaxation and 'play', as much ease as possible, and a sense that we are all – together – looking carefully at this giant poem. So it's a time during which we can begin to get a sense of the sound and meaning of each scene and character – as well as each other's personalities, quirks, minds, techniques. We also get a sense of the directorial concept, who the director is, and a chance to ask questions about the play itself. I encourage everyone to participate in the discussion since it will be the only time as a company we will address the play together.

As the table work comes to an end, and we've read and discussed the entire text together at the table, we read the play through for the first time without stopping. Before we begin this, I encourage the actors to go full throttle, 'let it rip' – just to get it out of their heads and into the air we're all breathing. I also suggest that anyone who feels like it may, as they read, get up out of their seat and read on their feet, since a few days 'at the table', while useful, can result in actors' heads stuck too deeply on the page and not as aware of their bodies as they're going to need to be when staging begins.

Stephanie Shine: You know what I have started to do recently? My actors are often looking at me as if I am out of my mind. The first read through I don't do that anymore. So I say, 'Okay, alright, just walk it through'. So that right away, whatever you do, it's active.

Meaning and comprehension

Kent Thompson: I start to try to go through as specific on the text work as we can. We'll spend three or four days around the table. Because I find that many of us understand speeches of Shakespeare generally, but not very specifically. The best example I can use is 'If music be the food of love' speech in *Twelfth Night*. Many people, if you ask them what the speech means, they say, 'Well, this guy's love sick'. And I go, 'Well that's true, but what he's saying is specifically what? And paraphrase it'. And 'You'll never be as good at paraphrasing it as Shakespeare is at writing it, but paraphrase it'. So that we talk about that he wants his love to die. He wants to be surfeited with feeding. We discover all the various imagery in there. And a lot of times I find that professional actors have skipped that step a little bit. I try to get back to that, to really go into a text and try and figure out what it means.

Brian Kulick: The first thing I need to know for myself is what does every line mean? Give me a paraphrase! What does this word mean? At the beginning it's like, 'I'm sorry, what did you say? I'm sorry, could you say that again? I'm sorry the operative word is? I'm sorry. Does that word mean this?' Or, 'Could you colour this more so I understand what that meaning is?' It might as well have been opera. It might as well have been sung in Italian. For me, even to this day, my first plateau is comprehension – making it comprehensible and making it immediate – so that the actor can first understand it and then ground it.

Ralph Alan Cohen: We do the bookwork. It starts with a word for word paraphrase. We tell the actors change all the nouns, verbs, adjectives and adverbs to the closest alternative you can find. You can keep the proper nouns the same. All the prepositions can stay the same. What we are not asking for is, 'To be or not to be' means 'I'm tired of life'. We are asking for 'To exist or not to exist?' We want a word for word replacement so that the director can hear, 'Does the actor have in his head the right thing *and* the right syntax'.

Ethan McSweeny: We start doing a close reading where we're going to start and stop. We're going to just ask the questions, interrogate the text: 'What does this mean?' And 'If that's what that means, why do you say what you say next? How do these things function together?'

I trust that all of us can read the script and read the footnotes [*laughs*]. It's not my job to walk us through the footnotes. Ultimately I'm interested in what it means, but I'm really interested in what it does and what's happening. What is the action? How does it play? What does it do to the other character that makes them do something to you?

Tina Packer: I begin rehearsal with a process called dropping-in. This is going word-by-word through the text, sitting eyeball to eyeball with your fellow actor. It is a process that gets the actors to own the words and own them in relationship to the person they are working with. It is deep work. It is almost the opposite of table work – it asks the actor to be in touch with his/her body, breathe, let the sound of the word have an effect, see what's in the unconscious mind and then notice what comes up. We all notice what ideas and words Shakespeare repeats and repeats again.

Punctuation, scansion, language analysis

Darko Tresnjak: These days actors get different editions; sometimes people download things from the Internet. I do that so that I can realign the text when I'm doing the cut. You realize that based on where they got it, that their reading of the line can be completely different. It's broken up differently. Sometimes you go, 'Ah, that's beautiful, that's great. I'd have never thought of it that way'. And then other times you can go, 'Really I don't think that's a good idea. I think this way would be more rewarding for the audience'.

Barbara Gaines: The Folio punctuation is of prime importance when trying to understand a character. If you follow the guidelines within a monologue, the actor will automatically feel just how the character feels. It's actually a miraculous experience. If you give real time in rehearsal to a detailed exploration of his text, you'll find that you're watching life itself being born.

Brian Kulick: Recently I find myself obsessed with punctuation. I no longer trust modern edited versions of Shakespeare and find myself poring over the punctuation of the quartos and the folio. Reminding myself how lightly punctuated these play texts actually are and that the punctuation in Shakespeare's time was for the ear, rather than for the eye. Shakespeare sits between an oral culture and print culture. His punctuation is about what you hear. His punctuation is about weights and measures: a comma is a blink of an eye, a semi-colon a half breath, a dash is an acceleration, a period is a full stop. Modern editors over punctuate, there is a preponderance of semi-colons that means, if you dutifully observe all of them, you can add ten to fifteen additional minutes to a production. I ask myself, when an actor in Shakespeare's theatre saw a semi-colon what did he think? Take a half breath? Or is the semi-colon, as some scholars think, an indication for a change of thought. It is interesting that every time there is a semi-colon there is a radical change of thought or intention. I find myself using this as a shorthand for understanding the shifts and changes in the characters. Also, what about odd capitalizations of words within sentences, is that a hint of what words should be stressed? And what about spaces between words, is that a compositors error or an indication for the actor to have thinking time? Not to mention issues like: why in one scene are lines attributed to Robin Goodfellow and a few lines later to Puck? And why does this not happen in one scene but several scenes? Is this another compositor error? Or an indication for the actor that here he should emphasize aspects of his character that is more in line with the hobgoblin Robin Goodfellow and here he should be more lovable and antic like Puck? All of these issues need to be unpacked and teased out over table work.

Ralph Alan Cohen: In those same sessions where we do the paraphrase, we do the scansion. I've now added figures of speech to their scripts and I ask them each to overstress one pattern of a figure they have. Every time we have an irregular line, we ask why? Every time we have a 'thee' rather then a 'you', why? Or a 'you' rather than a 'thee'. Particularly when it's a shift. 'What's going on? Why did you go from the formal to the informal? What's happening here? Just think about it'. It gets down to choices. In my direction, mostly what I say is, 'I don't care what you choose, but have a reason why you did this. You just made a shift. Understand that you made a shift'.

Mark Lamos: While we're working at the table, I am careful to point out internal rhymes, repeated vowel sounds within a line or a speech, and the way consonants need to be sounded, as well. I want the actors to be aware of the art of the poetry – because that knowledge will actually serve their work in bringing the character to vivid life. The sibilants in 'To be or not to be,' for instance … There's a softness to the sound of the speech, all those 's's' … They are pointing the way to interpretive choices for the actor. 'To sleep, perchance to dream'. That internal rhyme: so beautiful, so useful: 'sleep', 'dream'. Or the great primary colours of vowel sounds in 'O for a muse of fire –' All monosyllables – which are important to note, since they always express high energy – they are the most economical words. O/mUse/fIre! Big bright sounds.

'But soft what light through yonder window breaks?' Only two words are disyllabic. And note the consonants, so delicate: BuT SoFT whaT lighT. Then the completely different sound of 'yonder window' with their 'n's' and 'd's', all leading to BreaKS. You can't speak such a line too quietly. And it's a question. The hesitancy of it, the sense of the speaker being open to the visual clues in a city night. This is what the verse tells you. For starters.

Story

Timothy Douglas: We read and then we sit and discuss at the table until we are done. The play tells us what to think. The play tells us what it needs from us. It's a group discussion. Everyone is there for all of the table work. By the time we get to the end of table work, do we agree on the basic story being told? We keep asking that along the way. And if we don't, we have very lively discussions with people weighing in on what they're feeling about the moment. Then 'Okay, now consider this. Here are the given circumstances of Elizabethan England, and here are the given circumstances of Tyre or Ephesus, or this imaginative world that Pericles lives in, or the protocol of this unit. Now tell me how you feel'. That's the given circumstances. And it keeps adjusting the conversation. Oh, it gets very fiery. Even the stage managers are involved and designers are there as well, and it's great!

Ethan McSweeny: I find that I don't like to get on my feet until I understand the story that we're trying to tell. After the inevitable first read through, I usually try to get everyone talking. I think one important thing is if you want people thinking about stories, you've got to get them telling stories. So sometimes I start with myself telling a story, and invite other people in and let it happen organically.

Getting the company on the same page

Lisa Peterson: I like to do table work. I don't think it's the place where you get the answers, but you ask the questions. Then you are all in agreement about what the major issues are.

Penny Metropulos: You come to an agreement about the text, the story, relationships and character. So when we get on our feet, the actors have knowledge of what the action is. It makes my life a lot easier, because the actors respond to action. If they know what their relationship is, what the thought is, and I give them the space, they can usually find their place in it.

J. R. Sullivan: I want everybody to acknowledge and be aware of the thinking that's going on from everybody about the play, to get on board essentially with the main idea, which is whatever conceptual approach is being taken to the play. But then to get up, to get it in the body, and get relaxed with that. The sooner the better.

Henry Woronicz: Text work around the table is invaluable for me, primarily because it gives the actors an idea of where you're going with the play, what moments in the play are important to you, what moments in the play you think should stand out, or what we can throw away.

Events, structure, energy shifts

Oskar Eustis: What's the event? Why are you talking now? Why are you expressing yourself in this way? What is happening? What is the action of the scene? Nothing particularly deep or archaic.

Once I understand that, and I feel like we viscerally understand what the event of the scene is, everything else is detail; everything else is easy. Until you understand that, you can't make any real choices. In some ways it is all testing and improvisational, discussing it and massaging it until you crack the scene open to try and understand the central event. And once you have done that, directing is going to be easier because you know what you are doing, telling the story in time.

David Ivers: I'm extraordinarily interested in structure. So I'm an insane maniac for punctuation. I'm an insane maniac for timeline. This equals this and structurally it's telling us this. That's the kind of table work we'll do. I won't do a lot of character table work, I'll do a lot of 'What does this structure reveal to us in terms of character? What does, referentially, being in front of the sea in this location for this play tell us about behaviour? Just what does it mean just to live in front of the ocean? To be in Illyria?'

With *Romeo and Juliet*, I just asked the cast constantly to remember the kind of energy that it requires to remind yourself to hold a grudge. What it requires of you to walk down the hallway and remind yourself, 'I'm not supposed to like that person because my family doesn't like them'. So we have a lot of conversations that I think then lead to an actual active performance.

Darko Tresnjak: Something that's extremely important to me in terms of forming a group, forming an ensemble, is to actually say: 'Okay, look for this in this scene, when Antony comes back. These are the choices that are going to be most helpful. I think this is how we shape it. This is what happens when Antony and Octavius and Lepidus leave the room. This is how the energy changes'. So I talk them through how I think the energy shifts. I bring in music and I bring in a lot of images and pictures or whatnot – literary references, so that they can pool it to help awaken everybody's imagination, to put us all on the same page.

Brian Kulick: I move from comprehension to a grounding of, 'What are you doing? What is the language doing?' And 'What are you doing with the language to get what you want?' And once I start to get that, I then start to see the larger structure of, 'Here is the unit shift. That's where this block is. Now look at this other block of action'. To finally understand that action has a metabolic rate. An action – if I wooed you – has a certain kind of rhythm, which is different than if I taunt you or accuse you. It creates a different speed of being, a new time signature. So what I'm trying to do at the next level of table work, after comprehension and actions, is understand how those actions create units of energy and what happens to those various energies over time; to discover whether there is a cumulative development or entropic decline? I'm following a trail where language leads to action, action leads to energy and that energy becomes a kind of rhythm. There is the music of the language that leads to music of the actions, once I understand both 'scores', then we're ready to get up on our feet.

Developing layers

Jim Warren: We will go through the text several times in each chunk. We'll take the first chunk of the play. We'll do the paraphrase. Then the next time through, we'll go back to the top of that chunk. If it's in verse, we'll scan it. I ask the actors, 'We're going to do scanning. You don't have to do blocking and moving around, but you have got to be on your feet. Scanning and knowing the rhythms of the verse – where's my character regular? Where is it irregular? It needs to not be "a table sort of thing". It needs to be an "in your body sort of thing"'. So we'll go through that chunk again using Shakespeare's words, but finding the rhythm and seeing where things are not regular.

And then we'll put the books down, and get up and do it again. We either repeat things from the Ren Run or the read-through, or I say, 'Before we do this chunk, you know how you've made that character incredibly broad and comic? We're going to go 180 degrees from that. That character needs to be more serious'. I'll start to give them direction as we then go through it again on our feet, but not moment by moment and setting in blocking. That means that we've [really] gone through it, in our table work session.

'Let's try to incorporate those things into another time through it on our feet, where you're also thinking about acting. You're also thinking about the intentions and what else is going on in the scene'. So that we get through the whole play doing each chunk those three times. Then we go back to those chunks again. 'Now we're going to start blocking and working'.

It generally takes us, depending on the length of the play, either two days, sixteen hours, or two and a half days, twenty hours, to get through the whole play.

John Neville-Andrews: I like to layer things. So, for the first layer, we get in and read the play, and we talk about the play. Maybe we'll do some table work if the play is rather complex. But even if it isn't, it's nice to sit around for a while and explore the text – if you can afford it in the short rehearsal periods that we get nowadays. If you can devote a few days to really discussing the elements of the play, the director can bring an in-depth knowledge of the script to the actors if they've not quite done enough research, but also you get to know the actors, their chemistry, and find out the research they've already come up with.

Michael Kahn: We sit around the table for about a week. Not always all together. We'll sit around the table for a day. Then I'll start breaking it up into scenes and start working through them, and working through them again. Then I'll bring the whole cast back together.

In the first week I really focus on, 'What are you talking about? What did you just say? What did you just hear?' It's so interesting to me that sometimes actors hear what they want to hear from another person, but don't actually hear what was said. They hear 'angry': they hear 'sad': they hear 'annoyed'. They hear something, but they don't hear the thought, the words. And if they don't hear the words, it's usually because the other person saying it doesn't need to say those words either. So we spend a lot of time on, 'What are you saying? Why are you saying that? What is going on? What is that *really*?' All of a sudden the play takes on a life and all of a sudden it seems clear.

It's quite exciting for everybody to see how different it is from the first reading to that last reading. By the time that we get to that last reading, the actors are already walking around. They're on their feet, moving next to the person they talk to. Then we know we're ready to get on our feet. But I don't block the actors to start with. I say, 'You come in from there. You come in from there. We'll see what happens and then we make a plan'. I don't say, 'You need to walk here, then walk there' – any of that stuff anymore. I see what the impulses are.

Going back to table work

Bill Rauch: The table work will continue on well into the rehearsal processes, even though we're not around the table. We can still be able to talk about what actually is at stake here.

Kent Thompson: I often encourage the actors, if a scene isn't going well, to sit back down at the table. There's an awful lot of attention that I give to phrasing and operative words and how you communicate these best. I feel like the maestro in an opera company that's trying to teach them music. But I'm trying to get beyond that. I'm trying to get back to the emotional story of the journey of the character.

Stephanie Shine: [After exploring the text on our feet] we will go back to the table. I am a technician that way with the text. We will sit back down and we will figure out what is happening within the verse structure. I expect my actors to know what they are saying. I'm not there to say, 'You're saying this'. Instead I say, 'Gee, look at what's happening there? You've got a comma and a semi-colon that is stuck all into one sentence. What's going on there? What's happening with the iambic pentameter? Suddenly you're speaking in twelve beats, and you are having to do a lot of elision. What is that?' So that we start to get to know the characters as well as the tenor that Shakespeare feeds us. We might spend another two days doing that kind of work.

Image chains

Des McAnuff: One of the games we play during table work is to track image chains. Alfred Hitchcock does the same thing visually that Shakespeare does with language; think of the clocks in *Rear Window*. We sit with the actors and create categories of imagery, constantly on the hunt for hidden meaning. We might start with the categories of birds and then subdivide that category into songbirds and birds of prey. We will ask the characters to call them out and one of the two of the younger actors will notate every discovery. It is not enough to simply understand the images that appear in the text that you speak individually as an actor, you must have an understanding of the entire matrix before you can gain an understanding of how you fit in to the complex world that Shakespeare is creating. On some plays we've catalogued dozens of categories of images and icons. Larger hidden meanings can be contained there.

With *Romeo and Juliet*, we followed day and night as two groupings. After the death of Mercutio, all of the imagery inverts. Night, which has started off as a friend to the lovers, thinking of 'the mask of the night', suddenly becomes a threat. Everything turns topsy-turvy. This is a clear indication that Shakespeare is switching genres. You could argue that the first half of the play is essentially a comedy until the deaths begin and everything goes haywire. It is crucial for the whole company to do this kind of textual investigation if the abundant fruit of Shakespeare's plays is to be tasted. It is important to point out that this is only the beginning of the process, all of the imagery needs of course to be personalized or the work onstage is stillborn. Nonetheless, the best way to begin the process is by acquiring knowledge. Knowledge should never be feared. It should be embraced. And ultimately checked at the door.

Robert Blacker: I am going to jump in on two things and then get back to text work because I think that will be the most interesting thing.

In terms of images in the play, we work with living writers all the time. Des McAnuff is a writer, so this is enormously helpful in terms of our work on Shakespeare. There are two kinds of images that writers may come up with. The conscious imagery that they are creating through the play, such as 'night' and 'day' in *Romeo and Juliet*, is clearly conscious. There is also a certain kind of imagery that seeps in that the writer may not even be aware of. There is a good example in *The Tempest*. Jan Kott pointed this out in his collection of essays called *The Bottom Translations*, not in his original essay on *The Tempest* ['Prospero's Staff' in *Shakespeare Our Contemporary*]. He pointed out that there are odd, frequent references to *The Aeneid* in *The Tempest*. The most famous is where the one character [Gonzalo] talks on and on about Dido. That's the principle one. There are others, but they're not organized in a particular way, that they seem to be conscious references. Why does Shakespeare have them in the play? Writers, as they write plays, have ideas swirling around in their heads. In his head he keeps thinking of *The Aeneid* because of its detail of somebody moving from the old (Troy) into the new world (Italy). The old world and the new world are major aspects. Kott was so brilliant to see that in so infrequent and a handful of references. Swirling around in Shakespeare's head is old world and new, and that's why he keeps going back to that.

10

Staging the Play

As a younger director, I would plan everything out. Now after you have designed it, you know what imaginative world this is going to play from. It's important to know where they enter from and where they exit to, but after that, just let it happen. Let them work it out. All we have to do is come in with ideas and a care to work together on it, and to bring that honestly and forthrightly to each other. And then remarkable things can happen. The ensemble ideal lives anytime we do a Shakespeare. The best idea in the room should be the idea that is used.

J. R. SULLIVAN

At some point, directors must shift from talking about the play to staging it. Gaines likes to have the actors 'get up and explore the space as soon as possible' following actor impulses. Mullins has movement exercises he introduces during table work to prepare for that moment of standing up. McSweeny does what he calls an 'expert run-through', a no-pressure reading with actors moving around freely on their feet. He sets the performance area with chairs or what is available in the rehearsal room and encourages the actors to perform the play. Kahn also works with the actors' first

FIGURE 15 As You Like It, *directed by J. R. Sullivan, Oregon Shakespeare Festival, 2007. Danforth Comins as Orlando and Tod Rjurstrom as Charles the Wrestler. Photograph by David Cooper.*

impulses, looking for 'logical connections' in their movement to support the story.

Here we see various degrees of and rationales for blocking, from pre-blocking to completely improvised staging. Tresnjak and Ivers prefer to block quickly. This is so the actors have plenty of time to settle into the staging. Tresnjak works on 'enriching' what he has while Ivers likes to have 'play time' with the actors. Monte prepares extensive pre-blocking ahead of rehearsal, but is willing to 'discard' any of it when something superior is discovered. She also likes to create maps of the play's world and storyboards to generate a visual arc. Cohen blocks very quickly and reminds us that his actors have already staged the play themselves in their Ren Run, a device comparable to McSweeny's expert run-through, but without the table work.

Several directors like to sketch the staging by rough blocking a movement frame for the production. J. R. Sullivan points to the floor plan and uses 'a broad outline' to stage; like jazz, he considers how 'it plays together' with the actors. Woronicz uses 'large sketching' and advises directors that the verse work will largely be forgotten when the actors are first on their feet. Conlin has staging ideas for 'key moments' of a scene, leaving the blocking otherwise fairly free. The goal of her staging is to ensure the relationships and actions are 'clear'. Peterson will start in this manner, but also warns her cast that their initial explorations 'probably won't be the version that we'll end up using'. Zimmerman uses this approach except when a scene has a large number of actors who need to be blocked. Thompson creates staging that communicates the nature of a moment or character to the audience and is also readily identifiable. McSweeny has the model at his side during blocking rehearsals and refers to it frequently. He establishes a structure of entrances and exits but plays off of everyone's ideas. The structure can be changed later as he works toward specific 'attractive stage pictures'. Mullins gives his cast very general stage directions, such as: 'You never want to stop holding onto the person that you're doing the scene with'. He then has the actors follow their impulses, and refines the blocking while still focusing on the storytelling. Frank confides that staging can be 'creative chaos'. He warns that the director should not start staging until they 'really know what it is' they are staging.

Many directors favour organic blocking, including Packer, Zipay, Rauch, Douglas, Lamos, D. Sullivan and McAnuff. Packer does not block *per se*. She arranges the actors, who must be off book, into a circle and then has them move from their impulses. Zipay also wants her actors off script 'so that [rehearsal] moves right away into a physical connection with the language'. For her, staging comes out of the 'physical, visceral, emotional'. Rauch encourages his actors to improvise, and sometimes uses viewpoints to assist him in creating the staging. Douglas works entirely off of actor instincts. Lamos is 'spontaneous' in his blocking. He believes that 'movement and staging will reveal themselves' if the actors comprehend the dialogue and know why they say it. D. Sullivan hates to block but admits that 'with Shakespeare, you just have to' stage. His strategy is to 'ignore how scenes start' and work on 'the meat of the scene'. McAnuff says that 'working with good actors ... the basic designs stage themselves'.

Rauch, Mullins and McAnuff believe that the designs impact the staging. Rauch discloses that many staging decisions are made in the design process. Mullins informs his designers of specific design moments he wants to see with the actors. McAnuff describes his planning process that happens after each rehearsal using a set model or a rehearsal room floor plan tapped out. Together the stage managers, assistants, musicians, technical director and production manager 'map out the basic staging' moment by moment with one caveat. great staging ideas also come 'spontaneously' from the actors that can supplant the planning.

Managing scene transitions is an important part of staging Shakespeare, as the plays call for numerous location changes. Zimmerman really enjoys transitions and particularly loves to stage 'those little gaps in the text that call for staging'. Monte boasts, '[T]here is a very special technique and art in the ability to transition from one scene to the next seamlessly and flawlessly'. Conlin cautions that transitions must overlap in order to not slow down the production. Douglas agrees that scene changes 'cannot stop the show'.

The last section of this chapter offers additional staging advice. Conlin eliminates unnecessary movement during the final stage of rehearsals. Metropulos discusses the imperative of preparing to stage fifth acts. Neville-Andrews shares how he moves in rehearsal from instilling general meaning to an increasingly more specific idea of each moment. Lamos enjoys the 'visual sweep' that staging Shakespeare demands. He works to find 'stage pictures that tell the story' and that portray the 'dynamics of power in a scene'. McSweeny argues for an extra fifth week of rehearsal that would abet the entire organization. Because things have to be decided so early, he gets through as much of the play as possible in that first week.

That allows him to give notes to the shops so they have more time to prepare changes or additions. Burdman shares some of his distinctive staging techniques he has developed in his site-specific panorama theatre.

Moving from table work to staging

Barbara Gaines: Once text work is underway, I have the actors get up and explore the space as soon as possible. It's important to connect the text with action, so movement – even if it's random – begins to create impulses inside of the actors. Movement frees the actor from thinking too much about all our text work; it stimulates action and truth. I have ideas for staging long before rehearsals begin, but during early rehearsals I'm more interested in where the actors want to go. Often their instincts provoke my ideas to shift and grow.

Paul Mullins: I usually do table work the first week. We do some movement things that don't actually have to do with the play in particular. It has much more to do with moving around the stage and people being with each other in a way that is outside of sitting at a table. Sitting at a table for a week is great, but then there's this huge hole in getting up. Suddenly you've done this thing. You know these people at the table, and suddenly you have to walk in front of them. So I like to make sure that we've done some of that. We know each other a little better than just on the paper.

Ethan McSweeny: I do a series of steps to wean us off the table. If the script and design are appropriate to it, I often do what I call an expert run-through. After finishing the table work, we just get up and I say, 'This is the set. You guys make it up. Go! Nothing's right, nothing's wrong. You can't do anything wrong. You just do the play as though you know what you're doing'. I get to see how the cast will use the space in ways I expected or didn't expect. It teaches me an enormous amount about the physical space very quickly. It teaches me a lot about different members of the company, too.

I have a target that by the end of the week, we'll do either the expert run-through, or sometimes a read through with no tables where I just say, 'Here are more chairs than there are actors. You can move around. Move into groupings, but you don't have to'. I always make it voluntary: 'If you want to' because some people aren't ready to. On *Midsummer*, the set wasn't particularly conducive to the expert exercise so I simply sat the cast in a big circle and the most magical thing happened during the play within the play when the mechanicals got up and spontaneously performed it for their fellow players, facing away from me, and I was watching the company watching them. I don't think we ever truly forgot that moment and it informed how the court watched the play from then on.

Michael Kahn: An actor can get up once he knows what he's doing. Since they actually know what they're playing, I'll set the stage and then see where they go. I'll remember where they go. Usually a lot of things that an actor does off first impulses are often very good. They'll go away, and we'll do other things, but I'll remember. Then eventually I'll block it, because they need some plan – even if you change it. That happens a little more regularly with me now, probably the second time I get to it. But I'll go ahead and see it about three or four times. We won't just do it once on our feet. And they'll start playing around.

[What I look for and focus on is] storytelling, logical connections. Eventually I'll worry about focus and things like that. Storytelling means that to tell the story you have to know where the story is being told. So if somebody's got a line to somebody else, I'll probably work it out that they're not too far from them and their timing is in sync [*laughs*]. And I'll therefore find out why they got there. I'll never say, 'You have to be over there because you have a line to say'. I'll say, 'What happened earlier?' I find that fun now. It's like puzzles. Playing. I think that's something I'm good at.

I used to hate the beginning of blocking. I always felt this huge responsibility to do the blocking my own way. And now that I know I don't have to worry about that, and I also know I know how to do it, it's much easier. I used to be a nervous wreck the first day of blocking. I used to make everybody leave the rehearsal hall. I'd get so tense. Now I just laugh and say, 'I'm just going to get tense!' to everybody. 'But you know it's just the first day'. Because actors feel stupid too, standing up for the first time. So now we're at a point where they don't feel so stupid anymore.

Blocking

Darko Tresnjak: Often the expression 'blocking' has become a dirty word in American theatre. But when you're working with a cast of twenty-nine people, I block. I stage. I have ideas about physical reality. I think the ability to stage and to block is a craft and it's a gift. I make no bones about it. I'd rather spend most of the time with the text, and then most of the time after that, enriching things. The actual act of getting it up on its feet happens very quickly.

David Ivers: [First there is] a lot of discussion. And then I like to get on our feet and I like to get it roughed in, on the stage, and blocked quickly so that we have time to go back and work. That just comes from my preference from when I was an actor. I want as much play time as possible. So I tend to stage things pretty quickly and go from there.

Bonnie Monte: I block things like you would not believe, in tremendous detail prior to going into the process. It sits here and I use it to guide me throughout the process. But it is a collaborative art form and so 90 per cent goes away or gets changed throughout the process. Without it there, I don't have the play in my head. It forces me to have an extraordinary level of specificity when I go in.

I go in with it with much more of a level of specificity than they do. Even though I am willing to throw it away the minute I find something better or an actor brings me something better. That is the collaborative part of the process. I go in knowing what that moment is about, what I am ultimately endeavouring to do with that. It is so helpful in the beginning of the process. When people say, 'Why am I coming from there?' 'Because that's where the stable is'. 'Oh, that's where the stable is. How did you know that?' 'I know that because I have the whole world imagined out'.

I have been known to draw incredible maps of the entire landscape. When we did *The Cherry Orchard* I came in with these incredible watercolours of the entire estate. Everything goes on the walls. The walls were covered in my rehearsal. Then the actors get so excited because they are like, 'That's not where the cherry orchard is, Suzy'. They'll go to the next one. The estate becomes theirs.

And then blocking the script, sometimes it will take two hours to block one page, depending on the complexity. Other pages, I just write, 'Play around with it'. I know that that will have to be something really organic that the actors and myself find together. I know that they will come in and have to exit to the left. I'll keep it very loose.

It's like creating a storyboard for a movie, because each moment is a shot. For me to think of it otherwise is crazy. Every artist is different. I have no judgement over what other people do. I don't sit there and say, 'But that's not how I envisioned it!' I have a plan and a map. Occasionally I will say to an actor, 'That's taking the play down the wrong road. You can't do that. Please try it this way to see how that works out'. So I am as dictatorial as I need to be, but I don't know that anyone would ever call me a dictatorial director.

Ralph Alan Cohen: Let's say we have an hour of rehearsal; we'll spend forty minutes on table work and the last twenty minutes – after the paraphrase, the scansion, the rhetoric – we will go back over it. We'll start and say, 'Okay, let's get it on its feet. Let's look at some of it'. But remember, these same people have already done their Ren Run. It's been on its feet. They have blocked it somehow or another. They understand not to play proscenium. They understand to play it thrust. They know, 'Act on the diagonal'. They are used to turning their backs on the audience when they need to. So the blocking process is fast.

I tell our actors, 'I want to keep it on the stage'. There have been times, though, when we've had actors all around the perimeter of the stage, and that's when the play *per se* disappears, and it becomes a show about actors proving they can break the fourth wall and be in the audience. Something has to keep happening in the world of the play, not only in the audience around it.

Sketching a structure or frame

J. R. Sullivan: 'This is the floor plan. This is where you come in. This is where you go out. Let's see what happens in between'. I'll stage it roughly, just a broad outline of it, to see where it goes. But I also want to follow their impulses. So I spend a lot of time doing that, watching them work, and then we shape those, follow those, find where it plays together. That's where it should be like jazz. We just play it together. It sounds simple, but it's hard to build it.

Lisa Peterson: I am a sketcher in rehearsals, meaning I don't plan anything out ahead of time in terms of staging. I let the actors know that the first try probably won't be the version that we'll end up using. I am sketching, erasing and re-sketching. I like to work off of actors' impulses, so I am watching.

Sometimes the collaboration is between what their impulse is and what my thought is about how to stage something. Some things go easy and some things just never feel right.

Mary Zimmerman: Act I, Scene 1 is on call for the first hour. Then I call Act I, Scene 2 for the second hour. Then Act I, Scene 3 for the third hour. The people in that scene come in. The first half of that first individual rehearsal, we'll usually just be seated and we'll chat, chat, chat; read, read, read. We might go off on a million tangents about the play. The very next pass on that scene, we're on our feet and I'm figuring out the staging, which I do in the room. Unless there are twenty-seven people in the scene, I tend to, in my head, have a place to start, just a tiny sketch. But I feel it out with the cast in the room, what they seem to want to do.

Henry Woronicz: I tend to think it is large sketching. I talk to the actors about that. I say, 'We are going to get a rough frame for what this scene might be in terms of discovering the blocking'. Movement *is* an expression of character. I don't like to block it too finely too soon, because I want things to be able to evolve as they go. So I talk to the actors about 'Okay, we've got this big piece of paper out and crayons and we're doing a sketch, and seeing how it fills up the paper, and then we'll slowly fill in the lines and go from there'.

When you get up on your feet the first time, you don't worry so much about [the language]. You let the verse just fall apart a little bit as actors are trying to find a moment. Then you say, 'Eventually, we are going to take all the air out of that, but for right now keep finding the reality, the emotional reality about what this scene might be. But eventually know that that scene is going to want to fly. That it's an aria. It is going to want to go. A rhythm, find the rhythm and the rhythm will take you someplace'.

Kathleen Conlin: I never lock into it, nor do I have it all blocked out on paper. I do have ground plans with me. I do mark specific moments that I know have to look a certain way. At the end of the day's rehearsal, we have synthesized my preparation with the actor's instincts.

I'm always very concerned about whether the relationships are reading, whether the basic actions of the scene are clear. I really hold to that truth that every scene has some kind of beginning, middle and end. Even if we violate the beginning, middle and end, it's there somehow. We have to make sure that that beginning, middle and end *play* in some way before we move on. Creating an 'event' for each scene becomes the building blocks of the production.

Kent Thompson: In staging it, what I'm trying to do is constantly try to make it into something we will recognize immediately as an audience or as a character. That 'Oh, we know that moment'. Whether it's Orsino running in with a sword, shadow sword fighting with himself before the play starts, and somebody then runs in with a full-length mirror. Right away you got that image of a self-involved person. So I am looking for those things that will give us a key into ultimately letting the actor do it. Because I don't want the audience thinking twenty-five minutes into the play, 'Oh, that's a great directorial [conceit]'. I want it revealed to them.

Ethan McSweeny: I often tell the cast, 'I'll probably do anything to stave off the first day of staging' because then everything that's been pleasantly non-literal, gets very real. Then you have to get into the nitty-gritty physical detail. When you start staging, you discover at that moment any compromises you might have made in the design, or challenges you might have presented yourself in the design. I also spend an unusual amount of time looking at the model. I get it near me. While they're reading a scene, very often my head is in the model to start picturing where I think it could be and how it could work. Then when I look up at the tape-down, I can really see the model and the theatre.

I will always have an idea, but I try also to encourage everyone to have ideas too and to try their ideas. I want them to try my ideas, too. We can all bring it. I usually have a good sense rhythmically of entrances and exits, of where I think those are coming from and going. And I believe that we need structure. Make a structure and then we can change it. I will remind the actors of that: 'We're going to do this, and then it'll change'. It's good to have something to start changing. Kind of like it's good to put the light cues in the board, even if they're going to be different later. You can change a cue that exists, but you can't change the absence of something. To borrow a phrase, 'nothing comes from nothing'.

In the trial scene [*The Merchant of Venice*], I didn't really know what I was going to do. I kept looking at the model box and I set up the tables and chairs and I thought, 'I could do a pattern of chairs'. Then the day came when we were going to stage it and I realized I still didn't really know what I was going to do. I told everyone, 'I don't really know what I'm going to do. Let's just start'. I think sometimes you just start at the beginning. I gave everyone entrances, some of them have stayed the same and some have changed. Drew had the idea of Bassanio showing up late, and that did something to us. Then I thought, 'Well, if this is all impromptu, it can't all be setup before. We'll only get out what we need'. We needed the strap. I'd littered the stage with crates, just in case we needed stuff. I was like, 'Well let's just grab those crates and we'll put it on that'. I knew I wanted Tubal to bring in the scale that had already been established on his fruit cart. Then we realized, 'There's a lawyer coming and they've got books. We'll get them out at a café table'. Then 'Well, we'll need to figure out how we're going to look like we're really going to kill Antonio'. Derek said, 'It would be great if I was really tied to something. I really want to start feeling more and more fear as this goes along'. So we invented the chair.

By the time we were done with it, we went back and looked at it, I said, 'Well that has a shape'. And then we started shifting elements around, because I like there to be attractive stage pictures as I think we come to the theatre for a certain amount of aesthetic beauty of different kinds. There can be all kinds of beauty, but I like them to be compositionally elegant. My staging, once we're done, once we've gotten in the theatre, it's exacting and precise. There's room to fill in the emotional areas, but I'm pretty precise in the stage picture. And the lighting is always very tailored in my shows. Eventually you can't move too far left or right [*laughs*] because then you'll get out of the light.

Paul Mullins: There are times I don't know anything, and I'll say, 'Where do you want to come from. What do you want to do? Do anything you want'. Or I say, 'I'll think you guys come from back there, and I think that you need to do it over here. Do whatever you want'. Depending on the play, I'm not too much of a director who likes to dictate things.

I often say, 'Let's see what happens while you do this. You might learn something. Maybe the scene takes place, but you never get closer than across the room from each other. Or the scene might take place, and you find you never want to stop holding onto the person that you're doing the scene with'. How do we tell the audience what's important? Movement interests me because it should illuminate what you're saying. If standing still, sitting still, illuminates what you're saying, then good. If everybody on the whole stage stops when you say something: 'That must be important', then good. It's all about storytelling. How do we tell the best story?

David Frank: If you have done the thorough table work, established the geography and the core story, sometimes it is disarmingly simple. You'll be sitting there reading and discussing the text. An actor will get up because they can't make that reading work without getting up. Then someone else gets up, and the next thing you know, persuasive staging patterns are beginning to form right in front of you. The rest is solving traffic problems.

But it doesn't often happen that easily. Sometimes creative chaos is the best precursor to a thoughtful plan. Very often, the best moments emerge from controlled and disciplined improvisation. Sometimes a scene bends quickly to our collective will, and at other times it seems to take forever. And there are times when you need to set a rough staging just to retain what you have explored to date – you know it is not the final product, but the rough blocking is a way of recording your early exploration and making preliminary decisions. And in the back of your mind, there is always the clock, and the ever-diminishing hours, before you face that first audience. But being too aware of the clock presents another set of perils.

For me, it can be dangerous to stage too precisely too early. The desire to get the scene blocked can result in setting the story before you really know what it is – you risk cutting off the best source of ideas – a company of creative, collaborative actors. It is a trap I have periodically fallen into. You can't complete the staging until you've collectively discovered and agreed what the story is.

Organic blocking; improvising the staging

Tina Packer: We work in a large circle. The actors follow their impulses. (I never block. I do stage eventually as we get into the final weeks.) We discuss what's happening. All voices are heard. We begin to look at the structure of the verse more deeply, see what we need to support the actors to get to great depths within themselves. We work on the fights, the dances, do individual voice and text work, the designers start to design somewhere around here, its becoming obvious what the most important points in this story are, I develop more deeply the turning points in the play, so the story gets even clearer. And then it comes together as a collective act – one we have all made, all bought into. Many different points of view about the Nature of Man and society – but with a coherence we hope Will Shakespeare would be proud of! And then we offer it to the audience

Joanne Zipay: When I stage, I stage plays without book in hand. Actors should be off book, knowing the lines from the first rehearsal so that it moves right away into a physical connection with the language. We have a movement consultant, and a coach who works with the company on Alexander technique. We have a voice coach, a fight choreographer. Everybody is in rehearsal with me from day one, working together. We're working with movement patterns. We're working with the movement director on the physicalization of the character. She coaches the actors more specifically on their gestures, manners and movement. So it comes from the table right into a very physical connection – physical, visceral, emotional. You have to begin at the very start of the rehearsal process. Books get in the way of the commitment and the connection and the internalization of understanding. You're living it.

Bill Rauch: Ideally, I like the actor to improvise their way through the entire scene, improvise staging without me stopping them, all the way through once. Then I'll talk about things that I saw. Actors will talk, 'I felt really great!' Or, 'I felt really lost in this section'. Then we start dissecting why or what it's about, or trying new things. I really value organic blocking that comes out of actor improvisation and discussion. When I say 'improvisation' you understand I don't mean without the use of language, but improvised movement.

Once in a while I'll borrow a viewpoints technique. We'll do seven snapshots. Have the actors come up with telling the story of the scene with images. I'll leave the room so they can do that, and then come back in. I'll see those. Not often. But I'll use that technique occasionally because it's really fun and really useful, when I get really stuck, when I feel like we're getting lost.

I've learned over the years that constantly changing all of the blocking is no good because the actors don't have a foundation of 'This is my movement pattern through the scene'. Then they can't dig deeper in terms of their emotional choices sometimes. I would say blocking tends to be pretty fluid in the process that I do, but I also really value setting things and saying, 'We all agree this is the blocking for the scene'. So we can ask, 'Is this going to serve the emotional journey of the scene?'

Timothy Douglas: I work and stage at the same time. I work on the scene while I am staging. I am not an advance blocker, unless I absolutely have to be – if there is a time limit, a crunch, or if there are certain scenes that of course dictate it. In terms of blocking the play, I don't do it. I insist that actors move in whatever way they feel motivated to move. 'Follow your instincts in the room. Don't worry about playing in front of an audience. Just move when you feel like moving, and we are going to work on the scene'. I go through the entire play once like that.

After we've been through the whole play on our feet, that's when I like people to be off book. We continue working on the scene. While we are working through the play this second time, then I actually start making the staging 'audience friendly', and theatrically worthy based on the organic experience that the actors have. So, yes, I am making it theatrical, but the foundation is already in their body. Everything has source from the body. I just don't believe in the thought of 'putting on'. It didn't work for me as an actor, and absolutely does not work for me in the directing mode.

Mark Lamos: When I begin staging on my feet, I improvise. I don't write anything down beforehand. Poet Joseph Brodsky wrote, 'Every choice is a flight from freedom'. So I don't want to limit what might happen with the confluent energy of actors-text-director.

When we begin staging, I rough things in very quickly, asking the stage manager to be ready to write down everything that happens, without stopping. I don't pre-plan any staging, I'd rather it be spontaneous. If I've studied the play well, and the actors have some understanding of what they're saying and why, the movement and staging will reveal themselves as we start to work. If the ground plan of the set design is sound, we'll know it by the end of the first day of staging. I tell the actors to move when they feel like moving – I want to give them some ownership and latitude as we begin this crucial process, since I know we will revise later. Right now, I want to instil confidence. Let's prime the canvas. I also want to *watch* something as soon as possible. I'm at my best when I can stop talking and look at something, so I need to get the scenes on their feet.

Daniel Sullivan: I don't really like to block a play. I do less of it the older I get but with Shakespeare you just have to. It's far too complicated for the short rehearsal times we're allowed in this country. You have to have a fairly strict plan just to get it all done. But I will very often just ignore how scenes start and just work on the meat of the scene and not worry about the traffic of getting on and off.

I don't really like it when actors make notes in their scripts as we work. Just like in teaching, I don't like people to write down what I'm saying. I don't feel connected because everyone suddenly turns into a scribe and I don't feel like they are taking in what I am saying, they're just recording it. Most importantly, I'm going to change everything anyway, so why record it? By the time we open, your script will be illegible.

Des McAnuff: I find more and more, working with good actors, that the basic designs stage themselves. If you have a good design team, and you have good actors, you really don't need to come in. I used to put little pennies on [a mock-up] and I would have the whole damn thing worked out. I'd go in there and this person would be a nickel because there were thirty people onstage. I think I had forty when I did my first play at Stratford. Then you realize that not only is it unnecessary, it's just a bad idea. If you spend your life in rehearsal, then it should be pretty natural to move things around. And, the fact is that the actors would rather work that way, for the most part. There are very few actors who would want to be staged in some way as if it is the re-creation of some ballet. Most actors want to feel like they are involved in the collaboration.

Designs and blocking

Bill Rauch: A lot of design decisions were made in the design process, a lot of blocking decisions, too. That's probably why I love the design process so much. So many decisions about staging are being made by how you design the set and where what is going to happen.

Paul Mullins: I'm the type that just usually there's going to be five or six things that design wise I know that I want to see. There are some moments that, because the designers and I have made choices, which you have to make before you get to rehearsal (so that things can be built) there are things that I know about staging that will matter.

Des McAnuff: Every production requires its own approach to staging. Productions can get on their feet in a whole host of different ways. I have found that it is important to do a great deal of planning. At the end of every rehearsal, we all get together around the scenographic model or, even better, at the side of a taped out version of the set in the rehearsal room. We then go through the upcoming scenes beat by beat. My assistants are there, the movement people, musicians, stage managers, often the technical director and production manager. I try to map out the basic staging. On a musical, it is to counts. On an epic play it generally corresponds word by word to the unfolding text. We create a road map together. This is, of course, after many months of earlier preparation but once again, in our collaborative art form, it is important to get the whole team on the same page. Ultimately though, this only produces a backup plan. The ideas that spring forth in the rehearsal room itself are by far the most valuable. The best work often comes spontaneously after all the preparation has been transcended by the actors and everyone else in the room.

Transitions

Bonnie Monte: I think that there is a very special technique and art in the ability to transition from one scene to the next seamlessly and flawlessly to the point where the audience is almost absolutely unaware that you have evolved into the next scene. But yet you do it so perfectly that they completely buy into it and they know exactly where they are. They know exactly where those characters are. And yet, you've made it happen almost magically. There is tremendous technique involved in doing that and that takes a long time to perfect.

Kathleen Conlin: Of real interest to me is devising more strategies for stage-worthy equivalents of the cinematic 'dissolve'.

Timothy Douglas: No matter what the scenic elements are, I insist that they cannot stop the show. It cannot stop for the time it takes to shift. We have to shift and move at the same time. Most of my productions have moving parts, except maybe necessary furniture. It's got to all be about the storytelling and the connection. I insist that the storytelling be as transparent as humanly possible. Not that I don't like scenery. I love playing with the toys, and having the palate to paint with, but never at the sacrifice of the story.

Mary Zimmerman: Transitions are one of my favourite things in the theatre. To make them poetic and beautiful and worthy of our attention, rather than, 'Someone's moving the furniture off. Don't look!' Make a little production of it. Incorporate it into the pleasure of the play, the vision of it. Very often in Shakespeare, I'll make something a song that maybe wasn't a song. That's true in *Pericles*. Two or three of the galley passages are songs. I love staging those things. I love all of the strange things that Shakespeare asks you to stage. Like Jupiter descending. In *Pericles* he asks you to stage Pericles arriving at the door. During Gower's monologues, there's supposed to be dumbshows. It literally describes them and they're very rudimentary, so I don't quite stick to them. I love staging the back-story. Illustrating that. How to do storms at sea and how to do different countries in a really quick, visual, indicative way? Dances, the little court dance. I now have a choreographer.

In *Pericles* I made up a transition I like a great deal. Normally in *Pericles* they say, 'Let's go watch the jousting'. Then the very next line is, 'Oh, the jousting was great!' Generally the thing that comes in between those two lines is the competition of the knights, the jousting is staged. I always joke that perhaps because I'm a girl, I'm not interested in the jousting on stage. So in our production they all go off stage to see the jousting, and then music comes up and a long table is elaborately set as evening falls. Clearly something is meant to come between the king's last line and the very next line, the king speaking again and saying, 'That was great'. Clearly there's to be some sort of event. But we took the event offstage and just had this table being set with great flourishes of the tablecloth and a highly choreographed procession of delightful things to eat and table settings and so on; people at work in that concentrated way that can be so beautiful – beautiful and joyful. Show time passing. Show a little bit of the backstage.

I think in Shakespeare, there are always those little gaps in the text that call for staging. That's one of the many reasons why directors love Shakespeare, because of the entire, rather epic sometimes, visual apparatus. 'How am I going to stage all of those storms and dances and fights and armies marching by? Ghosts appearing. Jupiter descending. Diana descending. What's that going to look like?' That's where all of your cunning has to come to bear.

Mark Lamos: The plays have many different rhythms. Scene must follow scene without pause. But the rhythm of the concluding scene is in contrast to the next one. I'll often have actors begin a new scene as actors from the previous scene are exiting. It's like a jump-cut in film. I want to pull the audience's attention away from the action they've become involved with and get them focused on a new scene. Tumbling events. As in life, one scene overtakes another. This, too, propels the action and the narrative, keeps the audience in the grip of the play, while introducing new music, new rhythms, indeed new characters. The music of Shakespeare is varied and filled with vitality, even in its most contemplative moments. Soliloquy is followed, often, by tumult. Private moments are followed, often, by mass action, bustle, noise. Let the new energy *overtake* the old. It's like a composer who strikes a minor cord in a flow of E major. Bang. New scene. New characters. New energy. The actors entering must have a sense of 'Hey, now watch *us*!' If we wait for the director to create an elaborate new *mise-en-scene,* our natural inclination, as an audience, to remain within the flow of the muscular drama, is diverted. We stop listening and instead watch. Gaudy directorial devices – most especially annoying scene changes – get in the way of the play's natural energy. It's a gift to us that Shakespeare wrote most of his plays for a stage without scenery. Too many of us don't trust that gift and the rewards it can produce. The characters generally note *where they are*. 'This is the forest of Arden'.

Additional advice on staging

Kathleen Conlin: I always over-block. Even though we work in this organic way, I always have way too much movement. Then, I spend the last final weeks of rehearsal eliminating and getting it pared down, so it's as precise as possible. It's bloated first, where it's really messy and lots of movement all over the place. Every time there's a beat change, somebody's moving on stage. Once it becomes more internalized, then we start paring it away so that, hopefully, we get a very clear visual image for the scene that has vibrancy.

Penny Metropulos: If you have not figured out something about your fifth act when you walk into rehearsal, you are going to be in trouble. Fifth acts of Shakespeare will kill you. They will eat you alive. They have rather big jaws that come after me. Even if you don't know the specific answer, you have to have a good general idea, because you are going to come to it and it is going to be hard. It is when everybody's onstage, and the most complicated resolutions take place. It is where your conceptual thinking about the play will be most challenged, whether it is the mystery or the revelation, the dark ending or whatever. It's hard. Sometimes it seems as though it can go on for days. But you better face it early.

Mark Lamos: The work of staging begins with a close and long and slow study of the text. It continues in conversations with designers and hearing actors speak the text at auditions. These help me understand the text better.

I enjoy staging these plays because they offer so much in the way of visual sweep. No scene is very long, and so the constant variety the plays call for – the manipulation of crowds swirling onto a space where a soliloquizing actor is thoughtfully – or resolutely – exiting, for instance. These kinds of moments give me a lot of pleasure as a director. I enjoy creating stage pictures that tell the story, demonstrate the dynamics of power in a scene. I constantly revise the staging, right up until the last minute, as the acting and intentions become clearer and the actors and I understand the play more deeply. Usually my revisions simplify the initial staging; they rarely become more baroque or complicated.

Ethan McSweeny: *Merchant* was four weeks in the rehearsal hall, one week of technicals, with an invited dress at the end of it that was functionally a first preview. Then one week of previews with the press attending on Sunday night; so we are pretty much locking the show by the third preview, making only very few nips and tucks on the fourth and fifth. That was okay, maybe it was a little bit of a rush but that is not uncommon in our contemporary theatre with its need to find cost-savings at every turn.

Much Ado (the year after *Merchant*) had five weeks in the rehearsal hall. I think that makes a big difference and that it's really necessary on a Shakespeare. That said, I just directed *The Tempest* with the *Merchant* calendar, and that production involved a number of additional elements including flying and puppets. Of course, these days even having four weeks in the rehearsal hall seems like a luxury. But the plays are big. Ultimately, I think the fifth week benefits the producing organization, because it's not just the actors who need it, it's the prop shop and the costume shop and the scene shop, because ideas emerge during the week of table work and the initial stagings and those departments need time to respond and invent and build and create them. When you don't have that fifth week, you end up in a scenario where you've already made so many choices up front that you just can't allow as many choices to be made in the creative process of rehearsal. Or you have to try and police them.

My strategy for that now, in my first round of staging, is broad strokes. We get people in and we get people out. We don't spend a long time on the details, in part because everybody's holding a script in their hand anyway, and someone says, 'Well I don't know, this timing doesn't seem right'. I go,

'Well, nothing we're doing is right, yet'. I try and get through a good chunk of the play in the first week on our feet so that I can have it invented as much as possible, so that the prop shop has another week to try and start doing it.

Stephen Burdman: We've developed staging techniques, specifically for [panorama theatre] modelled on late nineteenth century banana crosses. One of the things I say to actors is, 'If it feels completely wrong, it's probably completely right'. For example, you do love a scene with an actor and you *never* look at them. In *Much Ado About Nothing*, Beatrice and Benedick would look out and they would only look at each other when they weren't speaking.

We do a close up effect that is reminiscent of our modern audiences watching TV or film. Then they have this very intense thing because they are privileged to watch the actor have an emotion. So the best seat in the house is not actually the actor's. It's now the audience's. It makes it harder for the actor, especially with modern training. But once they understand the technique, they come to love it. They find the incredible freedom in the restriction, knowing that they have to open up in such a way that they've never opened up before. So this is reminiscent of the nineteenth century when you're playing with no mikes to twelve hundred, fifteen hundred people in these giant acoustically sound theatres. But in our case it's not acoustically sound.

11

Speaking Shakespeare's Language

If I don't hear it, then I'm not happy. You cannot make a vocal or movement choice that keeps me from hearing the words.

RALPH ALAN COHEN

Directors seek different characteristics in Shakespearean language, the performance of which requires a technical skill set above and beyond most other kinds of acting. Mullins observes that not all actors have the skills or understand the complexity of Shakespeare's language. McSweeny says that actors need to regularly exercise their Shakespeare 'muscle' in order to be competent with the work. Eustis likes his Shakespeare to be 'well spoken' and 'thoughtful'. Shakespeare's playwriting is so strong, he 'demands you rise up to his level'. Lamos states that the actor must understand the difference between 'size' and 'bombast', vocally demonstrating 'largeness of soul' and an allowance for 'quiet moments'. He believes once you discern the form you realize the freedom. Buckley contends 'the language comes from a character's strong sense of self and clear objectives'; Shakespeare paints 'real people in extraordinary circumstances'. Douglas says, 'The more personal it can be for each individual, the more illuminated the

FIGURE 16 *Much Ado About Nothing, directed by Benjamin Curns, American Shakespeare Center, 2014. Photograph by Lindsey Walters.*

story is going to be'. One of his concerns is that actors '*stay on their voices*'. The voice is 'the actual vibration that carries the emotional content and hits your body and resonates … where that emotional content lives in you'. D. Sullivan does not care for regionalisms with Shakespeare, but realizes how difficult communicating class and portraying comic scenes can be 'without entering into a regional sound'. Rauch seeks an American approach to language, not some 'watered down version of how the Brits do it'. He and D. Sullivan dislike mid-Atlantic speech.[1] Monte advises that the more you know the rules, the easier it is to know '*when* to break them and *why* you should break them'.

Frank states that the actor needs 'good phrasing skills'. Zimmerman notes that the syntax is 'backwards' and the metaphors 'keep adding to themselves'. Frank asks actors to focus 'on the detail of the word – why those particular words in that particular combination'. Like Frank, Kahn believes he is responsible for making the actor understand 'emotionally and intellectually and situationally and physically – to *have* to say what the character says and not something else'. Both recognize the great difficulty actors face in order to work 'at the top of [their] game' with excellent breath support, articulation, emphasis, rhythm and pacing abilities. Frank also encourages playing images '*genuinely* on the moment' with 'spontaneity and specificity'. Similarly, McAnuff borrows an approach learned from Michael Langham: 'living thought' suggests there is 'no separation between the word, the thought and the emotion'. Packer believes the actor must use natural breath to own the language using all parts of themselves.

Zipay warns directors not to work on the poetry. Deciphering the rhetoric, the argument will be more useful. Everything else comes from this: stakes, action, intention as well as the poetry. Metropulos also believes rhetorical wisdom comes from the humanity of the characters. Oratorical structures communicate how the characters think.

Lamos marks stresses and operatives directly above each verse line. Cohen directs his actors to emphasize the last 'stressed syllable' of each line. Kahn, however, never tells his actors to stress specific words. He achieves stress through questions such as 'What did you say? ... Why did you say that? ... Why is that word there? ... Why do you think that's stressed? Why do you think that word's at the end?' He finds that the actors can build strong connections when understanding the reason for the stress.

Rhythm is rarely talked about by acting teachers, but hardly ever ignored by directors. Rhythm and pacing are important factors for Woronicz, D. Sullivan, Kulick, Lamos and MacLean. Woronicz is interested in the rhythms of the play and how the verse informs us about the character 'when it goes into prose, when it goes into verse'. D. Sullivan says the actor needs to develop an awareness of how their lines connect to the rest of the text. Often the actor wants to pause before speaking, to take in what has just been said, but that destroys the text's forward driving rhythm. Kulick depends on actors who understand the language 'on an iambic level'. He is fascinated with the 'rate of utterance,' the changing tempos of the text. Also he looks for where the rhythm breaks and what that disruption indicates in a specific moment. The difference between Shakespeare's polysyllabic and monosyllabic words adds to the 'musicianship' of the performance. As a director, Lamos works toward a 'natural-sounding *flow* ... that comes off like real speech'. Cohen dictates to his actors that there should be no pauses before or after a character's cue line. When actors take pauses, they work against the text's pace and risk the audience's getting ahead of the actor's thoughts and becoming bored. MacLean cautions that a Shakespeare production feels long when 'the action is unclear and the acting is unnatural and obvious'.

Douglas believes a strong emphasis on the physical and emotional aspects of performing the language is crucial, especially for actors who can get obsessed on technical analysis. '[T]he best thing I can do for them is to get them more in touch with their bodies'. Similarly Kulick discusses a 'particular energy that's trapped by Shakespeare's language. The challenge is to gain access to it and release it. When you unlock it, you unlock the play'. For *Romeo and Juliet*, he discovered it was duelling, which then became the 'DNA of every scene'.

Finally, Frank counsels that working on the details of language ends with run-throughs and the later stages of rehearsal. You have to trust that the foundation is there. There are other problems to be solved.

Qualities and objectives

Paul Mullins: As actors and directors, we're in lots of plays. You are hardly ever in a verse play, much less a verse play that is brilliant and poetic, and has to do with playing poetry in front of people. There are poetic writers, don't get me wrong, beautiful modern playwrights who write poetry, but they don't write verse, which is a different thing completely, a different technique to do it, a different knowledge – being able to be equipped as an actor to say it and as a director to guide that. You'll always have actors that are better at it than others. How do you, as much as you can, even that playing field? How do you better guide them to be as good as they can be?

Ethan McSweeny: Being capable of using this language and working it is a muscle. If you don't exercise the muscle, it's very rare that you can just drop in and be good at it. It's important to see actors who have the muscle trained and disciplined and ready. When you do, it's amazing how vibrant the material can be. When I see people who don't have the muscle for the language, that's less interesting to me.

Oskar Eustis: I really dislike Shakespeare when it is not well spoken. I really dislike Shakespeare when it is not thoughtful. This is the problem with Shakespeare. Shakespeare is so smart and he's so good at what he does, that he demands you rise up to his level. I'm talking as if the plays are a person. But the plays tend to resist people who approach them too cavalierly. They tend to not reveal their riches. And indeed they tend to make productions look bad unless you approach them with a serious degree of thoughtfulness.

Mark Lamos: It's also important that actors who speak Shakespearean verse understand and trust what I can only call *size*. I don't mean bombast. I mean a sense of largeness-of-soul. They need to think of their voice as being an extension of their muscles, not just their mind – the voice is a natural extension of the body, *as well as the mind*. Speaking onstage is a physiological act.

There are quiet moments in the plays, of course, and often these are the most powerful. They too require a sense of size that few modern plays do. The actor must be able to gather the audience members into his confidence as he begins, say, 'How all occasions do inform against me/And spur my dull revenge'. 'How'. 'Spur'. 'Dull'. Words that require a full sound, a weight of meaning.

Poet Paul Muldoon says, 'Form is a straitjacket in the way that a straitjacket was a straitjacket for Houdini'. Exactly how I feel about working with verse – and music. When you understand the form, its rules, the rigour of form, you discover freedom.

Kate Buckley: What Shakespeare has done is to give actors a bazillion human choices. Too often I see Shakespeare's language being pontificated on the stage. I hate that. They are real people in extraordinary circumstances. I don't remember who taught me that, but I often think about that in rehearsal. Shakespeare's language isn't precious. It comes from a character's strong sense of self and clear objectives.

Timothy Douglas: The more personal the moment can be for each individual, the more illuminated the story is going to be. Shakespeare is the most perfect text for it. There are no holes to fall into. If one is being fully present, allowing whatever emotional life experience to be triggered by the given circumstances of the text, and allow the text, to fully express this very real feeling that has been triggered by the enormity of what Shakespeare has set up, it's very vulnerable. It can be very risky for some actors. That's why Shakespeare is so perfect, because if an actor is willing to 'go there', there's not going to be an edge to fall off of. You are being taken care of all the way through.

I am constantly having to remind actors to *stay on their voices*. A habit in modern communication is that when I am starting to feel intense emotion, [his voice goes quiet and intense] I often go to this place. [He returns to his regular speaking voice.] And this is mostly influenced by film and television, but it's also crept right into the culture. People get emotional and 'I have to stop. I can't show it'. But that's not natural to the body. When emotion comes, when it is a heightened experience, the body organically wants to open a path and have it be released. That's a very animalistic thing. But we have learned to shut it down and not let it out. This has epidemically translated to the stage. I don't let any of my actors ever whisper. When I have a playwright who has in a stage direction, 'This is whispered', I try, as hard as I can to find another way until I am convinced that the only successful way that it's going to work is in a whisper.

In verbal communication we primarily respond to the actual vibrations – which 'carry' the emotions – coming forth from the body, and not to the words themselves. It is the vibration that carries the emotional content and hits your body, and resonates with your body where that emotional content lives in you. And after this initial contact, it's the words that help the brain to get the picture of what we are talking about. But in actuality I am responding to the vibration. To 'go off' the voice instantly distorts the communication that was actually in-process. Most often it habitually happens midway through a line. I scream in rehearsal, '*No! Don't do that*! You had me, but then I just fell out of my chair when you backed off. It was going so well!'

Daniel Sullivan: I'm not exactly certain after all these years what the term 'mid-Atlantic' means when speaking Shakespeare. Soft 'r's', I suppose. But that approach can cross over the time zone very quickly and everyone is doing a sort of muted English accent. I say pronounce those 'r's' – insist on them. We're doing American Shakespeare.

The trouble comes when actors have to portray the lower classes in Shakespeare. What should country people sound like if everyone is speaking in American accents? I believe it's possible to achieve an unsophisticated and less inflected delivery that suggests class without lapsing into an American regional dialect.

Bill Rauch: Obviously the ability with language is important. I will say that my tastes lean much more toward a more aggressively contemporary, a more aggressively American approach to the language than a more classical approach to the language. I think in my years here at OSF I have learned to appreciate more and more well spoken verse, clearly spoken verse. Our Director of Company Development, Scott Kaiser, is a real genius when it comes to trusting the verse and helping the actors trust the verse, that meaning and emotional connection come out of trusting the language and trusting where the accents fall. As I mature as an artist, I am more and more interested in trusting the verse than I was as a young artist.

With that said, I would much rather hear a more contemporary approach to a line than a more classical with a capital C approach to a line. Always! I'm talking about the fact that, as Americans, we should not be doing Shakespeare in a watered down version of how the Brits do it. I don't like mid-Atlantic speech. I especially get impatient when I hear a character that Shakespeare has clearly painted as a low-income character, and they're speaking with an elevated British accent: 'because it is Shakespeare and that is the way one is supposed to speak Shakespeare'. I feel we have to, like actors, be making direct connections with his language so that the audience can make direct connections with the language

Bonnie Monte: It seems like the more you do know about the punctuation and the scansion and the rules, the better you are at knowing *when* to break them and *why* you should break them. Because I think breaking them should happen far more often than people do it. But you have to be pretty confident about why you're breaking them and when you should, so that you can then explain it to the actor. So then it makes sense emotionally and motivationally. 'It doesn't sound right!' (which you can say on occasion). Sometimes I'll say, 'You know what? It just sounds better the other way. I don't really have any kind of technical reason I can give for that'. In part because our ears are different 400 years later, what we hear, and the words have different connotations. So to some extent you have to feel free to break the *rules*. But there are rules. It's poetry. It has a rhythm. It has certain things that you have to pay attention to.

Phrasing and word choice

David Frank: I have a verse workshop that I sometimes spring upon the unsuspecting. I call it 'Tools, Not Rules'. Long ago, I learnt that every time you pronounce *a rule*, you keep stumbling over potent exceptions. Nonetheless, I think you can identify some tools that are extraordinarily powerful and applicable to many situations. Some of the skills are obvious, although difficult to master: good phrasing skills can make the syntax of a sentence immediately apparent; without those skills it is easy to lose even the smartest audience. Another core technique involves focusing on the detail of the word – why those particular words in that particular combination? Figures of speech, rhetorical devices are central to Shakespearean verse. It often pays to play the metaphors and similes literally. Make each of them a little story with their own shape. Don't let them drown in the general point they are illustrating. Let the audience have the joy of unlocking the images. You paint the images, the audience sees what you paint and gets to interpret it. If you go straight to the interpretation, monotony threatens. Two pages reduced to a continuous expression of the same emotion can send anyone to sleep. In my experience, this approach makes dense verbal texts much more accessible to an audience. And you begin to answer another critical question: 'Why all those words?'

In some respects, this is all highly technical, but ultimately, it isn't at all.

Mary Zimmerman: Not everyone these days is well versed in reading poetry. Shakespeare makes up a lot of words. A lot of words have fallen out of use. His syntax is quite backwards from what we are used to sometimes. There are long metaphors that pile out, that keep adding to themselves and then are picked up by other people later on.

Michael Kahn: I've learned a lot through teaching. I've learned a lot about verse. I've learned a lot about structure. And I keep changing. Four or five years ago, I thought people who did end stopping were just little fascists. Now I find that involving myself in that (without saying that's the only thing you can do) actually helps. So I keep learning, partly through working with actors whose technique has come from John Barton and Peter Hall and other people. I have a very specific idea about Shakespeare that I think I'm able to teach – going moment to moment, and knowing exactly what's going on, and why a full stop is there, and what a transition means, and what might happen from the other person when that's there, so that a speech has a reason to keep on going, rather than thinking it's just written there. This is what I do and have come to believe now.

I don't think it's as easy to do as it sounds. The actor's job or the director's job is to get that character and that actor to the point – emotionally and intellectually and situationally and physically – to *have* to say what that character says and not something else. That doesn't mean you say it because Shakespeare wrote it. You say it because what is *going on* means that is what you *have to say* – whether it's intentionally or whether it's from the given circumstances or whatever it is. That takes a lot of rehearsal and a lot of playing around – a lot of going up and down a bunch of different roads until you find out *why* you have to say this.

I honestly believe if audiences don't understand the play, it's not their fault. It's not their fault that they didn't go to college or they didn't read it yesterday. It's our fault. We've done something to get in the way of the communication.

'Just saying the line' is not what I mean. 'Just saying the line' can mean nothing. Actors today understand that the reason you need consonants – you need breath control – is not because of some totalitarian idea of acting Shakespeare. If you are trying to make your emphasis only by being loud or soft, who knows what you're talking about? If you feel to be clear you have to talk slowly, no one can follow you either. Yet if you want to keep the thought going and stay in the rhythm of the verse, if you don't have final consonants, they won't understand what you're talking about either, if you're going reasonably swiftly. So it requires all of the energy at the top of one's game as an actor and a director. Then I think the audience can actually follow you and it's clear.

Sometimes I take it as a compliment (sometimes I think it's not) when people say, 'That production's always really clear'. I know what I do to make them clear with the actors, but it's not about spelling it out. It's about making sure that this moment is fully done, and that it's not ignored – what's going on at this moment. So it comes from the last moment and leads to the next one.

David Frank: To really make an image vivid for an audience, the actor has to be truly 'in the moment'. He or she has to honestly 'see' the image as if for the first time. Merely regurgitating the external symptoms of the idea or image is never enough. This understanding brought me back to the basics that I learned from the work of Viola Spolin – spontaneity and specificity. But when working on the plays of Shakespeare, these values are applied directly to the language that is Shakespeare's method of accessing our internal condition.

I do think you can make an audience appreciate intuitively how strikingly fresh and original a particular combination of words can be. But that only happens if the actor is genuinely *on the moment;* as always, it is about really listening and really talking. Not delivering just the external symptoms of the idea, but landing the idea itself. The goal is simple although the execution is hard. Create an urgent picture of all the details and resonant implications of the language, and transmit that to another character, or to God, or to the audience, or even to yourself. The goal is communication. The method is words. For me, when that happens, the two traditions fuse.

Des McAnuff: When I was doing *Henry IV Part 1* for Joseph Papp in Central Park in 1981, I had my students from Julliard play the so-called Mechanicals. I had worked with a remarkably talented class over the previous two years and they created a mighty foundation for the cast at the Delacorte Theatre. Val Kilmer, one of the brightest of the bright, suggested to me that the approach I was using to the text had some similarities to Michael Langham's approach. Michael was the head of the Julliard School and had become a good friend. I nodded in agreement with Val and then immediately went to Michael Langham to try and find out what Val was talking about. I asked Michael to tell me about his ideas on Shakespeare's texts.

Michael described to me a concept called 'living thought'. He said that this was all that was essential to know about acting Shakespeare. Like all simple things, it is much easier to describe than to actually do, but when employed successfully, it is truly magical. It can open doors for actors like Alice in Wonderland. In a nutshell, it says that there is no separation between the word and the thought. Ultimately, there is no separation between the word, the thought and the emotion. The key principle is that Shakespeare's texts are about thought and not conversation. Every line is a rolling series of discovery. Over time, I have found 'discoveries' is inadequate as a description, so I tend to use words like 'revelation' and 'epiphany'. I later went onto work with Michael Langham and John Hirsch, who was at that time the Artistic Director of the Stratford Festival in Canada. I got to work with actors in auditions with these masterful directors. The two of them had developed living thought to the point where it was practically a science. I had the extreme luxury of directing actors in their presence and developed my skills under their tutelage as we worked a whole host of actors that wanted to be in the company.

When you witness actors that are really capable of embracing living thought – Christopher Plummer, John Vickery, Roberta Maxwell, Martha Henry – it is extraordinarily impressive. It is exhilarating. The complexity of the ideas of the play and the matrix of the clashing points of view are so alive that you find yourself in the middle of something that feels like extreme life. These are real techniques but they are not limiting techniques. What you do with living thought has everything to do with who you are and what your experience brings to the table, the blood pumping through your veins and your own ideas and your own sense. When actors find this, it is like watching someone come face to face with a long lost twin.

Tina Packer: Breath, breath, breath and more breath. For the actor to have an instrument (the body, with all its elements vulnerably alive) that actually reflects what he or she is thinking and feeling. If the actor doesn't own it, and express it, the audience doesn't get it. Vowels and consonants affect our thinking – and have done for thousands of years. To be able to wrap our spirits and intellects to Shakespeare's great thoughts – and let them be a part of our lives! To know language comes out of our desire to communicate – with mind, body, soul, sexuality, sensuality, spirituality.

Rhetoric and language structure

Joanne Zipay: Rhetoric, the understanding of how the language is structured, how an argument is structured, is a thousand times more useful to an actor than poetry. When you look at everything that characters say as an argument, you begin to understand stakes, dramatic action, what people are fighting for, action/intention, objective – all the acting 101 stuff. It's immediate and you can talk about it and the shifts in it. But if you're 'being poetic,' it's unplayable, and an audience becomes uninterested. And that's what takes us back to that horrible Victorian idea.

I agree with John Barton: find the argument. When you find the argument, you find the character. And the poetry emerges. So in the dramaturgical work that we do, it's finding out what's at stake in every scene, what you're fighting for in every scene. And the stakes are always getting higher, every moment, and that's what's exciting. I feel that when people walk out on stage and say words that aren't connected, there's no way an audience is going to find anything interesting in that. The choice of words is an active process.

Penny Metropulos: I always try to come in looking at the text for what strikes me on the human level. The rhetorical language, the elevated thought comes out of that. It reveals everything about the character. It is completely natural to them. It's the way they think.

Stresses and operatives

Mark Lamos: When studying the play, I write the stresses out over the lines of verse. 'To BE or NOT to BE, that IS the QUES-tion'. Obviously, the actor's not going to use all those stresses, but seeing that they are there provides a map for him to work out his interpretation of the line.

Ralph Alan Cohen: I think that Shakespeare always cared most about the last word of a line. Americans tend to drop the last word of their sentences, and that habit is particularly dangerous when you're doing Shakespeare and he has built so much into the last word of lines and sentences. So I ask my actors especially to embrace the last stressed syllable whether or not it's to end a thought or launch the next line.

Michael Kahn: I question a lot: 'What did you just say? What was that? Now wait a minute, why did you say that?' And when I hear that there's no energy in a line from an actor, I know that they have no reason to say it. Or if the stress is in the wrong place, it's not that I think they don't know how to scan. It's that I think they don't know why they're saying what they're saying. So I'd never go back and say, 'Well look. You're stressing it wrong,' I'll say, 'Wait a minute, why is that word there?' And then immediately those stresses usually work logically. Or I'll say, 'Why do you think that's stressed?' Why do you think that word's at the end?' Or I'll say, 'What kind of what?' Or, 'Who?' Or, 'It's what?' And then all of a sudden they'll see that. Or I'll say, 'Dropping the ends of the line – it's not that it's so much a technical issue, but what is that word there? Why do you think it's there?' And then all of a sudden we won't be dropping the end of the line. We can still see the end of the line and still get through the thought. It's not as if actors are taught, 'Well, the thought goes to the next line'. You don't worry about that. The truth of the matter is that it is a line of verse, even if the thought keeps on going.

Rhythm and pacing

Henry Woronicz: I think a lot has to do with the rhythms of the play and how the language reflects the rhythms of the play. About how the verse also indicates what the character might be dealing with and pointing those things out, when it goes into prose, when it goes into verse – how that might reflect what is going on in the scene. When there are incomplete lines, when lines are completed from one actor to another, leading a first line and trying to keep a certain forward motion to the language. It has a meter and it has a rhythm like a score. Not as strict as a musical score, but it is analogous.

Daniel Sullivan: Very few American actors work the same way or put their performances together at the same speed. So it can sometimes be difficult to connect the necessary rhythms that connect speeches, particularly those in blank verse. It is often the understandable instinct of the actor to think about what has just been said before responding. This, in most cases, is deadly in Shakespeare. When playing a verse scene, your responsibility is not only to your own words, but how your words connect to the whole. Your words ARE the thought process. You don't need to think about it before you say it, and if you do take a pause to have a thought before you speak, you will most likely destroy the rhythm of the verse and the exciting gallop of the music will tumble to the ground. In my experience, it's very hard to get it moving again.

Brian Kulick: I'm particularly interested in this issue of rate of utterance. What is the metabolic rate of a given Shakespearean line? I think one of the problems that happens, in a certain kind of Shakespearean production, is that the actor or director can have a tendency to standardize the line, to give it an iambic regularity, when there is more variety than one might suspect (i.e. trochees, pyrrhics and spondees). There's a lot more movement and variation actually happening in the line than they're allowing.

There's a wonderful book by George Wright, *Shakespeare's Metrical Art,* which de-mystifies the whole business of metrics and the impulse that one has to 'make it all iambic ally scan!' That sudden nervous desire to fit everything into De-dum De-dum, De-dum. But what one needs to be awake to is, not when it is regular, but when that regularity breaks down, to realize that iambic pentameter exists to be broken. Where it breaks is where the real meaning is, where the real energy is. When it becomes a trochee or a spondee tells you something. The iamb, De-Dum, mirrors the rhythm of our own heartbeat, it suggests what is natural; so when you encounter a trochee, Dum-De, the very inversion of an iamb, it is as unsettling to us as a heart attack. It goes against our very nature and it can tell you that something very important has happened/is happening to your character. Lear's 'Never, Never, Never' is a series of trochees, a figurative breaking of his heart.

So I try to encourage an actor to look for when Shakespeare breaks out of the iambic rhythm and what that might mean at that given point in the line. Shakespeare gives an actor a tremendous amount of information with metrics, alliterations, word choice, spacing, etc. It's very moving and unnerving to discover how much acting information is imbedded in every line of Shakespeare.

Borges said that Shakespeare's language is a fight between Latinate and Anglo-Saxon words. It is those moments when Shakespeare pits the polysyllabic (Latin) against the monosyllabic (Anglo-Saxon). A great example is in *Macbeth* where a fevered messenger verbally paints an elaborate, polyphonic picture of terror – only to be followed by Macbeth's ever so blunt: 'It was a bad night'. It is the movement from artifice to reality; the play of syllables becomes a metaphysical insight into the shifting modalities of understanding being.

Mark Lamos: In verse-speaking, I work with the actors on breathing and rhythm and most of all achieving something that has a natural-sounding *flow* to it that comes off like real speech. I believe in long lines, thinking in a long line, choosing the fewest number of words to stress. I trust the slight end stop after five beats of iambic pentameter. Shapes of phrases emerge as we work on breathing, consonants, vowel sounds and the poetics of the writing. I firmly believe that pronouns, especially personal ones, must not be stressed, though there are a few – a very few – exceptions to that. One is in the first speech of *The Merchant of Venice*: 'In sooth I know not why I am so sad. / It wearies me, you say it wearies *you*'. The iambic stress tells you that you can stress the final 'you', and of course it makes the most sense to do so. But most of the time, if the actor attempts to reject stressing the pronoun, he will discover a line's truer sense.

Ralph Alan Cohen: I don't like pauses. I don't understand pauses. One or two silences may be golden; after three they turn to lead. I don't want my audience, two and a half hours in, to wish they were going someplace else. I want every minute [filled]: 'After two hours, you better really have a reason for the choices that made it go a minute over two hours'. The note that they're going to get from me the most is, 'NPB: there is no pause before your line, no pause after the cue and before your line. I don't know why you are pausing here before this'. At the same time I say to them, 'If there's space while you are giving the speech, I don't care. It's getting your cue immediately. I don't want *not* to hear you talking'. It's my belief that an audience that gets ahead of an actor's thinking gets bored. I think they turn off the thinking machine. They sit there waiting for them to get to where they are. So I do like for the actors to stay ahead of them.

Calvin MacLean: With few exceptions I think, the reason why a production of a Shakespeare seems long is because the action is unclear and the acting is unnatural and obvious, not because the language is inherently difficult. I did a *King Lear* which ran under three hours, and we didn't cut very much of the play. Transitions were brisk, language crisply spoken. It was speedy. It was efficient. Often productions are lengthened by inefficient action or generalized acting. Getting the action right, phrasing the verbal action accordingly solves much of the problem with an audience understanding Shakespeare's language.

Physical language

Timothy Douglas: Myopically, to emphasize the technical aspect devoid of the emotional and physical is actually exacerbating the union that must be present in the work. I am most often working with actors approaching Shakespeare, whose response is akin to, 'Oh my God. I've got to analyze the language'. When approaching that mindset, the best thing I can do for them is to get them more in touch with their bodies.

When the mind and body are once again in harmony, I can hear it. The actor can too, usually.

Brian Kulick: There's a particular energy that's trapped by Shakespeare's language. The trick is to gain access to it and release it. When you unlock that, you unlock the play. Look at the language in *Romeo and Juliet*, what is it like? How do thoughts and speeches and scenes build through language? What is it analogous to? Soon you realize, it is just like a duel. Every speech, every scene has a sword-fight-like-build, reaching that moment when the fight gets carried away, out of control and something very unexpected and potentially dangerous can happen. That is the deep structure of the world of *Romeo and Juliet*. Duelling infects everyone's psyche, it is not just how they use swords, but also how they use words, build arguments, horse around, make love – everything is informed and infected by this a culture of duelling. It has become part of the DNA of every scene. It impacts the text from a macrocosmic to a microcosmic level; right down to the versification itself – everything is always spiralling out of control like a sword fight. Once you start to understand that dynamic, you can then start to shape it.

Later rehearsals

David Frank: Everything I advocate is at least partially untrue; worse, you have to figure out for yourself what works and when. Although I am confident these techniques are useful in the midst of rehearsals, once you start run-throughs, broader truths have to take over. You have to surrender to the greater story, and trust that the precise moment-to-moment work you have done will be there, without you thinking laboriously about how to achieve it. And passion must fuse with precision if the best work is to emerge.

12

Middle Stage Rehearsals

I used to produce looks of askance: 'There's Shakespeare time and there's real time'. 'What the hell do you mean by that?' was the usual response. 'I mean this entire speech that takes three minutes, dare to think of it as two or three seconds of human experience that needs two or three minutes in order to communicate our common understanding of how it feels. Think of the sublime recognition scene in Twelfth Night. It makes no sense as you try to flesh it out with realistic, chronological detail. You have to trust Shakespeare and the power of poetry. When you think of the sequence as a single glorious moment, so intense it has frozen in time, it can work brilliantly.' And, of course, it still has to be both specific and spontaneous – heart wrenchingly true, not pedantically realistic.

DAVID FRANK

What gets the director's focus after the first phase of rehearsal is over? Here directors describe a number of possibilities. Woronicz focuses on 'how a story is told'. This includes attention to 'beginnings, middles and ends; the rhythms of

FIGURE 17 Richard III, *directed by Brian Kulick, Classic Stage Company, 2007. Michael Cumpsty as Richard III. Photograph by Joan Marcus.*

the story, the rhythms of performance' defining the specific tempi that dominate each scene. Kahn works on 'layering [the performance] with more complexity' by digging deeper and discovering richer choices in each moment. He provides two examples from his *Macbeth*. D. Sullivan develops behaviour in the actors by assuring the scene is 'constantly in motion', never set. He abhors the view that behaviour somehow gets in the way of the language. Gaines also works to instil behaviour that will highlight 'the language and intent of the characters'. The conflicts between character intentions help her create 'visual pictures' that buttress a scene's 'interior needs' and 'universal gestures' that communicate the production's central moments to the audience. Frank believes the director must find 'a source of tension in each scene or in each big speech'. He shares an example from his *Henry V*. Another factor is pointing out the pressures of time. Kulick asks, 'Have I found a way to activate the scene that grounds it for an actor and explodes it for an audience?' Peterson searches for 'positive objectives' to 'work against the tragedy'. Next she develops each character's arc. At the same time, she finds operative words that help establish a through-line of the play. Towards the end of rehearsals, Kulick works on shaping three arcs: the characters', the acts' and the play's. J. R. Sullivan warns that there are long scenes in Shakespeare 'that will elude you'. Often he realizes that he can be the obstacle to solving the problem. Also he works to 'groove in' the actors' performance to instil 'ownership and an enthusiasm for it and a pleasure in it that maintains through a run'. He believes much of the process is simply problem solving. Conlin, like McSweeny, works with the set model and costume sketches in rehearsal and reminds the actors how the designs will influence the performance. Ivers focuses on clarity of storytelling and 'how characters catapult other characters through the play'. Metropulos urges the director to develop 'fearlessness' to 'trust that I know what I am seeing in my head', yet recognize that this process is also a collaborative one.

Gaines, Kulick, Frank, McSweeny, Lamos and Shine contend that analysis of the punctuation and language in Shakespeare can provide clues to playing the character and the moment. Cohen argues that the actor must embrace, not resolve, the character's contradictions and let the audience project their own arc onto the character's actions: 'I think the moment is all that matters'. In a criticism of the American method, Serban points out that the character is so much more than the actor; the performance should move the actor beyond themselves toward something 'higher' than themselves. McSweeny believes Shakespeare is good at characterization because he has empathy for all of his characters. He can project himself into their circumstances and record their actions and speech. Thompson believes a character's thoughts are born at the moment when they are uttered. The actor's goal is to see how immediate he or she can make each moment. Esbjornson states that actors have considerable intuition: 'If you are in sync with them and if they trust you, actors will protect the choices that you've created together and will calibrate and build their performances in just the right way'. Sevy checks in with his actors to find out what in the character is 'resonating ... where they're making a connection'. Sometimes he is able to nudge them towards a perception; sometimes the awareness is awakened in him and leads him down another path. Lamos looks for similarities in scenes and characters. He observes 'Shakespeare's fascination with the idea of perception ... characters are [always] watching each other'. He gives specific instances from *The Merchant of Venice*, *Twelfth Night* and *Hamlet*. He warns of the importance of setting aside character preconceptions to successfully work with the actor before you. This is especially difficult for him when he has already directed the same play before.

Is there subtext and motivation in Shakespeare's plays? On the one side, Bishop warns that the actor must not 'complicate' by looking for dimensionality and motivations that are not there. Similarly Zimmerman declares that 'there is no unknown subtext' and that previous history and actions do not really exist for characters. D. Sullivan admits that American actors can 'work against the clear intentions of the scene' if they get too 'inward'. Yet he maintains that subtext 'dictates behaviour'. It is 'emotionally about what's the temperature ... what the connections are between the actors'.

To shape his production, Kulick divides it into two sections. Part one is the first three acts and by the end of it 'the audience should be hooked'. Part two explores a different landscape that has 'another time signature, a different metabolic rate ... new rules'. The play starts in a theatrical mode and by the end of it, the world has become much more real. Both parts must be carefully wrought with his audience, the final 'player'.

According to Lamos, run-throughs mean that 'you see the production begin to take on a life of its own ... a controlling entity that we all have to listen to, we all have to watch'. Tresnjak checks to see 'how it all hangs together, what falls into place', and then begins to work through the play once again, focusing on whatever issues have emerged from the run. There is little agreement on when to do the first run-through. Frank and Douglas run an act or section as they work through the play. Zimmerman does a run by the end of the first week. J. R. Sullivan has a run roughly ten days into rehearsals. Peterson runs at the end of the second week. McSweeny at the end of week three and D. Sullivan postpones the first run until as late as possible in the process. Like Frank and Douglas, he runs sections before then. Lamos has 'the first run-through just for "family"'. The second one is open to theatre staff; he knows he now has to 'defend and clarify my work'.

Directorial purposes for runs include: answering as many questions as possible, 'once everyone is seeing the rest of the play' (Zimmerman); 'to know what the goal is' and not worry about a lot of detail, (J. R. Sullivan); 'so I can start to do triage' (Peterson); to get a sense of the flow before tech (McSweeny); and to 'see 'how things begin to fit together' (D. Sullivan).

Warren discusses the difference between group notes (things that can be worked out in the space) and individual notes after a run (individual technical acting issues). Conlin advises the director to adjust to how each actor works. McSweeny cautions that it's 'not just *what* you say, but *when* you say it'. Buckley finds 'I don't believe you' is a useful note to give an actor; she has never been challenged on it. Peterson does not like written notes, but responds to 'the tone and body of the thing' in person with the group. She finds actors respond well to 'straight-forward' technical notes such as 'Pick up your cue'. She believes in working notes 'on our feet'. Zimmerman lets the actor know she has witnessed when 'they have taken an adjustment from the day before'. Like Buckley, she prefers action instead of discussion.

What are the director's strategies for managing the production and scheduling rehearsals? D. Sullivan remarks 'The surprise of rehearsals is always the rate at which actors work'. McSweeny shares the challenges of steering large productions that require some logistical skill. He remembers the tracking charts he did as an assistant for Michael Kahn, which now have become a vital part of his process. Zimmerman discloses how exhausting rehearsals can be as she is constantly 'in a state of attentiveness, on high alert' at all times. Both MacLean and J. R. Sullivan impart how they try to work through the play three times before tech rehearsals. MacLean first works on staging, then revising the staging and 'the rhythmic structure', and finally he focuses on clarifying the 'through-line of the action' and the flow. Kulick discusses his ideal schedule, aiming to 'activate the scenes through physicalization' during the first two weeks. After this, he has two weeks to 'explore'. He likes to have three runs in the final three days before tech. Conlin notes that in rep situations, like at Utah Shakespeare, sequential work-throughs are important for everyone to always know where they are — including herself.

After the first week

Henry Woronicz: I think a director has to develop the skill to understand how a story is told: the beginnings, middles and ends; the rhythms of the story; the rhythms of performance. Shakespeare was very attuned to the rhythms of an audience, to the rhythms of performance. There will be a scene that tumbles along and then there is a slow scene that happens. He was brilliant at it in terms of the form of the way that a poet would put language on a page. I think a skill that a director has to develop is one of telling a good story. It's a technical skill, to bring an act to a conclusion, to start the second act with something that gets the audience back into it, and then to wrap the play up.

Michael Kahn: You keep refining it. You keep layering it with more complexity. I mean you find things that are in the moment. You find things that are not suggested by the first logical response to it, but there's something else going on, making the situation more complicated or complex. Finding other levels of what's going on between people, any number of things, and then making certain things more theatrical. I had forty-three ideas for the witches this time around. It just took me about three weeks to go through them. When a rehearsal's going well, everybody's inspiration and imagination are starting to work. Including mine. And I trust, just like actors, that my unconscious begins to be valuable to me.

I remember when we were doing *Macbeth*, the character Seton developed through rehearsals. He originally played the bloody sergeant. Not as Seton, but it was the same actor. I thought, 'No, that's too close'. So I took the bloody sergeant away from the actor. But then I thought, 'Well, even though Seton doesn't have anything to say in the first two scenes, he's going to be connected to Macbeth all the way through. I need to find a reason for him to be in those scenes, even though he's not talking'. Then finally I thought, 'What happens to Seton at the end? Nothing'. And I thought, 'He should die'. So I said to Macbeth, 'I was just watching the "Tomorrow and tomorrow speech"'. I said to him, 'I think you should kill Seton'. That came like in the fourth week of rehearsal. I just trusted that, wherever it came from – in my head or from my soul – it didn't come intellectually; it just somehow came. Patrick Page [Macbeth] thought it was terrific. Then he went and thought, 'Well, okay, maybe I'll kill ... maybe I'll think about killing ... maybe that's what I think life is ... maybe I think about killing myself after my wife's death' – which I hadn't thought of. And then he did that and I thought, 'Well that's really interesting'. It came out of, 'How would I pull out the knife?' But he immediately transferred it to, 'I have the knife'. So who knows where that came from? But that was how we layered that speech. He has that speech about life's not worth it. It's this famous speech, and we kept going, 'Oh, I know ... !'

So that's what I mean by layering. We had discussed what the speech meant. Originally it had been up on the stairs. And

I said, 'No, that's too far away. We've got to bring it down here. Maybe it'd be nice if you sat on the edge of the stage, a player strutting, you know. If you were there, that might be nice'. So it developed. We understood what the speech was about and then all of a sudden it was a lot of things like that happening.

Daniel Sullivan: Once we're on our feet, I try to keep the process constantly in motion. Plays are about behaviour and the most deadening kind of Shakespeare is the kind that's afraid of behaviour; as if the behaviour somehow distracts us from the beauty of the language. People in Shakespeare's time had lives as complicated and eccentric as our own, more so, in fact, given how short and brutal life was 400 years ago. I can't imagine people stood about declaiming.

Barbara Gaines: As the actors develop their impulses I'm always open to new ideas, but eventually I take a more active part in the staging. I look for the human behaviour that supports the language and intent of the characters. Each character wants different things from the other, so you need to sort out the clashing intents and theatricalize them physically and vocally. I try and connect a visual picture that supports the interior needs of the scene. I'm always looking for universal gestures that will clarify moments, so if the language escapes the audience, they can understand the moment based on what they're watching.

David Frank: You've got to look for a source of tension in each scene or in each big speech. Sometimes it's so simple, it escapes you.

There's a notoriously difficult passage in *Henry V* when Hal confronts the traitors. Hal and his army are just about to embark for France, and suddenly they discover that three trusted members of the king's entourage, Scrope, Cambridge and Grey, are traitors who have succumbed to bribes. There must be two pages there where Hal rages at them. If it's just anger, it gets terribly dull. But Matt [the actor playing Henry] discovered how the tension was within himself. He couldn't leave it alone because he couldn't understand it. By creating a series of embryonic false exits, he gave it an immediate storytelling tension. Simple discoveries like that can lead to thrilling rehearsals that make all those words vivid and necessary.

Usually, you have a notion going into rehearsal of what you think it's going to be, but very often you realize somebody has a much better idea. Eventually you learn that being open to discovery is a key to creativity. It doesn't mean you don't have to really understand in your mind what the staging potentials are, what the key moments are.

Above all, I ask myself, 'what is the source of the tension and how does that get communicated to an audience? What is the role of time? Are we in a rush or are we at leisure? What scenes, what speeches are *less* important?' Because if everything is a peak, all you have is a high plain.

Lisa Peterson: I'm busy mining the positive objectives, especially in a play like [*Othello*]. I found that's what keeps the story moving forward, when it's all about a kind of descent. So trying to find – particularly with Othello and with Desdemona – the ways in which their characters work against the tragedy. Why is it that Desdemona continues to press Casio's case? It comes down to Othello and Desdemona, and trying to figure out a way to think of that as a positive: 'What's real? What are your positive objectives? How is this marriage working? What isn't working about the marriage?'

This is a process of discovery, looking for the arc for every character. That isn't something that I worry about too much at the very beginning, oddly enough. It's something that comes in the middle to the end. That question of, 'Okay, you start here and you end here. Is that the biggest arc we can make?' With Iago especially, it's a little tricky to structure, to not think of it as all the same thing all the time. Sometimes it's easier to see the arc when the play is up on its feet.

With Shakespeare, I am always listening, in terms of through-line, for the operative words – the words I would really like the audience to track through. In this play 'will' is one. Iago uses that a lot in relationship to everybody. Othello uses it in relationship to Desdemona's impulsiveness. So somebody's 'will' and what that is doing to them and how that is operating in the world.

Then there is each actor's own peculiar insecurities, those certainly come up. In that middle period, I found myself responding and doing that dance of encouraging, critiquing, trying to help them find ownership of the character. And let go of fear. This is something unique to this play. It's true of *Lear*, but less so. *Othello* is a scary play to perform. Even though they are strong actors and want to make bold choices, there was a deep-seated fear on the part of the primary players. We would come to that last scene, and there was a sense of dread. I thought that that was in the way, sometimes, of us figuring out what was happening in that scene. It's purely scary: scary for Desdemona, scary for Othello. It's just scary.

Brian Kulick: I feel like at three weeks, you discover what the play really is. Then you've got to shape it. That's your next two weeks. The first few weeks you are working on moments in isolation of one another, exploring what each individual moment can bare, then you run through all those moments and begin to think about what these moments add up to, how they build. That is when you begin the shaping phase, building the arc of each character. The arcs for me are the last pieces of the equation. The arc of the character and the arc of an act and the arc of the play really get shaped in those last two weeks and further refined in previews with an audience, that is where the final tuning happens.

I also try to find a psychical vocabulary for the play. The 'dance' of each scene. I need the scenes to be activated through physicalization. So that if you didn't understand the words of the play, you would understand the production just through its physicalization. One of the things that drives me insane about classical theatre is the 'stand and deliver' approach. It's almost as bad as opera. Where the actor just stands there and says a whole beautiful speech dead centre, and then another two people arrive and stand dead centre and do the same thing. Still as oaks, with not a wind in sight to even rustle their leaves. It drives me crazy! There is a dance that's happening in the scenes. There's another story happening, a story of forces and forces in collision with one another. How do you physicalize that? How do you visualize that? How do you manifest it? And how can you create a physical or movement score so that the actor can connect to it – not only on a cerebral level, but on a very visceral level?

The success or failure as a director in a room is, 'Have I found a way to activate the scene that grounds it for an actor and explodes it for an audience?' If I haven't, then I feel like I've failed slightly in my job. It doesn't mean they have to be constantly moving or constantly be busy, but they have to be constantly meaning – both in terms of the action that they are playing and the movements that they are taking on, so that everything has a potential to mean.

J. R. Sullivan: In Shakespeare there is always some 550-line long scene. And there is always one or two that will elude you. And it probably ought to. It just escapes comprehension. It escapes our full realization of it. I think in *As You Like It*, originally we had a tough time with the wooing scene, culminating in the marriage. But also [we had] a little bit of difficulty with the foresters and Jacques and the Seven Ages scene. And that surprised me. I thought, 'Oh, we'll get there'. But then I realized it was me. It's like that phrase, 'If something's boring you, it's probably you'. If you're not getting something here, it's probably you. What are you missing here? And there are more dark complexities to that whole thing leading up to the Seven Ages speech, that are not coming from Jacques. I didn't quite get that in this play. But I like to go with the flow on this. You see what is going to read and what isn't. And then you're building on the instincts of the actors. It's equally important not to over think something.

And there is also an art to timing these things so that the director's sense of their full comprehension of it is kind of timed so that they arrive at something at the appropriate time in the process, because that's where you learn it best. That's what I mean by 'grooving it in', too. It's a path that they find, but you have prepared it. Their act of finding it has been, I think, an ownership of it and an enthusiasm for it and a pleasure in it that maintains through a run. And that's where we are directors and not dictators, guiders and not conductors. Conductor in the sense of maybe a tempo and a rhythm, but not in a sense of, 'This is what you do'. Let them have their thoughts. And we must realize that they do put it on, on their own.

So I think that the way you deal with the problem solving in a rehearsal process is the same way that it is in a tech. It is just the sequence of solving problems. And where the scenes are going to be problematic, for whatever reason – should it be something personal or something difficult about the text, something physically demanding, whatever it is that is going to emerge – you have got to be ready to deal with it on a case-by-case basis.

Kathleen Conlin: I keep the physical model on the rehearsal table all the while we rehearse. I usually also have all the costume drawings in the rehearsals as well. I don't wait to put details like that in the production during tech week. I try to build that into what we are doing, so that we are constantly making references to, 'Now, remember you're really on the steps in this scene, even though we're here. So notice what that's going to do in terms of the quality of that scene. That you're going to be running up, running down, running up, running down. Get that in your body now, because it's going to affect the way you play this scene'. We constantly keep going back to that and try to employ as many of those elements.

David Ivers: Here we have so little rehearsal time. What we say here is we're long on weeks and short on hours. We're lucky if I get to do a full pass of the play as a work pass and then we're more into stumble-throughs and runs. It's rough. I mean it's the real rep.

[In work-throughs, I look for] storytelling. Are we lining up key storytelling components so that that's clear? I'm always looking and listening for clarity. I don't want our audiences or me to be doing any translating of 'I think that's what that meant'.

I'm also looking for how characters catapult other characters through the play. 'What are the actions you're playing and you're doing that serve the other person's journey?' And I'm really interested in muscular, lean, moving productions of Shakespeare's work that get at the central issues that he wrote about.

Penny Metropulos: I have to trust that I know what I am seeing in my head. It may not all be there at week three or week five. And I even may think, 'Oh my God! I wonder if it is going to get there?' But I know where it is going, and I am trying to share that all the way along the way. It's a challenge, whether you're working with two actors or fifty actors, to say [*laughing*] 'Look! It's in my head'. Every day when something is brought to me: 'Here's the design, here is this new idea about character, here is a prop, here is this accent' – whatever it is, I am saying 'yes' or 'no', depending on what is in my head. This is where the real fearlessness of being a director comes in.

There are times when everybody thinks you are crazy, because everyone wants it to look the way it looks in *their* heads, and all the way along the line, you are compromising your image in some way. As soon as you work with another human being, you are compromising. It is never going to be exactly what it was in my head to begin with. To me that is the beauty of the theatre. That's what makes it extraordinary. I hear an actor say something and I think, 'Oh my God, that changes the entire colour of this. Hold it! We've got to go back'. Just like that. In the beginning of the design, a costume designer shows me something, or gives me a piece of research and its like, 'Oh my God! This is incredible'. That is what collaboration is.

Barbara Damashek, this wonderful director, this fabulous, lovely woman, used to say, 'You know, we always must give up our little darlings'. And we do, all of us, along the way, we are giving up our little darlings. I think in the end, you are looking at something that is an approximation of what your dream was originally. In some ways, it has gone far beyond your expectations and in some ways it falls terribly short. The reason that I became a director is because the process and the collaboration are so fascinating to me. The final step is discovering whether or not that idea, that we all contributed to, is going to make enough sense that it will communicate with all the people watching and effect them.

Character issues

Ralph Alan Cohen: I love contradictions. I am not at all afraid of a contradiction in tone, even a contradiction in character. I think that contradictions are at the heart of these plays. If you are angry one moment and happy the next and sad the next, I think an audience will put that together. That's not narrative to me; that's character. So don't ever argue to me, 'I did this then and this moment is something different so I think I ought to make it fit the other moment'. I think that the moment is all that matters. I tell them, 'It's not your job to find the arc. Give me the moment. Make that moment as exciting as you can make that moment, and the audience will find the arc for you'.

Andrei Serban: Whenever I work with the actors I tell them, 'The character is larger than you. It is more intense than you. It is deeper than you'. Consider the bad example of The Actors Studio approach: 'Hamlet is you'. If Hamlet is me, there is no difference between me and Hamlet. If Hamlet is at my own level, it's of no interest. If Hamlet is up there and I'm here, I am trying, through the process of discovery to find how to understand his uniqueness, he is so much more intelligent, complex, sensitive, courageous, noble than I am. In doing that, I'm trying to open myself to something that is higher than me. In that way, there is a meeting between me and the character somewhere in the middle. Rather than say, 'Hamlet is me', please say 'Hamlet is the ideal'. Every actor must have an ideal. One cannot be an actor (or a human being for the matter) without an ideal. Make the character your ideal. Look up to him, not down. Don't bring him to your confused, weak level. Get strength from him. Even if he is called Iago. Iago is necessary, he is a needed force for the truth to come to light. Playing Iago is a big challenge, an opportunity. Think about being human, what a complex word *being human* is!

Ethan McSweeny: I find indecision interesting for characters. As we know, Shakespeare was an actor, and as a writer, I think that just like an actor, he finds ways to love or at least understand each of his characters. This is why he almost never writes an uncomplicated hero or villain, he is always thinking, 'What would this be like if I were in this situation?' Even in the face of using an anti-Semitic conceit, inherited from Marlow, in *The Merchant of Venice* out comes Shylock's, 'Hath not a Jew eyes … ?' It's a great example because that's just how Shakespeare wrote. He wrote from the place of, 'I wonder what I would do here? Or what would this feel like?' He would just start thinking that way. I get interested in thinking about the characters that way.

Kent Thompson: I am a great believer that Shakespeare writes in real time. In other words that the thought comes at the same time as it's said, that there's no pre-thought. It's not the modern theatre. Unless he explains it, or unless it's in the writing, whether the line is too short or you know. I think that they're speaking what they're thinking and feeling. So I try to get the actor back to some of the basic issues with acting, that sometimes are easy to forget with Shakespeare. Which are, 'Oh my God. This is what happens and this is what you say'.

Now, what does this mean about your character? So you're Viola. You come in. That shipwrecked scene. You've barely made it to shore. You think your brother's dead. In sixty or eighty lines you've determined, 'I'm going to dress like a guy, a eunuch. And we're going to have a future. And I'm going to devote myself to time'. Well that says something fundamental about your character, that you're willing to trust the time, trust the fate. So what I keep going back to is the character logic. Once we've started to excavate the text, how does it feed into your understanding of this person as a human being? And how *immediate* can you make it in the moment, what you're coming up with? That's a process that will go on through opening night, sometimes through an entire rep season.

David Esbjornson: If I have failed to consider some important aspect of a characterization or overlooked an important dramaturgical clue, it will often be revealed by our collective investigation. Actors are quite used to trying a variety of things and then are asked to abandon those choices for the greater good. There is no reason why directors shouldn't do the same.

In general, I find actors to be the most open-minded and perhaps bravest of all theatre artists. They astonish me with their intuition and what they are willing to do to make their characters come boldly alive. If you are in sync with them and if they trust you, actors will protect the choices that you've created together and will calibrate and build their performances in the just the right way. They will not only deliver the production, but once they find the audience, they are capable of taking the work to a whole new level.

Bruce Sevy: I'm interested in how the character is resonating for the actor, places where they're making a connection. I try not to have too strong a feeling about, 'I know it needs to go like this and like that'. Or 'That's the high point'. I'll have a certain opinion about that, but I watch as much as I tell, and shape as I go. I think it is important that they not be my puppets. But I'm taking in what they're bringing, watching them make discoveries, asking the same questions that I may have asked earlier when I was working on it, how that is fitting. And I adjust things, if I think something is happening. I'll go, 'Oh wait! That's better ...'. Really the whole process of rehearsal for me is a mixture of that. I don't just set it on.

Mark Lamos: In a Shakespeare text I seek similarities, first of all. There are elements in every scene of a Shakespeare play that reflect or examine elements he's already presented. It's like looking at a cut diamond. Each facet reflects the light differently, but each is an expression of the diamond itself. Another metaphor is the wheel. Each spoke of the wheel is joined to the axel. They all, together, carry the cart. Shakespearean scenes are often, I feel, a variation on a central theme – or set of self-relating themes – that keep examining the same idea over and over. Each scene in a Shakespeare play relates to one over-arching central idea, but in a delightfully different way.

Here's a case in point: the Gobbo clowns in *The Merchant of Venice* are a father and son. The son makes fun of his blind father. At first we may wonder what these two funny guys have to do with a play about Portia and Bassanio, Shylock and his daughter. Well, for starters, Shylock too is 'blind' to his daughter's intentions, blind as well to the wisdom of the boy (Portia disguised) who will quietly cause his downfall. Levels of perception are key as well to the relationship of the two lovers, based on the idea that one cannot tell a book by its cover. Beauty and richness (as in the gold and silver caskets) can blind us to the truth, the essence. Bassanio's ability to *perceive* the truth allows him to choose the right casket.

Every play of his I've ever worked on demonstrates Shakespeare's fascination with the idea of perception. In so many of his scenes, characters are watching each other. Perceiving. Seeing. Trying to understand what they see. In

Twelfth Night, for instance, the three clowns watch Malvolio make a fool of himself as he tries to work out the 'script' they've written for him. Meanwhile, we are watching them. And we are watching a scene about a man's blindness.

Think, too, of the Mousetrap scene, the play-within-the-play in *Hamlet*. Claudius and members of the court are watching actors acting in a play; Hamlet, however, is watching Claudius to see if the way he 'acts' tells him (Hamlet) the truth. We, in kind, are watching not only The Mousetrap, but also a key member of its audience, *and* its director – Hamlet – watching that audience member. Perception, the truth of what we see, can be the foundation of any production of *Hamlet*. After all, the protagonist spends most of the play not being at all sure that what he's seen (his father's ghost) is in fact real. He can't kill Claudius – as his father's spirit has ordered him to do – until he works out the truth of the accusation that has, after all, come from beyond the grave. Or from Hamlet's tortured mind ... He senses he may be going mad.

It's as if Shakespeare spent his entire life investigating the act of seeing and perception, constantly trying to test the characters' – and the audience's – suspension of disbelief. As each of his plays was a new experiment for him, unlike anything that he'd written previously, he constantly sought ways of understanding reality. Is reality what we perceive? Is behaviour how we 'act'?

Subtext and motivation

André Bishop: I think the trouble American actors have in Shakespeare is that sometimes they attach too much importance so their inner psychological ladders, that they sometimes want to complicate the Shakespearean character unduly. Which modern plays do, to try and find, 'He does this, but it's really because of this'. Sometimes Shakespeare's characters are kind of two-dimensional or one-dimensional. There is no real psychological explanation for Iago's villainy. Yes, he might be jealous of Othello. I've read endless theories.

You cannot attach psychological realities to a lot of *Cymbeline*. On the other hand you've got to act it. You have to justify it to the audience. When Martha Plimpton has to throw herself on a headless dummy, we know it's not a person whom she thinks is her husband because he is dressed the same way (and fortunately both actors are more or less the same size). She has to make us believe she believes it, or we are lost. I mean it's just hilarious. Her need as an actor to somehow find the motivation and justification and all that, beyond the artifice, is very real.

In fact, there's no point, in my opinion, in delving too far. I realize that the modern American actor needs that in order to act, because that's part of American training. 'Why am I doing what I am doing? What is my motivation?' But sometimes in Shakespeare that can trip you up, because there isn't a whole lot of motivation. [The actor playing] Iachimo has a tendency sometimes to over think Iachimo. So we get into this whole thing – it's like all in his head because 'he repents at the end and he is really in love with him'. He sometimes overcomplicates this villain, who is kind of just a villain and then in the end repents. I think that is a danger over here of some directors also.

Mary Zimmerman: I think we know what the characters in Shakespeare are thinking because they tell us. If they don't tell us, it probably is not there. Actors sometimes get caught up in wanting to really work their character and find out the subtext. I would almost say there is no unknown subtext in Shakespeare. Someone like Iago might be lying in a scene, but we know he's lying because he told us exactly what he was going to do before the scene started. It's very rare that, in some undisclosed way, someone has actually got some ulterior motive. When people try and lard a scene down with that, put a kind of contemporary gloss on something – like a contemporary idea in psychology and 'they couldn't possibly mean this' – it just muddies up the waters so extremely. My approach with Shakespeare is so simple. It's 'Find out what it literally means and do that'. I'm actually overly glib about this, I know.

There's a duster scene in one of the plays I've done where two people come on and talk about stuff out loud which in real life they would know and not have to say aloud. They would not articulate the events in the overly explicit way it is written. The actors kept saying, 'Why are they saying this?' I said, 'For the audience!' They would say, 'But since I already know this, am I not trying to get something out of him by repeating it?' I'm like, 'No!' They'll obfuscate. 'Where are we coming from?' I'm notorious with the actors. I say, 'You're coming from the greenroom. That's where you're coming from'. Now, I will obviously answer that question if it needs to be answered for the actor, and I do understand that it does; but I honestly think for Shakespeare, the offstage, backstage life of the character does not much exist. What is important is spoken. I'm old-fashioned that way.

Daniel Sullivan: You know to me life is subtext. So I don't understand the idea that there is no subtext in Shakespeare. The inward looking American actor, very often in playing the subtext or constructing a subtext in a scene, can be destructive if he or she works against the clear intentions of the scene. Very often actors will make those kinds of choices. But I don't know what guides behaviour if it isn't subtext. What else is it? Certainly Shakespeare very often in direct address to an audience will reveal that to some extent. What's going on with Olivia in those scenes? It's all subtext. They are not saying on the surface what they are feeling. We impute to them those feelings. How do we do that? We do that because we know what the subtext is. So to me they're very, very strong in subtext.

It's 'What kind of tensions physically? What kind of behaviours?' It's also very much about the subtext. That is, it's very much about emotionally what's the temperature of the scene, what the connections are between the actors. Very often you can read that. Even if it were in a foreign language, you'd understand what was happening. Getting that right and precise and absolutely clear, I think, is very important. It is very much playing on top of the scene so you are playing the clearest thing in the scene. You're not buried in subtext somewhere. It's to make the subtext legible is what you are trying to do.

Shaping

Brian Kulick: Shaping Shakespeare is an interesting process. The first movement (made up of the first three acts) is about ninety minutes of masterful plotting and by the end of that third act, the audience should be hooked. That is what you are working toward, getting them hooked enough that you can give them a break and know they will come back to see more. Why do we want to come back? Because at the end of the third act of a Shakespeare play, the world as the characters have known it has usually been forever altered or destroyed or (in the Romances) a new world is literally discovered. We come back to see these characters in these ' brave new worlds' and whether or not they will be able to survive them. These are worlds where now Lear has lost his kingdom and his mind, Tybalt is forever dead, or everything Leontes loved has been ruined by him. Now what? What is life like under the sun of this new reality? These new worlds have another time signature, a different metabolic rate. They have new rules. In rehearsal we must learn them. And as we move closer and closer to the end, these new worlds seem more and more real. That is the journey of Shakespeare play; it starts off as theatre and ends in some very real place. At the end of the third act, the illusions of the characters are destroyed and reality begins to seep in, or madness or wonder – something new that grows and comes to fruition in the second half of the evening.

We have to learn to shape these two worlds (the world of act one and the new world of act two). The final arbiter is the audience. They collectively can help us find the proper metabolic rate for both acts. This is what I call the endgame of a production and it is played with a third and very important player: your audience.

Run-throughs

Darko Tresnjak: After staging it, I like to do a run or two – just to see how it all hangs together, what falls into place. And then we go back to working it scene-by-scene. Going, 'This fell into place; this is great. This needs to be tweaked. This part needs defining'. It's so many different criteria from that point on. What feels honest? What feels alive? What feels ready? What is wonderfully unpredictable? What is confusing?

Mark Lamos: You begin to see the larger picture once you have the company stagger through the show without stopping, though they may still be calling for lines occasionally or forgetting some blocking changes. I ask everyone to be ready to advance the action, be prepared for entrances, etc. This is when you see the production begin to take on a life of its own, and you have to be *observant* – you have to be very aware of where that life is going. Note it, don't control it. Let it be what it is. You can edit once you let it happen before your eyes. It can be a very painful day! But for better or for worse, the architecture is rising, the beams are almost ready to be screwed in. The play itself, the production itself has become a controlling entity that we all have to listen to, we all have to watch.

David Frank: I try, however bad it is, to run an act or two acts, whatever seems to be the convenient portion, as we go. With multiple plays in rehearsal, our schedule is odd, we have plenty of weeks but not as many hours as one might want. Occasionally, the designer run is the first complete run ever. This is a pity, because run-throughs mark a new stage of rehearsal. We all learn different things about story, pace, variety once you start to put it all together.

Timothy Douglas: What I usually do when I am conducting the initial staging, I'll block an act, after which we will stumble through it. When we start putting the whole thing together we learn so much. I find myself often saying to myself, 'Oh. Okay Tim. What were you thinking?' So then we work carefully through the play again, all the while addressing the questions that come up from the prior round. If there is not time for another work through, then we will run it everyday, as these crucial rehearsals depend upon our ability to zero-in on things that need the most immediate attention. And then we nip and tuck our way through previews through to opening and always rely on that elusive and wonderfully consistent 'magic of the theatre'!

Mary Zimmerman: I start stringing scenes together and say, 'Let's run what we have'. I'm a huge believer in runs. I'm not kidding you. By the end of the first week, I'm doing a run of Act I. By 'Act I' I mean our entire Act I up to intermission. Part I. The next week we might be doing Act II, running that. And then by the third week I'm running the show, once a day. I believe that so many problems, so many questions take care of themselves once everyone is seeing the rest of the play – when they're beginning to feel in their bodies the arc of what they have to do in those two and a half hours. They just become familiar with it. A whole huge part of the process of acting is, 'What the hell is my next scene?' It's getting to that point where you're simply in it and you know it from beginning to end. You have the confidence of where you're going, where you're starting, what the journey is, and where you're ending up. So much of that is solved by running it. I hugely run.

I think actors are kind of shocked how I force them through a run of an act really early. I think much earlier than a lot of people do. These things are meant as a whole, and the parts all inform the whole.

J. R. Sullivan: I work pretty fast that way. I like to do it within the first week and a half, in about ten days, so that everybody gets to put their arms around it. It doesn't have to have a lot of detail. It has a kind of overall shape. It's like a story when you're writing. You want to know where you're going with it. You don't know how you're going to get there. You're going to have a lot of things to overcome on the way. But it's to know what the goal is. You know what you're going for. You have a final image in your mind. It's a final line or a final thought simmering there. You know it at the end of the day. But it's what's in the day and how to get there, is the thing.

Lisa Peterson: Normally for me, it would be the end of the second week. No matter what, I would always do a stumble through of some kind at the end of the second week, assuming that I've got a four-week rehearsal period. So I try to do a very early stumble through of the whole play as quickly as I can, even if it's a big old mess. And so I can start to do triage: 'That scene isn't working, and it's a big problem. That other scene isn't perfect, but it's less urgent that we figure it out, it's okay for now'. I try to do an early stumble through before going back a second time through scenes. So: roughly stage it, stumble it and then see what we've got.

Ethan McSweeny: One of Michael Kahn's greatest skills is his ability to watch a play as though he doesn't know what's going to happen next. I've always tried to do that too, or rather I don't try so much as just sort of let it happen. When I'm trying to decide what's wrong with the focus on a scene, I just watch where I'm being guided with my eye, and if I don't feel that I'm looking at the right narrative point, then we need to fix that. That's when that audience member sitting on one's shoulder is really useful, helping tell you where to look and to listen. Because listening is as important in a Shakespeare play, and listening not to the story you *think* you are telling as a director, but the one that is actually being told. Looking at the characters, is their behaviour psychologically real? Do I understand these choices? Are things being answered for me by choices of behaviour or delivery of the line?

On the four weeks in the hall schedule, I do a rough stumble through at the end of the third week. It can be painful (for everyone) but it does help diagnose what we don't know. Then in week four the pattern becomes notes and scene work and another run, and notes and scene work and some other things. I like to try and get a couple runs in while we're still in the rehearsal hall, if only because once we get into the tech, we may not get another run in for almost a week, and I want the actors to have a sense of the flow and the experience of how the play works for their character when its barrelling forward. For Shylock, how does it feel to come into the trial scene when you've had the experience of the daughter being abducted at the end of Part I as opposed to coming into the rehearsal where you have to create that experience for yourself?

I'd love for the first run-through to end a week. I love to get to the stumble through. It's three quarters of the way into the process. First stumble through is just a disaster, but you know that's going to happen. Then I like to do the same thing with a tech.

Daniel Sullivan: I'm running sections, usually. I try not to do a run of the play until very late in the process, but I have a pretty good idea from running sections of the play how things fit together. Actors also vary in how clearly they can see the whole at this stage. Some actors think like directors and can see what is emerging. Some don't have any sense of this and are merely concentrating on the task at hand. Once I've cobbled together at least two-thirds of the play, I begin the run thru process.

Mark Lamos: I try to keep the first run-through just for 'family'. Maybe just the dramaturg. The second can have more folks in attendance: dressers, production managers, management staff, etc. At this point I begin to take notes from those who watch, and I bring these observations back to the process as we continue rehearsals. I have to defend and clarify my work now. This is very useful. As unsettling as it may feel to allow people into the room to watch what you've all achieved, just their presence alone will make many things about the production clear to you, because you are seeing it, to a certain extent, with their eyes.

Giving notes

Jim Warren: Once we start running stuff, I write notes for actors on separate sheets of paper, anything I can explain as simply as, 'You're trailing off on the ends of lines in this speech. We need to hear those final words because they're really important'. Anything that I can communicate easily by just handing that out, I'll write, hand those out. Then, on another sheet of paper, I'll have the things we're going to work. So we'll do a run or a dress or parts of the play. I'll hand out notes, and then we'll work on our feet with the things that are too complicated to write on a piece of paper. Or things that involve so many people like the storm in *The Tempest*. I couldn't just give notes to an individual. We really have to run that thing.

Kathleen Conlin: The more I know the actor, the more I'll know, 'This is the guy that I'll just stop and talk to him. Then he'll do something'. Somebody else, I won't even bother to talk, because it'll just get them all confused. I'll simply say, 'You know, if you really just keep moving, whatever the motions, keep moving, keep moving, keep moving. When you get to line 23 when you say such-and-such, bring yourself to a dead stop. See what happens'. Sometimes a discovery will happen in that that will inform the scene. So it's really adjusting to the way the individual actors work.

Ethan McSweeny: To me, a big part of it is not just *what* you say, but *when* you say it. When is it a good time for an actor to receive a note? When is the right time to get in and work on something because everyone will be focused and receptive? When is it right in tech to work patiently on a lighting cue? I am always mindful of trying to make the work being done efficient and artful.

Kate Buckley: Sometimes it's as simple as saying, 'I don't believe you'. I have never had an actor respond negatively to that note. If it comes down to giving that kind of note, 'I don't believe you', they recognize that within themselves, and then make a correction. If I am having a serious problem, it is a matter of digging more deeply into the text with an actor in a one-on-one session. I encourage them to live in the words, rather than play an idea of a character's quality. Sometimes it doesn't work – for some, old habits die hard.

Lisa Peterson: I try to do verbal notes in a group. I like to have everyone sitting there. Note sessions are the time when the tone and body of the thing really become clear, because we can all talk about it. I am very leery of written notes. I used to do more written notes. I would handwrite them out myself. I don't do that anymore – too time consuming.

Technical notes are good. My experience has been that actors actually appreciate something straight-forward. 'Pick up your cue. Faster rate of speech'. Clarity notes: ' I am losing that word'. I give a lot of rhythmical, technical language notes. And those kind of notes are easier to give in a written form or through an assistant.

Then, so that it doesn't get boring, I try to balance technical notes with larger questions or discoveries. I'm always happy when I've had a discovery while listening to the play. I can share that with the actors: 'Here is an idea. I didn't realize until last night that such-and-such. Let's see what we can make of that. Let's spend fifteen minutes on every physical moment between Othello and Desdemona and see if we can't heat it up'. That kind of thing.

I do try to do as many working notes as possible. I would say, 'Okay, for these ten minutes let's focus on that on our feet', and I try not to do too much just talking at them. I try to work it out physically.

Mary Zimmerman: Usually after the first run I will only give positive notes. No matter what a disaster it was. I will only say, 'That was fantastic when you did this' and 'I loved how you did that like that'. Because I know I'm pushing them too early. I know it's too early to be really doing a run, so I only say positive things. I always note if they've taken an adjustment from the day before or whenever. They want to know that they're seen, that you are a consistent witness and that you are seeing what they are doing. That's really what they want to know. Observations sometimes are great for actors to hear that are sort of non-evaluative.

But [I give] all kinds. Like 'You're taking too much time with that. I think the next thing is what you should take time with'. We've done detailed scenework. Things that continue to be a problem I put on a list that we continue to work on. It all has to be done in the doing. I don't think you should get trapped into talking too much. If something isn't working, continues to not work, I'm not going to give a half-hour to it and say, 'You see, it's more like ... and then you should ...'. I don't do that. It's more like, 'We need to rehearse that'. Then I'm stopping them all the time and saying, 'Yes, yes' or, 'No, no!'

Rehearsal schedules and time management

Daniel Sullivan: Let's say you have a five-week rehearsal period, say at about three and a half weeks in I would probably do a run. Which would then leave me a week to work on what I learn from the run. And then I do another run. Then the last say two or three days in the room I would just do a run everyday.

The surprise of rehearsals is always the rate at which actors work. Usually three weeks into a rehearsal period you will have some actors still face in book, still trying to figure it out from the page. Other actors are completely free; they've been off book for a week and a half. So you have an odd, slightly distracted thing in front of you. Yes, you are looking at performance in some way, but you are looking a little bit past that, because you know people are at different levels, really. And you are looking more at how a thing fits together than you are at, 'Is that performance coming together? What do I do to fix that? How in the hell is that person ever going to play that role?' You know, [thoughts] that you have usually after the first reading.

Ethan McSweeny: I used to do these tracking charts for the rehearsal schedule when I was the assistant, so that I would know when was the last time we had rehearsed a scene, and make sure that each of them got four rehearsals before we moved out of the rehearsal hall. If you consider table work one pass through a scene, initial staging a second pass through a scene, you'll be lucky if you get two more rehearsals on it, in addition to runs. So four or five cracks is about what you're going to have. You have got to make them count.

Over the years, and the shows, I have become much better at anticipating where the problem areas are going to be and preparing for them. I don't think most people understand how much of directing is really logistics. For example, on *The Tempest*, we had mammoth puppets that could only be rehearsed off-site because they didn't fit into the rehearsal hall. But we planned ahead. And I think there were days were we were simultaneously rehearsing in seven rooms, which was a record at STC. These days, I also like to bring the cast together at the end of the week to outline where we are going to get in the following week so that they can be participants in achieving those goals.

Mary Zimmerman: My normal process when I'm doing a play that I am writing – adapting – from a non-dramatic text is to go in scriptless. I write the script every night – by myself. I don't sleep very much. The pressure is enormous. There's no play and we're going up in four or five weeks. I don't even know who's playing whom. But still, it does not exhaust me the way Shakespeare does. There's no day in Shakespeare where you go into rehearsal thinking, 'Oh, this is an easy scene'. There is no day off, no hour off. I am listening to every fucking word so fucking attentively. 'Is that clear? Is that clear? Is that both beautiful and clear? Is that expressing what is meant to be expressed? Does that sound like a human being?' You're in a state of attentiveness, on high alert, which it demands, and it is exhausting.

Also, in my other rehearsals if I don't have anything more to give them that day we break. We do these really short days a lot, even though the pressure is intense. I'm going home and writing or whatever. In Shakespeare, I use every minute of rehearsal. I never have a short day. You turn around and you've got the fifteen people coming in for this next scene. Then immediately after you have a very intense, hard emotional scene. Because it's so rich and so full and so dramatic, there's very little dross in there. There's very little chaff. It's 'on' all the time and you have to be 'on' all the time when you're rehearsing it. Ironically, it is more exhausting. There is less homework for me when I'm doing it, but it is so exhausting and so rewarding.

Calvin MacLean: I go through a play in rehearsal essentially three times prior to tech rehearsals, four times if you count the initial reading of the play with the company. That first time is when I'm really working out the geometry of the staging. Who's got to be in focus here, what might be going on in the background to reinforce the action, etc. During this trip through the play, I'm laying the groundwork with the actors on 'This scene is about this' and 'These are the set of intentions' and 'This is how it relates to the rest of the play'. We've discussed the critical point of view of the production and how it plays out in action.

Second time through the play, I'm revising or sharpening the staging to incorporate what we may have learned so far, attending to the rhythmic structure of the scene with the actors, trying this and that, searching for the tempo-rhythm with the actors. In some ways this is the most exploratory (and most exhausting) part of the rehearsal process. I like the actors to work off-book in this tour through the play, so this is where a certain amount of time is taken to stop and start for memorization.

The third time through is for me the most exciting part of the process. Often, it is the quickest as well, with me as a director responding more than initiating. If you think of the process as comparable to building a house, this section is when each room or scene takes on its individual character – and relates to the larger house. My contribution is to be sure that the through-line of the action is clear and focused, that things flow, that certain moments are well crafted. I am trying to sharpen and clean the order of the action so that an audience will see and hear without superfluous distractions. Cleaning and clarifying. Run the scene, notes, then run it again.

J. R. Sullivan: I like to do it three times. That's the magic number. That's always worked for me. You go through it once, and you throw out a whole chunk of it and start again. And then you throw out less of it and start again. And then you should be in some kind of good shape.

Brian Kulick: I try to shape the first three acts of a Shakespeare play into the first half of an evening and acts four and five as the second half. I do a week of table work and then get up on our feet and start exploring the text through physicalization. I try to make a first pass of the first half in a week. Sometimes you don't know what you really have until you've worked your way through the whole thing and seen it in a run through. So even though I want to stay in the first act trying to refine everything until it is perfect, I know that it won't really be perfect until the actors have had the opportunity to experience the second half and bring that knowledge back into what they are doing in the first part. So a week on the first half; a week on the second half. Look at them together.

In those first two weeks of initial staging I'm trying to activate the scenes through physicalization, I'm trying to understand the 'dance' of the scene, is the scene a game of cat and mouse? A bullfight? How does it move, when is it still, what does the opposition of movement and stillness tell me? Scenes in Shakespeare, like his sentences, can be built around antithesis – one scene will be static followed by another that is kinetic. I am interested in finding and playing the differences between scenes, what is high poetry and what is low comedy and not trying to blend them into some nice and neat middle place. Shakespeare is all about the play of differences, making meaning through difference, so I try to find the differences in tone, movement, behaviour and celebrate that. Then go back and refine with the knowledge gained from seeing a first pass.

That usually gives me two more weeks to explore before we hit tech. I like to try to have at least three runs in those last three days. At a certain point you can really only learn things by running the play. It is at this juncture that one focuses on the arcs of the characters and the play itself. Asking a basic question like: 'It started here, it ended there, how did it get there?' This last stage of work is all about shaping each of those phases in terms of rhythm, behaviour, tonality; making sure I have the proper distance between where the work started (*Romeo and Juliet* and *Othello* start like commedia plays) and where they end (both become tragedies). The key is being attentive to the nuances of transformation, the bridge that, plank by plank, carries us from one world to the other. Making sure those planks are secure for us to traverse such a distance.

Kathleen Conlin: I do work sequentially. If it's a musical comedy, if it has a dance, I can send the dance people out with the choreographer to start working on basic dance shape that may not be until Act Five. Other than that, I always rehearse in sequence. I think that's a decision I made once I started working [at Utah Shakespeare Festival], because our calendar is so tight. I want to make sure I'm providing as much context for actors all the time, so they're not spending the time thinking, 'Oh yeah, we did that then … How did that fit in?' They don't have time to think about that. I needed to put that into the process. I want actors to be reminded constantly of the momentum of the play.

PART FOUR

Finishing the Production

13

Tech and Dress Rehearsals

I like to be ready to get to techs – to not have techs destroy what we've done. I like to be far enough along so that when we get to tech, and I have to worry about other things, the actors can still grow in their roles. I like them to act during tech. They know I'm not looking at them so much, but I like them to be using their time on stage. It's continually refining it in some way, continually looking at those things that I don't think work, or that I can't understand.

MICHAEL KAHN

The last phase of production starts with the tech and dress rehearsals, a time when the designs and technical elements become married to the production. Shakespeare productions tend to be rather sizeable affairs involving a much larger than normal production staff and more difficult technical problems to be solved.

For Gaines, this phase is 'thrilling'. For Peterson it is 'the most creative time'. Buckley claims her extensive pre-production preparation assures smooth tech/dress rehearsals. Frank remarks how quickly problems can be solved in tech that earlier would have taken considerably more time.

FIGURE 18 Troilus and Cressida, *directed by Rob Melrose, Oregon Shakespeare Festival, 2012. Photograph by Jenny Graham.*

Not all directors enjoy these rehearsals. Thompson notes that the actors can feel abandoned by the director who suddenly has many more elements to be shaped. J. R. Sullivan confides that techs can be 'tortuous' because all the rehearsal room work can become unglued as the production moves from the truthfulness of the room to the technical theatricality of the theatre. Kulick adds that actors, who are just beginning to find 'competency' in their acting, must now append foreign design elements to their work. He finds preview audiences to be invaluable in coalescing the new elements into a performance for the actors. Being outside in Central Park helps too because 'having night fall as the dramatic tension rises ... focuses everything'.

For original practice directors, tech is a simpler process. Cohen says that because their theatre does not use lighting design or computers, they do not really have a need for technical rehearsals. Zipay, Shine and Warren also express that their technical rehearsals are less difficult than non-language based theatres. Zipay uses considerable music so it becomes the most taxing element in her techs. With all the challenges of that week, she feels productions 'grow immensely' because the director now has split focus and actors are freer to explore. Shine's tech goal is simple: 'continuous storytelling'. If there is a problem that arises with a scene change or what have you, she is quick to go on stage and tell the actors to 'focus'. She does not like pauses, a sentiment she shares with other original practice directors like Cohen. Warren notes that at American Shakespeare Center, costumes and set pieces are introduced 'as soon as they're ready', so that aspect of tech/dress is not an issue.

Several directors use tech rehearsals as an opportunity for making changes in the acting as well as the designs. Since so many other changes are being introduced, it can seem a logical time to introduce additional adjustments. Lamos informs the entire company at the beginning of tech that the actors will need to adjust to the space and to the design as much as the designs will. D. Sullivan reveals that he never stops altering the actors' behaviour. He also refines the staging to 'keep the thing as fluid as it was in the rehearsal hall'. Kahn has several goals: 'making it slick, making it clear, making it clean'. He also assesses the production to see if the story on stage matches the one prescribed to by the company. Peterson and Douglas use tech rehearsals to make cuts. Douglas also uses them to adjust to the rate of performance, whether the delivery is too quick or too slow. His aim is get the actor 'to keep speaking at the speed of the thought'. Zimmerman shares a strategy for aiding the timing of transitions by distributing music for transitions to the actors.

McSweeny provides an extended description of his techs on *The Merchant of Venice*. He discusses the complexity of making changes in large shows and substantial theatres. He also directs the actors to continue to work on their performances as they adjust to the costumes, props and other technical elements.

MacLean enjoys 'letting go' of the production. He wants to find that moment where 'everyone knows what they need to do to 'fix' things'. He then moves into an encouragement mode with the company and accepts that it is time for him to move on.

Possibilities

Barbara Gaines: Technical rehearsals are thrilling, for it's at that time that we create cues in order to create emotions. I still can't get over the joy when an image, lights, sound, costumes and actors all find a new language to clarify plot and inspire souls. There's nothing like it. It's pure magic.

Kate Buckley: I love tech. If we – the director, design and stage management teams – have done our work properly, if we have stayed in touch throughout the process (even if we live on opposite coasts) when we come together, tech can be a joy. Of course the actors become more energized once the lights, costumes and music are in play, but if pre-production work is thorough, it will pay off in tech. I've never had a tech crash and burn. Events can happen in tech with designers and actors that can improve the production beyond measure. It can be very exciting.

Lisa Peterson: Normally tech is the most creative time for me. That's the time when the thing becomes real in front of you. I make a lot of changes in tech. I restage in tech. I love keeping all those balls in the air at the same time, the design elements, the acting, the rhythm of it all.

David Frank: Later rehearsals – when dress rehearsals have been completed – can be immensely rewarding. It is a great time for detailed polishing. But if you still have big problems to solve, it has always struck me how very productive the few remaining hours can be. Everyone is quite familiar with the scene and usually everyone is highly focused on the problem at hand. What would have taken hours in the first week can often be accomplished in minutes in the last few days.

Problems/challenges

Kent Thompson: I think one of the useful sides of the technical process is that you have to deal with all the other elements. Actors sometimes don't like this because you disengage from the actors for a certain period of time. I find it very useful because then, when you see it again, you see it with fresher eyes. What I am looking for, again, is whether the elements that are arriving are consistent with the journey we have been taking in the rehearsal room. If something is wrong, then we need to figure it out. If something doesn't work, we need to figure out how we can accomplish that. It's usually the big test of the scenic design and the costume design.

J. R. Sullivan: Techs are torturous for me. I'm not one of these directors who likes to tech. I like my collaborators and the designers. It's not that. It's just that you watch everything fall apart. It's like everything you laboured on for five, six, seven weeks suddenly turns to shit. And it's of course because everybody's minds have shifted away from what had happened in those final moments of the rehearsal hall to this new reality. And everything is suddenly false. The clothes don't fit right, or they're not comfortable yet. And space is wrong. And everything is foreign. Everything is hateful to everything you've been working towards. The play actually happens in the rehearsal room. A play can happen there as an act of imagination. I mean you can see the whole thing. And anyone that's watching it there, especially within that community, can see it and know what it's going to be. And it has truth. You get into the tech and all of a sudden it's all false. And that's irritating for me. Again, it takes me a while to get over all that, and work-through it. But I know it well because I go through it every time – no matter what the play is, contemporary or classic.

Brian Kulick: Just as the actor is getting a certain amount of competency in playing this incredibly intricate and nuanced piece of writing, they walk into a completely new environment called a theatre. And if they are working with me, it is usually in a set that is not always very 'actor friendly'. There may not be a level playing surface, things are likely to spin and break, or fall, or spill. Suddenly the acting company has to learn a whole new script that is a technical or physical script, you've tried to approximate this in the rehearsal room, but it never quite captures what the real set will be. What happens as they are learning this new physical script, is that the textual script which they spent four or five weeks working on suddenly recedes at the very point where it's very important for them to feel like they own it. Will the company be able to get through to the other end, reach this final plateau, get to the other side of it? Or be gobbled up by tech?

What usually happens, thankfully, is the audience comes and helps pull them along. Their being present creates an adrenaline rush that can fuel the actors. Especially if they are that amazing audience that Joseph Papp first brought to Central Park. I've done three Shakespeare's at this magical space, where you have one of the most generous and diverse audiences in the world. They pull a company through to the other end and start to give them confidence. Nature also conspires to help the event, having night fall as the dramatic tension rises, which somehow focuses everything.

Original practice tech/dresses

Ralph Alan Cohen: There is no tech because we have no light design, no computer. We do a lot of previews and pay-what-you-wills so that we can see the play in front of an audience, and that's when we learn most about the play. We have to have the audience there, because the audience is so much a part of what is going on. But usually [technical needs] are evolving through each individual rehearsal because they are integral to the actors' work. For the most part, we already know who is doing the thunder sheet; we already know who is rolling the cannon ball; we already know who is doing all of that.

Joanne Zipay: I have a very tricky relationship with tech because in all actuality Shakespeare's plays don't really require tech. They can be performed on a street corner with nothing because the language does all the work. I have a problem with tech competing with the language. I have live music in all my plays, but I hardly ever underscore anything language wise. It's usually incidental or to highlight a battle scene or there's a song in the show. Some shows have more music in them. *Twelfth Night* has a lot of music. *The Tempest* has a lot of music. So it's an aural environment technically as well as a visual environment. Lots of times I will say to my designers, 'You know, I could do this whole show with lights up at the beginning and lights down at the end. So we have to talk about what tech is going to add to the show and how it's going to support it'. I've been very lucky to have wonderful designers that I've worked with over the years.

Things do happen. The show always takes a leap forward in tech. I feel like part of the reason that it's happened is because I don't have my full attention on it. The actors are putting things together. I was an actor for fifteen years. During tech week, it's maybe the first time that everybody's not breathing down their necks. We're looking at light levels and how the costumes look. The actors are dealing with many things for the first time – trying to make a crossover in the dark or how a costume feels when they sit down or stand up or God knows what. The focus goes off of what we've been so intensely focusing on. That often allows new stuff to come in. Shows grow immensely during tech week. But I can't allow that to be a time where I say I'm going to get work done. The work for me as a director has to be done before I go into tech. And I'm always working. The actors get notes all through tech. We rehearse. There are so many other things to focus on, so that week has to be a week of guiding things to come together.

Stephanie Shine: Our rehearsal period is four weeks, but that includes tech. We don't have a huge tech. We use live music and it's usually incorporated and produced by actors. Our sets are minimal and so is what we do with our lights. I am quite the original practice director. I don't believe in black outs. I believe in continuous storytelling. I believe in coming in with high energy mid-scene. For most scenes in Shakespeare, there's really a bit of a scene change anyway. So it's like coming in, topping the previous scene. I don't like pauses unless Shakespeare gave me a pause in the iambic pentameter. Our tech is really about putting on a play and adjusting to the space. I think what we're afforded is the opportunity to have a show that moves on stage as we've rehearsed it during rehearsal period.

I don't do tech like the normal people. If they get stuck with something, I am up there on that stage with my actors saying, 'Focus, focus, focus. Okay this is what I saw. Is this what you intended? Could it be stronger?' I use the tech process to continue working my actors because often there is the thought that, 'We're in tech, actors, it's not about you. It's me and me and me'. And my theory is 'All this is acting'.

Jim Warren: In an ideal world I'm able to work it so that they're rehearsing in costume pieces as soon as they're ready. They've got rehearsal pieces that simulate what they're wearing. They've got rehearsal stuff from day one, and as pieces are ready, they can wear them, so that it's, hopefully, never a big shock to the system. Even before dress rehearsals, we're running either halves of the play or the whole play a couple of times before we get to dress rehearsal.

An opportunity for improvement and change

Mark Lamos: I like tech rehearsals to feed the acting process, and vice versa. I always say to the crews on the first day of technical rehearsals, 'We're going to be working on the play as we go; we've gotten only so far without you, and now your involvement will take us to new levels – which will mean we will be changing a lot of things about the show because of what you bring to it. A gown, a cape, hat or glove can change the tempo or even the intent of a moment. As can props, lighting effects, etc. All sorts of new elements come into the production, into play. Play time.

Mary Zimmerman: The music cues are coming in one by one all the time throughout rehearsal and being reworked. As soon as we have them all, that's generally right before tech. You usually have the day off. I ask the composer/sound designer to make a tape or CD or a link to every single transition in order, any sort of pre-show needed or act music, every cue. Then the cast can listen to that on their iPods on the day off. They come back in and it's in them in a deep way. The transitions end up being perfectly timed. They know the music perfectly well. It's like the sound track of the show goes into them. It's very useful. There's a huge leap after they get to take those home and just have them in their head.

Daniel Sullivan: I try to keep working on performances in tech so that the actor doesn't think that technical considerations have entirely taken over. I try to keep the thing as fluid as it was in the rehearsal hall so that discoveries can be made from the first day of tech; you don't want actors just sitting in their dressing rooms, waiting for the work to get done. Performances need to continue to evolve in tech rehearsals.

Michael Kahn: I focus on all the technical aspects of making it slick, making it clear, making it clean. It's important to me that there be a real momentum. What I try to do is have an arc for a whole act. An act usually is three acts of Shakespeare. So eventually by the time I'm there in those rehearsals putting the whole show together, I get concerned about the arc and the rhythm of the whole act. Often you begin to feel that the tempo or the pace of one scene, or the change in between the scenes, or the dramatic points, need to be shifted a bit. And you'd better have a pretty interesting ending at the intermission.

Then I go back and look at the performances and try to see whether we're telling the story we've all agreed to tell. I can be criticized for the story that I think this is about, but at least I feel that that's what we've done up there. The technical stuff is a lot. It's music, sound, battles, lights, costumes, scenery, quick changes, projections – all the things that once you get into the theatre, become a new element that has to be dealt with and addressed pretty carefully. Then I can go back and just look at the play and look at the performances.

Timothy Douglas: I am a big 'cutter', meaning I am often removing things from the physical production if there's anything that's in the way once we've arrived at the eleventh hour and encounter anything that's 'slowing' things down. Also during tech, previews, dress I am also making sure that actors are not indulging empty pauses. I am fine with pauses on stage as long as they are 'filled' and 'earned'. One has to know the difference between communicating in the silence, and 'theatrically flatlining'. There may have been silence during rehearsals because the thought process was still authentically working things through. Literally, new neurons were being formed. But once there is that breakthrough of clarified communication, the actor doesn't require that silence anymore. The body has absorbed the benefits of that rehearsal and has entrusted its reveal to the organic brilliance of muscle memory for its full fruition.

A description of tech for *The Merchant of Venice*

Ethan McSweeny: We came in for a day onstage before we started tech at the end of the fourth week. Naturally it's an exciting time to see because you can't really tell, especially when you have a set with multiple layers like mine. The rehearsal hall fit about half of the set and certainly none of the stairs. So we were doing an enormous amount of guessing. I think you start to then respond to the space, and see which guesses were good. Are the strong points on stage where you thought they would be? I like to have a day or two on the stage just to actually put the production – the play we did in the rehearsal hall – put it on stage. If I have time, I try to not judge it until we've actually put it up there. Even though I suspect I'm going to change an entrance or an exit or some blocking, I'd rather put it on, and step back and look at it, then try and change it all while I'm up there. Sometimes you're a little rushed for time and you start skipping steps to make up time.

We started a tech on a Tuesday. We did an eight out of ten. We did two tens out of twelve on Wednesday and Thursday. I thought I would be able to get all the way through the play by the end of Thursday. Go back, review the transitions, and do a stumble through Friday. But we didn't get through the play until Friday at about 9 o'clock at night.

This is a big theatre. Big theatres are like big boats. They don't turn on a dime. If you want to get something for a scene, you have got to think two or three days out to give the note, to get the note to the prop shop, to get the rough thing mocked up, to get it in, to get it reviewed. Or the costume shop. They're battleships. They're wonderful and they're huge, but you have to work within the system. The Guthrie's like that. They're all like that. You have to give the organization time to respond.

I absolutely believe in continuing to act through and work the acting beats. The nice thing for the actors is that I've got other things to occupy me, so they can do some stuff on their own. I really don't think there's any reason not to. Frankly, I've rarely met an actor who didn't want to use the time that they had. Almost always you're meeting the real costumes for the first time and those are influencing you, the real props and how they function, and all that.

Moving on

Calvin MacLean: There is a moment in the latter stage of rehearsals or during dresses, that I hope to get to in each production I direct. This moment is quite private for me. It is a moment in which it seems to me that everyone knows what they need to do to 'fix' things. The production is well in hand; it is clear; all the pieces are put together pretty well. Actors and designers don't need a lot from me; they know what needs to be done. Some directors hate to 'let go' of a production and others are quite busy being sure that everything is right. I prefer the feeling of letting go. I feel more confident that the production is going well if I am in that place. People have a strong sense of what we are collectively doing. I then do a lot of encouraging, some 'directing', but mostly just trying to stay out of the way and start to take on the part of an audience member. Let folks get their work to where they want it to go. 'Miller Time'.

14

Adding the Audience

Theatre is all about collaboration. There is the collaboration between the director, designers, actors and the final and perhaps most important collaboration with the audience. They become the objective correlative and suddenly, through their collective presence you can hear the play anew, in a way you never heard it when you first read it alone in your apartment or around the table with a group of actors, or at a run through for the producer and the design team. They bring their world to Shakespeare's world and sometimes these two worlds rhyme in ways one can never quite fully anticipate. It is at moments such as this, that you realize what staggeringly transformational things can happen when Shakespeare and an audience meet.

BRIAN KULICK

As Kulick notes, the final stage of rehearsals is, indeed, about bringing the production to an audience. Before the official opening, some theatres have tryout performances or previews. There is no standard number of them in Shakespeare theatres.

FIGURE 19 *Photograph of the audience at American Players Theatre, Spring Green, Wisconsin. Photograph by Carissa Dixon.*

Some theatres have no previews; some have one; others have from two to five. D. Sullivan wants two weeks of previews to help him finish his work. A very select few (The Public/ Shakespeare in the Park, Lincoln Center), have a month of previews. Woronicz advocates that previews are essential for comedies, yet many theatres cannot afford to have many, so there is little time to adjust to audience reaction.

Directors find previews to be an effective tool in solving a production's problems. Zimmerman refers to previews as 'the greatest invention in the world'. Gaines says they are 'the biggest teachers' and as the first one begins, 'no fewer than ten thoughts come to me about what I've failed to do or new ideas that should be in the show'. Serban and Zimmerman maintain that they help the director look at the production with a fresh perspective. Lamos believes previews come at the end of a long line of negotiations, and signal a new phase when 'the audience begins *its* negotiations with the work'. He also says they are a 'living, breathing entity'. Tresnjak watches the audience closely for when they are 'engaged' by the play and when they are not. D. Sullivan monitors a preview to see 'when an audience breathes with a play'. He enjoys diagnosing problems, but finds actors reluctant to make different choices so late in the process.

Cohen and Esbjornson observe that Shakespeare actors have to adapt to working with audiences, as the plays were meant to exploit a direct audience/actor relationship. Esbjornson warns, 'You certainly won't succeed if you curtail an actor's ability to be spontaneous and responsive'. Thompson has observed that audiences do not all respond the same way from region to region. He discusses the challenge a director has in accurately assessing and diagnosing issues in a given performance. The less previews you have, the more pressured and difficult it is. D. Sullivan advices, '[V]ery often an audience will tune out or not respond in a place, but that's not the problem. The problem was the scene before'. Peterson reveals, 'I use previews pretty aggressively'. Esbjornson discloses, 'It is in the preview period that I have the confidence to make my most radical edits and dramaturgical choices'.

McSweeny shares how he approaches previews including giving notes, dividing up rehearsal time and handling transitions. He sees previews as the time to 'get back to acting and acting notes'. At some point he has the company do a speed through 'with full tech and all the actions and all the business'. He urges directors to work with the actors individually during this stage in order to best prepare them for opening. Finally, he gives the production over to the actors as his last act with them.

Buckley is most optimistic about her openings. She treats previews like openings so that openings become playtime. Although Frank has been opening shows for many years, he is still astonished by how much audiences teach him. J. R. Sullivan believes you want the 'high anxiety' of opening because it 'hones us'. but the director must provide a safety net for the actors who go to quite difficult places with 'emotional truths that can strike very, very close to the heart'. Bishop hates openings because everything is somehow 'false'. Serban also 'dreads' openings as he wants to continue to develop the production, while the actors see it as a time to freeze things or change them if the reviews are bad.

After the production has opened, Warren continues to give notes, because he does not truly know a production until it is played before an audience and he has a chance to observe their reactions. J. R. Sullivan says if a production is 'grooved in right, it will deepen in all the right ways and stay also on the path'. Buckley helps this happen by setting an appropriate 'tone in rehearsal', by allowing actors to discover it by themselves. She also works closely with the stage manager, with whom she continues to communicate during the run. McSweeny observes that a director on closing can see 'what you rehearsed well, and what you didn't'. He adds that performances should be 'getting deeper, but not wider as the run progresses'. A performance that varies by more than 45 seconds usually means air is being added back in. Bishop notes that he is 'constantly finding new things' and 'infinite layers' when he returns to see a Shakespeare production after opening.

Number of previews

André Bishop: We have endless previews. *Cymbeline* was previewed for four weeks. We have fairly long runs. Plays always get better, especially with something as long as *Cymbeline* is, and in verse. In the beginning previews, some of the actors were ahead of others in terms of verse speaking and comprehensibility. Certain parts of the house are more grateful on the ear than others. It took Martha Plimpton a number of weeks to get her intentions right so she could speak. So time is our friend. And we have a membership here, so we have fairly decent audiences.

Henry Woronicz: It's hard when you only get one preview when you do a comedy. You don't get the time to let the performance find the rhythms of the laughter, where we think they're going to respond, things that work and don't work. You don't know if a comic business works, or was it just off that night, or somebody in the audience coughed at the wrong time, or something else. You need a good four or five previews to put your comedies in the right place. But you don't get that here. You don't get that at a lot of places. You usually get three or four previews. Four is not bad. Five would be lovely, but that's hard.

Daniel Sullivan: Two weeks are good, I think. I believe you can still do good, important work in those two weeks. In Central Park it's more difficult because technical work basically stops at the first preview. From then on, you can only work during the day since you're performing at night and, of course, you can only use the lights at night. You have to have all the technical elements very quickly because it's all acting work from that point on.

Using and assessing previews

Mary Zimmerman: Previews you know are the greatest invention in the world. The audience tells you everything – what's funny, what's not, what's working, what's not, when they get ahead of you a little bit, when you're going too slow. You can find out little cuts you can make in previews to the story. They already know that. Timing issues end up being different. You adjust staging. Once you see it all flowing in front of an audience, you say 'Well that's not so good, is it?' or 'That transition is ass'. You start to see it with another's eyes. What comes back to you is the story because for weeks it's been a little hard to see the forest for the trees. You lose faith in even the simplest things like, 'Will anyone even *know* that Romeo and Juliet are in love?' You get so caught up in the moment and the tiny moments and the work of it that you think, 'Are they going to understand that he thinks she's dead?' You think the craziest things. But then you get very reassured. You just learn everything.

Far and away I'm ten times more nervous – and I think all directors might agree – on first preview than on opening. That first encounter with an audience, you don't know if they're going to like it. You like it, but you think, 'What if they throw tomatoes?' You literally have no idea.

Barbara Gaines: Previews are our biggest teachers. You learn from audiences very quickly what does and doesn't work. Most of us spend lots of time watching their faces, their body language to see what they're feeling. It never fails that, as I await the first preview house lights to go out, no fewer than ten thoughts come to me about what I've failed to do or new ideas that should be in the show. It springs from the fear of a room full of strangers judging our work, but that's directly connected with being more honest with myself, more rigorous with my ideas. No show I've ever directed has been perfect: I could have helped them all in some way after they'd open. I'm continually dissatisfied with *my* work in the shows – there's always more truth to unearth. I don't think I'll ever figure it all out. Perhaps that's part of the joy ... the joy is in the searching.

Andrei Serban: Once the audience comes in, I see it with different eyes. Always! I always see my productions through the eyes of the audience. What I discover is unbelievable. I discover things that I never saw before because I see with the audience's eyes. That's when, if I have a good amount of previews where I can clean up, I always profit from this a lot. If I can profit from reducing, eliminating a lot of the 'too-much-ness' (which we tend to put into it) the production will benefit. I would take 40 per cent off, if I could. Sometimes I'm not courageous enough or I don't identify with our own love of this and that.

Mark Lamos: Stephen Greenblatt has written a book called *Shakespearean Negotiations*. That's how I see the entire process. First I negotiate with a text. Then designers, actors, technicians, composers, coaches, etc. We are all negotiating every moment until the production is finished. Then the audience begins *its* negotiations with the work. It's a living, breathing entity that relies for its power on the contact with a live audience.

Darko Tresnjak: As we get on the stage and into previews, when is the audience engaged? When are we losing them in the story? The moment I get into previews (we don't have too many of them here) I try to split myself in half so one half is looking at the stage and the other half is looking at the audience. It's not about pandering to them.

Kent Thompson: Audiences across the country react very differently to Shakespeare. I have begun to believe that it is cultural. I think audiences here [Alabama Shakespeare] respond to the story; they respond to the character; and they respond to the language. That's part of the Southern oral tradition. In some areas of the country they respond more visually, and they don't care about the language as much. But for me the audience is a real marker about whether or not it's engaging.

The hard part for any director is to judge that one performance in context. Is the audience response accurate? What was the audience responding badly to? Were they laughing at the violence in the scene where Macduff's wife gets killed? We had two large school groups that first performance, and they laughed at that. I was trying to figure out, 'Is it the violence? Or is it the way that it's been staged?' What I ultimately thought it was, was that the actors were taking too long to build to the final moment of the scene. It wasn't that it was funny, but it allowed enough room for somebody to laugh out of nervousness. So they're a critical part of it, and the ebb and flow of how audiences respond to it.

Daniel Sullivan: In previews, the audience becomes your collaborator. The audience breathes with the play. They relax into it if it's good; they become anxious if they have difficulty entering the world you are constructing for them. I'm attuned to that in a very instinctive way and I make many changes during this period in response to an audience's response.

At the same time, on a separate track, I am still in rehearsal mode, still learning about the play, still making discoveries. I go back to the text to see what I am missing. Should I have taken that moment more seriously? Maybe we're playing this too heavily? I make cuts if a scene feels too repetitive. I love to experiment during previews. Actors? Not so much. You're late enough in the process that many actors have now set what they are doing in stone. Late changes can be difficult for them to make and they can sometimes need convincing that the change will actually make the performances richer. I always feel for them. It's not always easy to give up a part of your performance that you've come to depend upon. Maybe having been an actor makes me particularly empathetic in this moment, and though I communicate this understanding, I make the change nonetheless.

Ralph Alan Cohen: They learn how to deal with audiences not giving it back almost as well. The other night Lear says, 'Switch the Justice with the thief', and what Lear (James Keegan) does when he says that is, he comes down, indicates two members of the audience who were the justice and the thief. They just switch. And the last time he tried that the two audience members just sat there. He said, 'Switch the justice and the thief'. They finally did it and then the whole audience goes, 'Wow they did it'. And somehow that new relationship with Lear gets into the DNA of the production. That's the kind of thing we do so well.

We have workshops on audience contact. We speak a lot about being too intrusive or not. We think that the mad Lear is an okay place to be intrusive. That's the mad Lear asking them to switch places, and so we're okay with that. We try for the most part not to make our audience have to do anything, in particular have to speak. Moving out of the way, letting us have one of the gallant stools, that's easy, because that's just an easy move. But we also want them *not to speak*. We try never to require any language from them.

David Esbjornson: The presence of an audience is important in any theatre process, but I find it critical with Shakespeare. It is in the preview period where I have the confidence to make my most radical edits and dramaturgical choices. The audience teaches you so much. They will let you know exactly what is landing in the production and what isn't. If you can maintain a clear perspective about your original choices while at the same time gauging the reactions of the audience, the information will go a long way to further your storytelling.

At this point in the process, the primary relationship will be between the actors and the audience. Shakespeare's plays were written to function this way. There is no fourth wall, no pretending that people aren't sitting there. There is no place to hide, and the actors (especially the clowns) will thrive on this interaction. It can be challenging to make Shakespeare's humour work for a contemporary audience but you certainly won't succeed if you curtail an actor's ability to be spontaneous and responsive. A director must also allow for the juxtaposition of serious and humorous moments in performance. Even though Shakespeare provides obvious scenes of comic relief, careful investigation can often reveal the comedy inside tragic scenes and vice versa. This requires a specific calibration of the performances that can only be learned in front of a live audience.

For me, the real DNA of Shakespeare is the relationship between the performer and the audience. If a director can contextualize, motivate, interpret and craft a production, these great plays will appear to unfold with an effortless magic.

Lisa Peterson: I use previews pretty aggressively. Regularly those preview rehearsals are very key for me.

Ethan McSweeny: I think everything we do, prior to the preview, is educated guesswork. Then you have an audience. Your audience tells you almost instantly which guesses were good ones and which ones are not working.

My rhythm in previews is to take notes with my assistant during a performance, do tech notes after the performance, and then to do actor notes the next day. I like the time to digest my own notes. I often go down and check in with people at the end of the show, but I'm rarely ready to give notes at the end of a performance. The actors have just done this amazing thing and they're on one high, and my experience of sitting there and watching it is a very different focused kind of experience. I want to make sure I get as much information out of that preview as I possibly can, and then disseminate as widely as possible, so that all the departments can go and attack the problems and we can solve them the next day. In a preview rehearsal (which is usually four and a half or five hours) I like to do about an hour of notes with the actors, give the lighting and sound time to do some of their own cueing notes, and then bring us together for a combination of tech and acting.

Shakespeare plays have lots of transitions, much like musicals. I've always believed that the transitions should continue the narrative. It's never enough for me to just turn down the lights, have someone walk out, and then turn them back up. So every transition is an opportunity to tell a story. One of the biggest tools for doing this is tightly integrated lights and sound that move the audience's focus around the stage to the stories I'm trying to tell. I think that is why my work is often called cinematic, which I take as a great compliment. I'm keenly aware of moving the focus on the stage using the tools we have. The way I approach light and sound is almost as if it were a camera that can be used to pan, to zoom, to pull back. To some extent, doing a play as a director is creating one long uninterrupted take that you could release for an hour and a half without stopping. I challenge any movie director to ever do that.

One big element of transitions is the opportunity to feature music. The music tries to match the staging and then you try to match the staging to the music. There's this chicken-and-egg dance that you're doing because it isn't like an opera. It's not a set of fours measures and then this happens or that happens. I usually find myself needing to go back. We create the first round of transitions, and then we go back and we refine them and refine them and refine them. That's usually a big part of what ends up happening for me in previews, because you can't really start refining them until you've gotten all the way through tech. Also it's very important to me to get back to acting and to acting notes, responding to what we've learned from the audience every night.

Then I usually like to do a speed through at some point in that preview week. I find it's a good idea to blow the cobwebs out, get everyone to lean forward again. Sometimes it's like trying to get horses in the gate at a race. What you want is [*claps*] for the bell to sound and all the horses to jump out at their best. Some people are way early. Some people get in the gate and they're all ready to go, so you don't want them to stay in the gate too long, so you've got to back them out, walk them around and then put them back in. Some people just resist getting in. Every one of the actors has a slightly different response to how they're going to be ready, what you need to do to get them ready for the opening night, to release them into that.

My speed-throughs are not gibberish. It's with full tech and with all the actions and all the business. It is just permission to think faster than you would be willing to do in front of an audience. We did one yesterday on *Merchant* and the results were apparent that night. While we took very little change in the actual timings, there was a big change in the energy. But I have had shows that shed a crucial extra minute or two of accumulated acting that is just polite, patient and explicated.

I don't want acting to be any of those things. I want it to be impatient, vital, necessary and honest.

Just don't assume that you can treat every actor the same way. Listen to them, because they're all going to have a different moment where they need something, and you need to figure out what it is they need at that moment. I don't know if I have any better advice than that right now. If somebody is too patiently sitting in the gate, and their performance is starting to calcify a little bit, just give them a big adjustment and change it [*laughs*]. And don't be afraid! Previews are work. Final dress, like an invited audience or that first preview, is so mind numbingly scary. But then once you get into the groove of actually rehearsing during the day, and putting it on stage at night, I find that really fun! It's a lab. It's like, 'I want to try this little bit of an experiment. So you do this here. What did that do?' I like the lab of it and I like the work of it. I love getting to the stage where we're really refining things. You can feel it shift after a couple of previews.

I also believe, frankly, if I've done my job well, the baton has been passed to the actors. By the time previews are ending, one of the reasons that they're going to get rid of me after opening night is I'm not necessary. Whatever we've done, it's done. The steps that got us here are taken and you can't take them back anymore.

Opening

Kate Buckley: This may be an overstatement, but I think every company of actors I've worked with has been confident about going into previews. Therefore, opening night should be fun. Preview is my opening, and opening night is 'Let's play with the audience. Play with each other. Enjoy each other'. That is a goal – a strong ensemble.

David Frank: I have been doing this for almost fifty years and it still surprises me just how much you learn when you face an audience for the first time. After all those years of experience and hours of intense rehearsal, you would think you could pretty much anticipate the audience reaction. But you cannot. The director, producer, actors and stage managers all learn so much that first night. What I find most remarkable is how much we learn by the mere presence of a decent size audience. Before you even get to the moment in question, it suddenly dawns on you what will interest them and what they will need to know. Actors sense it too and immediately adjust to an audience's presence. That, of course, is one of the most exciting moments of all: when actors and audience learn things together on a great opening night. It is something that only a live theatre can achieve.

J. R. Sullivan: There is a character to it, to a play that begins in rehearsal, a tone and an attitude, an emotional temperature. These are things that I think we are responsible for. When it gets to a state of high anxiety, and we have these strangers come in and watch what we have been doing, that's something that hones us, reassures us. You want the high anxiety of that. There is an undeniable energy about opening nights. But at the same time, you want to know that there is a net, that there is somebody who is going to be there for you, that there is a support based on love, but also integrity, respect and admiration and caring. That starts in a rehearsal room, because you want them to feel. You ask them to feel secure in going to emotional truths that can strike very, very close to the heart, cut close to the bone. That's the danger of being in it. It can become a necessity for going there regularly. That can't happen, I think, without the support that comes from an ensemble, and an atmosphere that is supportive of that kind of adventurous and experimental and sometimes dangerous work. You've got a couple of guys, the Scottish king and queen. They're required to go places that are inhuman. There are lots of ways to do that. If you do that honestly, you better have the kind of support system I'm talking about.

André Bishop: We go through the opening night and the critics, which I just hate. I hate opening nights because I think it is kind of false. The audience is false. And I dread reading reviews. I'm always in a state of terror.

Andrei Serban: What can we do in six weeks rehearsal (minimum for a Shakespeare production)?! How to use the time well? Start with exercises, readings, discussions and all that. The scope in the first weeks is to purify, clean up, if possible, take away all sorts of preconceptions, clichés of our own memories of what the play is and hopefully discover the fresh play, the secret play, which is hidden (as Brook says) under the surface of the outer skin. Still, Shakespeare proves always slippery. We made some steps forward, that's true. We were prepared to shout 'eureka' but ... By opening night there's a sense that, 'Oh this play really needs to be discovered another time'. It's so ridiculous how it slipped through the fingers! Mr Will's is a bottomless pit indeed.

I dread opening night. I would never have it if I could. To me the opening night is when my work is finished. And more and more I don't want to go and see the show after that. The critics come and they write. If it's a great review, the actors don't want to change it because they think, 'Why tamper with success?' If it's a bad review, the actors want to change it because it's a failed project anyway. I believe in the continuous re-examination of something that is never never the final product. That would make everybody crazy. They would prefer that by opening night I would disappear in order for sanity to be brought in. Even five minutes before opening night, the official opening night, I'm still changing. Which makes some of the actors very upset, because there is never time to settle. There is never time to freeze anything. Freezing to me is death, but for some actors it's a saving grace. So that's a conflict.

After opening

Jim Warren: Because we involve the audience so much, we don't really know what our show is until it's with an audience. We get our staff and invite people from the community in, so that it's not a huge shock to the system when we get to a preview and we've never done it in front of an audience. We've had bits and pieces of audience before, sometimes a decent size. We may have planned, 'Alright, you're going to go to the audience on this line'. 'You're going to go to the audience on that line'. 'You're going to use this person as a prop for this'. Until we start doing that and seeing what that interaction is, we don't know the shape of our show. We have a lot of things in place, but the audience is a huge part of that. That's another reason that, not only do I keep giving notes once we get through those first performances, but I'll watch shows during the run and give notes, because things just tend to move a little this way or a little that way.

J. R. Sullivan: Openings are always exciting. There is an adrenaline rush to it. There is an undeniable energy to it. There's a focus to it. There's an excitement to it. All of those things coalesce. It can really be incandescent. But then they settle in, and the question is, 'What happens when they settle in?' If it's grooved in right, it will deepen in all the right ways and stay also on the path. And that's what you always hope for. It's whether you have laid that groundwork for them successfully, that they can't veer off and create something else.

Kate Buckley: I am strongly committed to the idea that a production needs to continue to grow and deepen from opening night to closing. If there isn't improvement during the course of a run, I am disappointed.

How you set the tone in the rehearsal room, how you can give them permission to find things on their own, how you work with your stage manager during the process, how you stay in contact with the stage manager during the course of the run, all contribute to a production's improvement. If any problems crop up, there should be a free flow of communication between all parties. I have gone back to see a show at the end of a run and found actors had discovered new things – nothing an audience might notice if they were there at opening and at closing, but a minimal change. This is thrilling because it tells me the actors never stopped enlivening the work. I *love* that. However, it's never about me, it's about the craft, the playwright, the audience; it's always about the work at hand.

Ethan McSweeny: I believe that a well-rehearsed play should grow deeper through the course of its performances. It can be a scary thing sometimes to go back (when I have the opportunity to go back) and see a final performance, because you can really see your work, you can tell what you rehearsed well, and what you didn't. If something has gone way off the rails, that's my responsibility. I talk to the cast usually at the end of the rehearsal process about getting deeper, but not wider as the run progresses. Time is only one measurement, but I watch the clock, and I know the run times, and when I read the stage management reports, if the play has deviated by more than, about 45 seconds from what our usual run times are, something's going wrong and that's not good. Air is being added back in. I like to challenge actors to think faster. Shakespeare thought incredibly fast. People have a habit of being pedantic with Shakespeare. Clearly, if they say in *Romeo and Juliet*, what is it about 'The two hours traffic of our stage' [*laughs*] ... in addition to the 'two' and 'traffic' alliterate (which is why he said it) they clearly took it at a pretty good clip, and that's exciting! We can understand it better sometimes when you put it together.

André Bishop: I think I go to see our Shakespeare productions more than I go to see any of our other shows because you are constantly finding new things. I think I sat through *Henry IV*

Parts 1 and 2 maybe fifteen times after we opened. I mean they were my favourite plays in the world. But every time I would discover something new, some scene that I hadn't quite registered or a speech that … It's like peeling an onion. They're just infinite layers. Which makes it all the harder sometimes to go back to contemporary writing because there aren't so many layers.

CONCLUSION

Working on Shakespeare requires the practitioner to work 'at the top of one's game' as Michael Kahn so aptly put it. As we have seen, the director must supervise a considerable number of complex and difficult issues not normally encountered when directing many contemporary pieces. These can include conflating multiple versions and source texts; assuring comprehension of the text's meaning; shaping the delivery of language, verse and imagery; supervising considerably larger character lists than contemporary plays have; establishing the story's setting – historical or otherwise; staging crowd scenes, dances and battles; handling scene changes and special effects, such as gods descending, masques and supernatural elements; and managing a larger team of professionals that include voice and text coaches, dramaturgs, fight directors, choreographers, sound and special effects operators. Directing Shakespeare is indeed an arduous process.

The complexity of these productions can reveal a great deal about a given director's beliefs, biases and craft more readily than can their work on contemporary productions. The challenges of directing Shakespeare can bring the differences as well as similarities between approaches and methods more clearly into focus. We can readily see the strategies employed by directors because the same canon of plays repeats over and over. The basic elements of production more or less remain constant while ways of addressing each problem vary considerably. We can compare and contrast director practices, and, hopefully, learn from them. In the process, we might discover new techniques that are available to us when encountering our next production.

It is my contention that an examination of directorial approaches and methods ought to take into account the director's beliefs about what their role should be in the production. Thus an informed assessment of a director's production work should consider views on function, as well as the director's values – the principles and standards used, consciously or unconsciously, to measure their success and achievement. The underlying beliefs exposed from such an appraisal have considerable influence on a director's choice of methods. Thus an individual's view of their role and principles reveals their aesthetic sensibility, and their aesthetic sensibility affects their choice of tactics and techniques. Perhaps we will be able to decipher the values and goals prescribed by a director when witnessing their next production and evaluating it.

We should not forget that the director's methodology often is in response to a specific production situation. Is the producing organization a large well-supported institution with considerable resources and ample rehearsal periods and previews (New York Shakespeare, Chicago Shakespeare, Goodman)? Is the producing organization located in the country away from large urban centres (Oregon Shakespeare, Utah Shakespeare, Alabama Shakespeare, American Shakespeare Center)? Is it associated with a university campus (Colorado, New Jersey, Illinois)? Does it have an associated training programme component (Shakespeare Theatre Company, DC, Shakespeare & Company, The Old Globe)? Is it dedicated to original practices (American Shakespeare Center, Atlanta Shakespeare Company at the New American Shakespeare Tavern)? Or is its mission to explore gender or race issues (Judith Shakespeare, L.A. Women's Shakespeare Project, African-American Shakespeare Company?) Is there a special community that is to be served by the organization?

How *can* the play be best communicated to a contemporary audience? It is *the* question that almost all directors ask themselves when approaching a production. Regardless of philosophy, style, approach or technique – or the specific circumstances of a producing organization – the director's intention generally remains the same: to discover resonances in Shakespeare's text that speak to their audience today. Many answers to this question can be found throughout this book. Collectively they paint a picture of the current US landscape for directing Shakespeare.

INTERVIEWS CONDUCTED

Albers, Ken. Personal interview. 6 June 2004.
Adams, Fred. Personal interview. 10 January 2015.
Adams, Fred and R. Scott Phillips. Personal interview. 29 June 2004.
Appel, Libby. Personal interview. 11 June 2004. Revised 4 January 2015.
Berger, Sidney. Personal interview. 13 January 2005.
Bishop, André. Personal interview. 30 November 2007.
Blacker, Robert. Personal Interview. 12 July 2008.
Bond, Timothy. Personal interview. 10 June 2004. Revised with new material 7 January 2015.
Buckley, Kate. Personal interview. 16 June 2008. Revised 24 January 2015.
Burdman, Stephen. Personal interview. 10 January 2015.
Caldwell, Raymond. Personal interview. 2 July 2012. Revised with new material 29 January 2015.
Carpenter, Karen. Personal interview. 6 July 2004.
Ciccolella, Ann. Personal interview. 10 October 2009.
Cohen, Ralph Alan. Personal interview. 15 June 2008. Revised with new material 29 January 2015.
Conlin, Kathleen. Personal interview. 1 July 2004. Revised 24 January 2015.
Craft, Barry. Personal interview. 10 June 2004.
Devon, Richard. Personal interview. 4 August 2004.
Douglas, Timothy. Personal interview. 30 November 2007. Revised with new material 18 March 2015.
Dreyfoos, David. Personal interview. 11 June 2004.
Edmondson, James. Personal interview. 11 June 2004.
Esbjornson, David. Personal interview. 9 August 2004. Revised with new material 6 January 2015.

Eustis, Oskar. Personal interview. 7 September 2007.
Falls, Robert. 20 October 2006.
Frank, David. Personal interview. 8 September 2012. Revised with new material 24 January 2015.
Gaines, Barbara. Personal interview. 3 June 2004. Revised with new material 17 January 2015.
Gaze, Christopher. Personal interview. 10 January, 2010.
Halberstam, Michael. Personal interview. 27 June 2004.
Ivers, David. Personal interview. 12 February 2015.
Kahn, Michael. Personal interview. 14 September 2004.
Kahn, Michael. Personal interview. 18 July 2008.
Kemper, Rebecca. Personal interview. 10 January, 2010.
Kinstle, James. Personal interview. 14 January, 2005.
Kubzanski, Jessica. Personal interview. 26 June 2004.
Kulick, Brian. Personal interview. 11 August 2004. Revised with new material 19 January 2015.
Lamos, Mark. Personal interview. 15 May 2008. Revised with new material 15 January 2015.
McAnuff, Des. Personal interview. 12 July 2008.
McAnuff, Des. Personal interview. 7 October 2008. Revised 31 March, 2015.
MacLean, Calvin. Personal interview. 26 June 2004. Revised 6 December 2014.
McSweeny, Ethan. Personal interview. 25 June 2011. Revised 28 January 2015. New material 4 February 2015.
Metropulos, Penny. Personal interview. 11 June 2004. Revised 24 January 2015.
Monte, Bonnie. Personal interview. 11 August 2004.
Monte, Bonnie, Personal interview. 24 January 2008. Revised 25 January 2015.
Mullins, Paul. Personal interview. 11 August 2004.
Neville-Andrews, John. Personal interview. 20 June 2012. Revised 20 January 2015.
Noel, Craig. Personal interview. 7 July 2004.
Packer, Tina. Personal interview. 14 January 2005. Revised with new material 28 January 2015.
Peterson, Lisa. Personal interview. 14 June 2008. Revised 17 January 2015.
Rauch, Bill. Personal interview. 2 August 2007.

Rauch, Bill. Personal interview. 17 June 2008. Revised 15 January 2015. New material 16 February 2015.
Seavy, Bruce. Personal interview. 17, June 2004.
Serban, Andre. Personal interview. 12 August 2004. Revised 17 January 2015.
Shine, Stephanie. Personal interview. 13 January 2005.
Sneed, Philip. Personal interview. 14 January 2005.
Sullivan, Daniel. Personal interview. 4 March 2008. Revised with new material 3 March 2015.
Sullivan, J. R. Personal interview. 1 December 2007. Revised 3 January 2015.
Syer, Fontaine. Personal interview. 6 June 2004.
Thompson, Kent. Personal interview. 18 June 2004.
Tresjnk, Darko. Personal interview. 5 and 6 July 2004.
Warren, Jim. Personal interview. 1 July 2011. Revised 25 January 2015.
Williamson, Laird. Personal interview. 12 June 2004.
Willis, Susan. Personal interview. 17 June 2004.
Wolpe, Lisa. Personal interview. 31 January 2009. Revised 4 February 2015.
Woronicz, Henry. Personal interview. 29 June 2004. Revised 25 January 2015.
Zimmerman, Mary. Personal interview. 15 June 2006. Revised 6 January 2015.
Zipay, Joanne. Personal interview. 9 August 2004.

NOTES

Introduction

1 At the January 2015 Shakespeare Theatre Association, estimates of the number of Shakespeare theatres, although varied, were slightly above this figure.
2 I was unable to see work directed by Sidney Berger, Stephen Burdman, Christopher Gaze, James Kinstle, Rebecca Kemper, Craig Noel and Joanne Zipay.

Chapter 1 Text and Context

1 Payne, B. Iden. *Life in a Wooden O: Memoirs of the Theatre* (New Haven, 1977), 120–90.
2 Barranger, Milly S. *Margaret Webster: A Life in the Theatre* (Ann Arbor, 2004), 59–150.
3 Barranger, 65–6.
4 Guthrie, Tyronne. *A Life in the Theatre* (New York, 1959), 191–2, 336.
5 Guthrie, Tyronne. *Directing a Play: A Lecture by Tyronne Guthrie.* Folkways Records, 1962.
6 Interview, 3 June 2004.
7 Interview, 16 June 2008.
8 Sturgess, Kim C. *Shakespeare and the American Nation* (Cambridge, 2004), 183–6.
9 See, for example, Little, Stuart W. *Enter Joseph Papp: In Search of a New American Theater* (New York: 1974), for a discussion of his thoughts about casting diversity.

10 Berry, Ralph. *On Directing Shakespeare* (London, 1989), 13–23.

11 Interview, 25 June 2011.

12 Dessen, Alan C. *Rescripting Shakespeare: The Text, the Director and Modern Productions* (Cambridge, 2002), 2–5.

13 Taylor, Nancy. *Women Direct Shakespeare in America: Productions from the 1990s* (Madison, 2005), 35.

14 Taylor, 13.

15 For detailed accounts of American directors see Karen Fricker 'Robert Lepage', 192–210; Patricia Lennox 'Joseph Papp', 307–22; Douglas Lanier 'Julie Taymor', 457–73; and Matthew Wilson Smith's 'Orson Welles', 493–508 in *The Routledge Companion to Directors' Shakespeare*, John Russell Brown, ed. (London, 2008). Also Franklin J. Hildy and Robert Shaughnessy have contributed chapters on B. Iden Payne, 323–8 and Tyronie Gutherie, 123–39 respectively.

16 Loewith, Jason, ed. *The Director's Voice. Twenty Interviews. Vol. 2* (New York, 2012), xiii.

17 Loewith, 163.

18 Loewith, 336–7.

19 Barry, Paul. *A Lifetime with Shakespeare: Notes from an American Director of all 38 Plays* (Jefferson, 2010).

20 Homan, Sidney. *Directing Shakespeare: A Scholar Onstage* (Athens, 2004).

21 Interview, 9 January 2015.

22 Interview, 15 June 2008.

23 Interview, 9 August 2004.

24 Interview, 11 June 2004.

25 Interview, 14 June 2008.

26 Interview, 20 October 2006.

27 Interviews, 2 August 2007; 17 June 2008.

28 Dated 19 January, 2015.

29 Interview, 13 January 2005.

30 Interview, 11 August 2004.

31 Interview, 18 June 2004.
32 Interview, 15 May 2008.
33 Interview, 20 June 2012.
34 Loewith, 365.
35 Interview, 17 June 2008.
36 Interview, 7 September 2007.
37 Interview, 16 June 2008.
38 Judith Shakespeare Company website: http://www.judithshakespeare.org/aboutus.html [accessed 31 December 2009].
39 These are observations from attending Shakespeare productions across this country over the past decade.
40 Interview, 12 July 2008.
41 Interview, 7 September 2007.
42 Rauch update, 11 December 2014.

Chapter 2 The Directors and their Aesthetic Values

1 Hobgood, Burnett M. and Thomas Mitchell. *Framework of the Director's Work in the Theatre*. Unpublished Manuscript (Champaign-Urbana, IL, 1987), 15.

2 Kott claims that Shakespeare should not be viewed as archaic: 'Shakespeare is like the world, or life itself. Every historical period finds in him what it is looking for and what it wants to see. A reader or spectator in the mid-twentieth century interprets *Richard III* through his own experiences. He cannot do otherwise'. *Shakespeare, Our Contemporary* (Garden City, NY, 1964), 5. Many directors and productions were inspired by his argument.

3 Spolin's *Improvisation for the Theatre*, first published in 1963, has had a revolutionary affect on theater training and especially improvisation, forming the basis for work at such noted companies as Second City in Chicago. She created many exercises, known as 'theater games' to develop and train

actors. Exploring 'where' something happens is one of the most important elements.

4 Packer had a close relationship with Kristin Linklater who worked with her company for many years. Linklater is known in particular for her *Freeing the Natural Voice* and *Freeing Shakespeare's Voice*. In addition, Packer developed a highly physical method called 'dropping in' that establishes strong emotional and body connections to each word.

5 Angus Bowmer started the Oregon Shakespeare Festival in 1935. His autobiography, *As I Remember, Adam* (Ashland: 1975) is an account of the founding and early years of the festival.

6 Neil Freeman's *Applause First Folio* editions (thirty-six plays) and his *Shakespeare's First Texts* (New York, 2000) have been a considerable influence on many practitioners.

Chapter 3 Developing an Approach

1 Interview, 9 August 2004.
2 Interview, 24 January 2008.

Chapter 5 Preparing the Production Text

1 See Rosenbaum, Ron *The Shakespeare Wars* (New York, 2006), Ch. 2, for a discussion of some of the issues with the source texts.

Chapter 6 Working with Designers

1 Barbara Gaines, Michael Kahn, Mark Lamos and Darko Tresnjak shared this observation with me and discussed its impact on how design meetings take place over the past decade or so.

Chapter 8 Beginning Rehearsals

1   She wrote two books on rehearsal: *Rehearsal from Shakespeare to Sheridan* (Oxford, 2000) and *Shakespeare in Parts* (New York, 2007) with Simon Palfrey.

Chapter 9 Table Work

1   Tina Packer interview (revised with additional comments), 28 January 2015.
2   The First Folio came up repeatedly in my interviews and readers will note the many references to it in this book. I have already mentioned the work of John Barton and Patrick Tucker whose work with the First Folio had an influence on American training programmes and Shakespeare theatres a generation ago. In addition, Neil Freeman's teaching at several American university training programmes and at Shakespeare & Company, has added to the enormous influence of the First Folio as a primary source on which to base the production's text.

Chapter 11 Speaking Shakespeare's Language

1   Edith Skinner taught mid-Atlantic speech at several notable universities including Yale Drama School, Julliard, New York University, Carnegie Mellon and American Conservatory Theater. She also disseminated her approach through *Speak With Distinction*, the first edition of which came out in 1942 (New York, 1990).

SELECT BIBLIOGRAPHY

Barry, Paul. *A Lifetime with Shakespeare: Notes from an American Director of all 38 Plays*. Jefferson: McFarland, 2010.
Barton, John. *Playing Shakespeare*. London: Metheun, 1984.
Bartow, Arthur. *The Director's Voice*. New York: Theatre Communications Group, 1993.
Berry, Cecily. *The Actor and the Text*. London: Harrap Ltd, 1987.
Berry, Ralph. *On Directing Shakespeare*. London: Croom Helm, 1977.
Brown, John Russell, ed. *The Routledge Companion to Directors' Shakespeare*. London: Routledge, 2008.
Dessen, Alan C. *Rescripting Shakespeare: The Text, the Director and Modern Productions*. Cambridge: Cambridge University Press, 2002.
Engle, Ron, Felicia Hardison Londre and Daniel J. Watermeier. *Shakespeare Companies and Festivals*. Westport: Greenwood Press, 1995.
'Festivals and Theatre Companies'. Mr William Shakespeare and the Internet. 2 February 2009. www.palomar.edu/FestivalsandTheatreCompanies [accessed 26 August 2009].
Fliotsos, Anne and Wendy Vierow. *American Women Stage Directors of the Twentieth Century*. Urbana-Champaign: University of Illinois Press, 2008.
Freeman, Neil. *Shakespeare's First Texts*. New York: Applause, 2000.
Freeman, Neil. *Applause First Folio Editions*. New York: Applause.
Hobgood, Burnett M. and Thomas Mitchell. *Framework of the Director's Work in the Theatre*. Department of Theatre, Urbana-Champaign, 1987.
Hodgdon, Barbara and W. B. Worthen, eds. *A Companion to Shakespeare and Performance*. Malden: Blackwell Publishing, 2007.

Ko, Yu Jin. 'Shakespeare Festivals'. *Shakespeare in American Life*. Virginia Mason Vaughan and Alden T. Vaughan, comp. and eds. Washington, DC: Folger Shakespeare Library, 2007.

Linklater, Kristin. *Freeing the Natural Voice*. New York: Drama Publishers, 1976.

Linklater, Kristin. *Freeing Shakespeare's Voice*. New York: Theatre Communications Group, 1993.

Loewith, Jason, ed. *The Director's Voice. Twenty Interviews*. Vol. 2. New York: Theatre Communications Group, 2012.

Morrison, Michael A. 'Shakespeare in North America', in Stanley Wells and Sarah Stanton, eds., *The Cambridge Companion to Shakespeare on Stage*, 230–58. Cambridge: Cambridge University Press, 2002.

Radio Documentary: Shakespeare in American Life. Folger Shakespeare Library. www.shakespeareinamericanlife.org/documentary/listen.cfm [accessed 3 September 2007].

Rosenbaum, Ron. *The Shakespeare Wars: Clashing Scholars, Public Fiascoes, Palace Coups*. New York: Random House, 2006.

Shakespeare in American Life. Washington, DC: Folger Shakespeare Library. N.p./n.d. www.shakespeareinamericanlife.org/documentary/listen.cfm [accessed 3 September 2007].

Shurgot, Michael W., ed. *North American Players of Shakespeare*. Cranbury: University of Delaware Press, 2007.

Stern, Tiffany. *Rehearsal from Shakespeare to Sheridan*. Oxford: Clarendon Press, 2000.

Stern, Tiffany and Simon Palfrey. *Shakespeare in Parts*. Oxford: Oxford University Press, 2007.

Taylor, Nancy. *Women Direct Shakespeare in America: Productions from the 1990s*. Madison: Fairleigh Dickinson University Press, 2005.

Thompson, Ayanna. *Colorblind Shakespeare: New Perspectives on Race and Performance*. New York: Routledge, 2006.

Thompson, Ayanna. 'In The Blood: William Shakespeare, August Wilson, and a Black Director'. In *Colorblind Shakespeare: New Perspectives on Race and Performance*. New York: Routledge, 2006.

Vaughan, Virginia Mason and Alden T. Vaughan, comp. and eds. *Shakespeare in American Life*. Washington, DC: Folger Shakespeare Library, 2007.

Watkins, Jeff. 'A Personal Perspective on Original Practice in American Shakespeare'. Winner of the Amy and Eric Burger Theatre Essay Competition. 2006. Paper.

INDEX

accents 247, 248
actors *see also* casting; rehearsals
   different needs from director 191
   difficulty of late changes for 316
   directors' approach to 27
   director's notes to 116, 120, 258, 265, 286–8
   insecurities 270
   note taking 233
   open-mindedness 276
   as source of splendour in Cohen's view 64–5
   veteran 170
   working with 186–92, 263–4, 265, 276, 319–20
Actors Studio approach 274–5
Adams, Abigail 13
Adams, Paul 15
Aeneid, The 216
aesthetic values 26–8
African American Shakespeare Company 22
Akalaitis, JoAnne 13
Alvarez, Frankie J. 26
American Players Theatre 2, 46, 310
American Shakespeare Center 16–17, 64, 66, 132, 182, 242, 296, 328
analysis of research 123–8

Andrews, John Neville
   on changes in Shakespeare production 78–9
   on language of Shakespeare 20, 79
   on table work 200, 213
Antony and Cleopatra 132, 137–8
Antoon, Jason 166
Appel, Libby
   on casting 167, 170
   directing credits 33
   on Peter Brook 9
   on Shakespeare in contemporary context 18, 28, 33–4
   on working with dramagurgs 131, 134
arc of a character 263, 269, 270, 274
arc of an act 263, 306
arc of a play 263, 292–3
archetypal symbols 91, 95
Arden editions 133
arguments over editing 139
Artzberger, Ryan 19
As You Like It 218, 271
Aspects of the Novel (Forster) 125
audiences *see also* previews
   director's concern for, in Cohen's view 65
   effects on actors 302

identification with
performance 188–9
sharing actors' experience
74, 311, 316–17
auditions *see* casting

Baitz, Jon Robin 47
Barillas, Christian 198
Barnum, P. T. 10
Barry, Paul 14, 15
Barton, John 9–10, 93, 102,
250, 254
Battery Park 111
Beaumont, Francis 64
Bensussen, Melia 13
Berry, Cecily 7, 10
Berry, Ralph 10–11, 18
Bishop, André
after openings 312, 324–5
on openings 312, 322
on previews 312
on subtext 264, 278–9
Blacker, Robert
dramaturg credits 51
on interpretive directing 51–2
on table work 200, 215–16
Blackfriars Playhouse 64
blocking
in approaches to directing
27
avoiding initial planning
186
design and 234–5
organic 219–20, 230–4
relation to table work 201,
203
varying approaches
218–40
Bloodgood, Bill 156
Blumenfeld, Mara 152

Bond, Timothy
on casting 167, 174–6
directing credits 79–80
on inclusive casting 32–3,
80–1
Bottom Translations, The
(Kott) 216
Bowmer, Angus 34
British directors 7–10
Broadway 8
Brodsky, Joseph 232
Brook, Peter 9
Brown, John Russell 13
Buckley, Kate
after openings 312, 323–4
on analysis 117, 124
on casting 167, 171
directing credits 61–2
on First Folio technique 31
on Gaines's Chicago
Shakespeare Theater
workshops 10
on historical context 21
on language of Shakespeare
241, 246
on openings 311, 320
on preparing the production
text 62–3
on rehearsal 182, 183,
184–5, 187–8, 192, 265,
287
on table work 198, 201
Taming of the Shrew, The
production 15
on tech rehearsals 297, 300
on working with designers
146–7, 149–50
Burbage, Richard 143
Burdman, Stephen
directing credits 70–1

INDEX 345

Henry V production 94,
  111–13
on panoramic theatre 31–2,
  71–2
on preparing the production
  text 132, 144
on staging 221, 240

casting
  inclusive approaches 32–3,
    79–85
  overview of directors'
    approaches 165–8
Cerveris, Michael 146
character
  arc 263, 269, 270, 274
  issues arising in rehearsal
    274–8
  motivation 15, 97, 264,
    269, 278–81
Cheeseman, Ken 166
Chekhov, Anton 175
Cherry Orchard, The 224
Chicago Shakespeare Theater
  34, 62
children's audiences 22
Cibber, Colley 34
Ciulei, Liviu 115
clarity, as director's emphasis
  64–5, 68
closet scene in *Hamlet* 137
closeup effects 240
Cohen, Ralph Alan
  on casting 167, 172–3
  on character issues 263, 274
  on developing an approach
    92, 93, 101–2
  on language of Shakespeare
    241, 243, 244, 254,
    257–8

on limitations of concept
  approaches 105
original practice views 31,
  64–5
on previews 311, 316–17
on rehearsal 182, 185–6,
on staging 225
on table work 199, 205,
  207–8
on tech rehearsals 298,
  302–3
collaboration
  in casting 174
  in design 103, 149, 153,
    161–2, 273–4
  in rehearsals 182–3, 186–8,
    263, 273–4
  in staging 223–4, 225–6,
    230–4
  with audiences 309
colour blind casting 167, 173
Comedy of Errors, The 50,
  102
Comins, Danforth 218
communities as interpretive
  contexts 22–4
complexity in Shakespeare 29,
  35, 41–5
concept 11–12, 14, 18, 53, 70,
  93–4, 103–6
condensing text 111
Conklin, John 158
Conlin, Kathleen
  on analysis 117, 125
  on casting 168, 176
  on developing an approach
    93, 103
  directing credits 74–5
  on physical interpretations
    of text 32, 75

on rehearsal 263, 265, 266,
    272, 286–7, 293
on staging 219, 220, 226–7,
    235, 238
on working with designers
    147, 155
contexts
    approaches to Shakespeare
        as 94
    contemporary 18–20, 33–7,
        62–3, 94, 101, 104,
        106–13
    dimensions of 18–24, 106–13
contradictions, in characters
    263, 274
costumes 17, 152 *see also*
    dress rehearsals; tech
    rehearsals
Craig, Noel 8
Cranston, Bryan 48
critical scenes 95–6
critics 322
cross-gender casting 83–4, 107,
    167–8
cues in Elizabethan theatre
    17–18
Cullum, John 146
Cultural Literacy (Hirsch) 85
culture, Shakespeare's role
    84–5
Cumpsty, Michael 262
Curns, Benjamin 242
current events 99
cutting text 134–40
Cymbeline 146, 279, 312

Damashek, Barbara 274
Dehnert, Amanda 26
dementia 108–9
DeMunn, Jeffrey 104

designers
    attitudes about 157–62
    dialogues with 154–7
    ground plans 148, 162–3
    influence on staging 220,
        234–5
    meetings with 149–54
    overview of directors'
        approaches 145–8
designer's theatre 12
Dessen, Alan 11–12
developing an approach 89–94
Dickey, Dale 43
dictating 27
*Directing Shakespeare:
    A Scholar Onstage*
    (Homan) 14–15
*Directing Shakespeare in
    America* 1–4
directors
    absence from Elizabethan
        theatre 17
    aesthetic values 26–8
    challenges of Shakespeare
        327
    views on role of 328
The Director's Voice, Volume 2
    (Loewtih) 14
discoveries in rehearsal 287–8
diversity in casting *see* inclusive
    casting
Donohue, Dan 120
Douglas, Timothy
    on authentic communication
        in acting 32, 72–4
    on casting 167, 171–2,
        173–4
    directing credits 72
    on language of Shakespeare
        241–2, 246–7, 258–9

on rehearsal 183, 184,
189–90, 192–3, 265, 283
on research 117, 123
on staging 219, 232, 235
on table work 199, 208–9
on tech rehearsals 299, 306
on working with designers
147, 156–7
Douthit, Lue Morgan 21
dress rehearsals 297, 304 *see
also* tech rehearsals

eclectic approaches 11
editing plays *see* preparing the
production text; text of
Shakespeare
Elich, Michael 15
Elizabethan Stage Society 7
Elizabethan staging
lack of scenery 151
original practice movement's
efforts to recapture 16–18
Packer's and Warren's
approaches 102–3
Poel's advocacy 7
scenes to facilitate theatrical
exigencies 136–7
emotional responses to
Shakespeare 31–2
empathy of Shakespeare 263,
275
end stopping 250
English directors 7–10
Esbjornson, David
on casting 166–7, 171
on developing an approach
89–90, 94
directing credits 36
on interpreting female
characters 91–2, 97–8

on previews 311, 317
on rehearsal 263–4, 276
on Shakespeare in
contemporary context
28, 36–7
Eustis, Oskar
on casting 167, 173
directing credits 84
in *Director's Voice* 14
on editing decisions 130,
132, 139–40
on historical context 21
on inclusive casting 33
on language of Shakespeare
241, 245
on limitations of concept
approaches 93, 105
on Shakespeare's role in
culture 84–5
on table work 200, 210
on tradition 24
on working with designers
146, 147–8, 149, 158
Evans, Maurice 8–9
expert run-throughs 217, 221–2

Falls, Robert 12, 19
female characters, interpreting
97–8
feminist performance theory
12–13
Ferguson, Jesse Tyler 166
first day of rehearsal 184–6
First Folio
influence on Buckley's work
31, 62, 117, 124–5, 150
influence on Gaine's work
199, 206
influence on MacLean 131,
133

influence on original
  practice movement 17
influence on Shine's work
  68
influence on Thompson's
  work 57, 125
influence on Warren's work
  135
Tucker's influence 17
fisherman scene in *Pericles* 193
Fleshler, Glenn 19
Forster, E. M. 125
fourth act of *Antony and
  Cleopatra* 137–8
Frank, David
  on analysis 117, 125–6
  on developing an approach
    92, 100
  directing credits 75
  on fusion of performance
    approaches 32, 76
  on language of Shakespeare
    242–3, 244, 249, 251–2,
    259
  on openings 311, 320–1
  on preparing the production
    text 131, 132, 135, 142
  on rehearsal 182, 185, 262,
    263, 265, 268–9, 282–3
  on research 115, 118
  on sense of time in
    Shakespeare 261
  on staging 219, 229–30
  on table work 198, 203
  on tech rehearsals 297,
    300–1
  on working with designers
    148, 158–9
Freeman, Neil 57
Fri, Sean 182

Gaines, Barbara
  on casting 165, 168
  Chicago Shakespeare
    Theater workshops 10
  on complexity in
    Shakespeare 29, 35
  on context 28, 108–11
  on developing an approach
    89
  directing credits 34–5
  King Lear production 94,
    108–9
  on preparing the production
    text 131, 132, 136, 140
  on previews 310, 314
  on rehearsal 183, 186–7,
    262, 263, 268
  on staging 217, 221
  on table work 199, 206
  on tech rehearsals 297, 300
  Timon of Athens production
    90, 94, 109–11
  in *Women Direct
    Shakespeare in America*
    13
  on working with designers
    146, 149
Gardner, Herb 47
gender-oriented productions
  casting approaches 33,
    81–4, 107, 167–8
  as interpretive contexts 22
Gielgud, John 34
given circumstances,
    approaches based on
    89–90, 94
Glymph, Avery 182
goals for rehearsals 192–5
Governor's Island 111–13
Greenblatt, Stephen 315

Groff, Rinne 84
ground plans 148, 162–3
Gurr, Andrew 135
Guthrie, Tyrone 9

Hagen, Uta 9
Hall, Peter 102, 250
Hamlet
   contemporary challenges 96
   Eustis on editing 139–40
   Lamos on editing 137
   LeCompte's production 13
   Packer's performances 102
   Rauch's production 120
   source texts 130
   Sullivan's, D., comments on meaning 47
   themes 278
   Tresnjak's production 116
   Webster's production 8
Hansberry, Lorraine 175
Harman Hall 161
Heald, Anthony 26
Henry, Martha 253
Henry IV Part 1 8
Henry V
   Burdman's production 94, 111–13, 144
   Frank's production 268–9
   Monte's production 130
   New York Classical Theatre production 22
   versions 135
Henry VI Part 1 252
Henry VIII 136–7
Hirsch, E. D. 85
Hirsch, John 252
historical materialism 84
historical setting
   developing an approach based on 89–90, 94
   importance to Buckley 62–3
   interpretive contexts 21
   Shakespeare's world 36
Hitchcock, Alfred 214
Holtzman, Jonathan 16
Homan, Sidney 14–15
humour 317
Hwang, David Henry 84

iambic pentameter 47–8, 58, 214, 256–7
ideals, characters as 275
ideas, sharing
   design 154–7
   in rehearsal 186–8
   on staging 228
image chains 200, 214–16
image clusters 127
imagery
   clusters 127
   communicating effectively 251
   interpretive contexts 20, 90–1, 95
   sharing ideas with designers 149
   table work focus on 200, 214–16
improvisation 99, 219, 230–4
inclusive casting
   racial and ethnic diversity 32–3, 50, 79–81, 167, 173–6
   women 33, 81–4, 168, 176–8
indoor theatres as interpretive contexts 22
insert scenes 132, 144

Internet research 115, 118
interpretation 97–100
interpretive directing 30, 48–56
interviews in this text 2–3
invisible directing 29–30, 45–8
Ivers, David
  on analysis 127–8
  directing credits 60
  on language of Shakespeare 30–1, 60–1
  on preparing the production text 131, 135
  on rehearsal 263, 272–3
  on research 117, 118, 122
  on staging 218, 223
  on table work 200, 210–11

Jacobson, Naomi 19
Jones, Dan 182
Judith Shakespeare Company 22, 81
Julius Caesar 26, 62–3, 96

Kahn, Michael
  on analysis 117, 123
  on complexity in Shakespeare 29, 41–2
  on difficulty of doing Shakespeare 327
  directing credits 41
  in *On Directing Shakespeare* 10
  in *Director's Voice* 14
  on language of Shakespeare 243, 250–1, 254–5
  McSweeny's work with 266, 284
  on rehearsal 183, 187, 262, 266–8
  on staging 217–18, 222–3
  on table work 200, 213
  on tech rehearsals 297, 299, 306
  on working with designers 148, 159
Kaiser, Scott 134, 248
Keach, Stacy 12
Keegan, James 316
Kenerly, Kevin 26
Kilmer, Val 252
King, Floyd 116
King Lear
  Burdman's production 144
  contemporary contexts 18, 94, 108–9
  Falls's production 12
  Gaines on editing 140
  involving audience 316–17
  MacLean's comment on themes 43
  MacLean's production 258
  Peterson's production 104
  racial diversity in casting 175
  Shakespeare's revisions 143
Koszyn, Jayne 13
Kott, Jan 28, 216
Kraft, Barry 134
Kulick, Brian
  on analysis 127
  on collaboration with the audience 309
  on developing an approach 91, 96–7
  directing credits 38
  on endless possibilities of meaning in Shakespeare 29, 38–9
  on language of Shakespeare 244, 256–7, 259

on preparing the
    production text 132,
    140–1, 143–4
on rehearsal 184, 194–5,
    262–3, 264, 266, 270–1,
    281–2, 292–3
on research 117, 118, 121
Richard III production 262
on table work 199, 200,
    205, 207, 211–12
on tech rehearsals 298, 302
Kushner, Tony 84

Lamos, Mark
on analysis 117, 124
on casting 165
on complexity in
    Shakespeare 29
on context of language 20
Cymbeline production 146
on language of Shakespeare
    30, 58–9, 241, 243, 244,
    245–6, 254, 257
on preparing the production
    text 130, 131, 132, 137,
    142–3
on previews 310, 315
on rehearsal 184, 192, 263,
    264–5, 277–8, 282, 286
on staging 219–20, 220,
    232–3, 237, 238–9
on table work 198, 199,
    200, 203–4, 208
on tech rehearsals 299, 305
on working with designers
    147, 148, 154, 162–3
Langham, Michael 243, 252
language of Shakespeare *see
    also* table work; text of
    Shakespeare

casting for ability with 167,
    170, 172
directors' views 30–1,
    55–64, 241–4
discoveries in rehearsal
    194–5
effect of overemphasis of
    design on 160
interpretive contexts 20–1
phrasing and word choice
    249–53
physicality 258–9
reading aloud 117, 123–4
spoken quality 244–9
stresses and rhythm 254–8
structure 253–4
Lao Tzu 46
Latino characters 107–8
layering 212–13
LeCompte, Elizabeth 13
Lee, Eugene 158
LePage, Robert 13
Lieberman, Andrew 161
A Lifetime of Shakespeare
    (Barry) 14
lighting 16–17, 71–2
Linklater, Kristin 72
living thought 252–3
Loewtih, Jason 14
logistics 290
Los Angeles Women's
    Shakespeare Company
    22, 82
Love's Labour's Lost 53, 93,
    102

Macbeth
contemporary challenges 96
Kahn's production 267–8
Monte's approach 91

rhythm 257
  Warren's production 16
  Webster's production 8
Machado, Eduardo 84
MacLean, Calvin
  on complexity in
    Shakespeare 29, 42–3
  on language of Shakespeare
    244, 258
  on preparing the production
    text 131, 132, 133,
    135–6, 138
  on rehearsal 266, 291
  on tech rehearsals 299–300,
    308
  on working with designers
    147, 152–3
Mailer, Norman 111
Major Barbara 158
Mann, Emily 84
Margulies, Donald 47
Maxwell, Roberta 253
McAnuff, Des
  on developing an approach
    92, 98
  directing credits 50–1
  on interpretive directing 30,
    51–2
  on language of Shakespeare
    243, 252–3
  on rehearsal 184, 194
  on staging 220, 233–4,
    234–5
  on table work 200, 214–15
  on tradition 24
  on working with designers
    147, 154–5
McDiarmid, Ian 90, 109–11
McLaughlin, Ellen 84
McSweeny, Ethan

  after openings 312, 324
  on analysis 118, 126–7
  on Berry's paradigms 11
  on developing an approach
    92, 100–1
  directing credits 68
  on instinctual and emotional
    responses to Shakespeare
    31
  on language of Shakespeare
    68–9, 241, 245
  on preparing the production
    text 131, 132, 133–4,
    141–2
  on previews 311, 318–20
  on rehearsal 184, 193, 263,
    265–6, 275, 284–5, 287,
    289–90
  on research 115, 116, 119
  on staging 217, 219, 220,
    221–2, 227–9, 239–40
  on table work 199, 200,
    205–6, 209
  on tech rehearsals 299,
    307–8
  on working with designers
    148, 161–2
meaning in Shakespeare 29,
  37–40, 204–6
Measure for Measure
  Kahn's production 41
  Oregon Shakespeare Festival
    production 50
  Rauch's context for 19–20,
    22, 94, 107–8
  Zimmerman's comments on
    complexity 44–5
Melrose, Rob 298
mental pictures 273
Merchant of Venice, The

contemporary challenges 91, 96, 97
cues 17–18
McSweeny on editing 141–2
McSweeny's production 116, 119, 132, 161–2, 228–9
tech rehearsal example 307–8
themes 277
word stresses 257
Metropulos, Penny
directing credits 59–60
on language of Shakespeare 30, 60, 243, 254
on preparing the production text 132, 140
on rehearsal 263, 273–4
on staging 220, 238
on table work 200, 201, 209
on working with designers 147, 153–4, 155–6
Mewbron, Rachel 182
Midgley, Patrick 16
Midsummer Night's Dream, A
Brook's production 9
McSweeny's production 222
Metropulos's production 156
Peterson's production 53
Sullivan's production 166
mixing approaches to directing 74–9
models
designing with 157, 159
as rehearsal aids 219, 263, 272
as staging aids 227, 228
Moeller, Jennifer 161
Monte, Bonnie

directing credits 39–40
Henry V production 130
on imagery in Shakespeare 90–1, 95
on language of Shakespeare 242
on meaning in Shakespeare 29, 40
on rehearsal 183–4, 190–1
on research 116–17, 120–1
on staging 218, 220, 223–4, 235
on table work 198, 203
Morgan, Bob 158
motivation of characters 278–81
Mousetrap scene in *Hamlet* 278
Much Ado About Nothing
Buckley's production 62, 150
Burdman's production 240
Curns's production 242
Esbjornson's production 36, 90
McSweeny's production 239
Muldoon, Paul 246
Mullins, Paul
on context of story 20
directing credits 63
on language of Shakespeare 31, 63–4, 241, 244–5
on rehearsal 184, 191
on research 117, 121–2
on staging 217, 219, 220, 221, 229, 234
music 303, 305, 319

Naked and the Dead, The (Mailer) 111

Nelson, Tim Blake 166
Neville-Andrews, John
   on changing approaches to Shakespeare 32
   directing credits 78
   on organic approach 78–9
   on staging 220
   on table work 200, 213
New Cambridge edition 131, 133
New York Classical Theatre 22
non-traditional casting
   gender in 83–4, 107, 168
   racial diversity 167, 168, 173, 174–6
   Zipay's approach 81–2
notes
   actors making in scripts 233
   after opening shows 312, 323
   on design 93, 103, 146, 147, 155
   giving to actors 116, 120, 258, 265, 286–8
   group vs. individual 265, 286
   during previews 318
   on run-throughs 286
   on staging 221

O'Brien, Ellen 13
O'Brien, Jack 158
Old Globe 8
older actors 170
Olivier, Laurence 34
On Directing Shakespeare (Berry) 10–11
openings
   after 323–5
   varying approaches 311–2, 320–2

opera set design 159
Oregon Shakespeare Festival 8, 26, 49–50
organic approach 78–9
organic blocking 219–20, 230–4
organization of this text 3
original practice approach
   Cohen's advocacy 31, 64–5, 101–2
   directors' views 31, 64–8
   general impact on Shakespeare productions 16–18
   tech rehearsals 298–9, 302–4
Original Shakespeare Company 17
Othello
   arc 292–3
   contemporary challenges 97, 269–70
   Peterson's production 53, 269–70
   Shakespeare's revisions 143
   Webster's production 8
   Wolpe's production 23
outdoor theatres 21–2, 71–2, 310

Pacino, Al 47
Packer, Tina
   approach to Shakespeare 32
   on developing an approach 92–3, 102
   directing credits 76–7
   Douglas's work with 72
   on fusion of directing approaches 77–8
   on language of Shakespeare 77, 243, 253

on rehearsal 183, 190
on staging 219, 230–1
on table work 199, 206
in *Women Direct Shakespeare in America* 13
Page, Patrick 267
panoramic theatre 31–2, 71–2, 144
Papp, Joseph 10, 13, 41, 252
paraphrasing 205
Parks, Brooke 26
Parks, Suzan-Lori 84
Pauli, Matthew 182
pauses
    avoiding 244, 257–8, 299, 304
    filling 306
    lack of, in Shakespeare 59
Payne, B. Iden 7–8
perception, Shakespeare's explorations 277–8
Pericles
    accepting on its own terms 44, 45
    image from Zimmerman's production 19
    non-traditional settings 22, 152
    staging 236
period analogues 11
Peterson, Lisa
    directing credits 52–3
    on director's point of view 53
    on interpretive directing 30
    on preparing the production text 132, 139
    on previews 311, 318
    on rehearsal 263, 265, 269–70, 284, 287–8
    on Shakespeare in contemporary context 18–19, 104–5
    on staging 219, 225–6
    on table work 200, 201, 209
    on tech rehearsals 297, 299, 300
Phelps, Gregory Jon 16
phrasing skills 249
physical directors 68–74
physical environments 21–2
physical language 258–9, 270–1
physical models *see* models
Playing Shakespeare (Barton) 9–10
Plimpton, Martha 146, 279, 312
Plummer, Christopher 253
Poel, William 7
point of view 93, 100–1
pre-blocking 218
previews
    benefiting from 313–20
    numbers 310, 312–13
    varying approaches 309–11
prisons, as interpretive contexts 22
problem plays 44
problem solving 263, 272
producing organizations 328
production text *see also* text of Shakespeare
    cutting 134–40
    punctuation 131, 133–4
    replacements and adaptations 142–4
    transposing scenes 132, 140–2

version and editing
considerations 129–32
punctuation
analyzing in table work 206, 207
discrepancies 199
editing 131, 133–4
pure Shakespeare 12

racial diversity in casting 167, 173–6
racial identity 19, 50, 94, 107–8
racially oriented productions 22
Raisin in the Sun, A 175
Rauch, Bill
on casting 167, 168
directing credits 48
on interpretive directing 30, 48–50
on language of Shakespeare 242, 247–8
on rehearsal 182–3, 186
on research 116, 120
on Shakespeare in contemporary context 19–20, 21, 22, 94, 106–8
on staging 219, 220, 231–2, 234
on table work 200, 214
on tradition 24
on working with designers 148, 162
read-throughs 203, 204
Rear Window 214
received traditions 24
rehearsals
after first week 266–74
approaches to middle phase 261–6

character issues 274–8
in Elizabethan theatre 17–18
first day 184–6
goals for 192–5
notes to actors 258, 265, 286–8
overview of directors' approaches 182–4
run-throughs 264–6, 282–6
schedules 289–93
shaping 281–2
subtext and motivation 278–81
tech 297–308
time allowed for 239, 272–3, 289–93
working with actors 186–92
Ren Run 185, 186, 218
Rescripting Shakespeare (Dessen) 11–12
research
analysis of 123–8
overview of directors' approaches 115–18
sample approaches 118–23
reviews 322
rhetoric 253–4
rhythm
in language of Shakespeare 243–4, 255–8
Shakespeare's awareness 69, 266
Richard II 8, 64–5, 121–2
Richard III
Burdman's production 144
depth of communication in 73
Kulick's production 262
Zipay's production 177–8
Rjurstrom, Tod 218

Robeson, Paul, 8
Romeo and Juliet
  arc of story 292–3
  Brian Kulick's production 244
  David Ivers' production 198
  deep structure 259
  imagery 215
  Ivers's analysis 127–8
  McSweeny on developing a viewpoint 100
  text clues to original performance 17
Rosenthal, Todd 149
rough blocking 203, 218–19, 230
Routledge Companion to Directors' Shakespeare, The (Brown) 13
rules on language 249
run-throughs 264–6, 282–6

Sanders, Jay O. 166
Savage, Lee 161
scansion 47–8, 206–8
scene-by-scene table work 198, 200, 202, 203
scene changes 7, 103, 220 *see also* transitions
scenery, paucity in Shakespeare's time 151, 237
scenes, adding 132, 144
schedules 289–93
Schlesinger, John 102
school audiences 22
Seagull, The 144
Sellars, Peter 54
semi-colons 207
Serban, Andrei
  on actors' relationship to character 263, 274–5
  on analysis 118, 128
  on developing an approach 92, 93, 98–100
  directing credits 37
  on meaning in Shakespeare 29, 37–8
  on openings 312, 322
  on previews 310, 314
  on rehearsal 183, 188–9
  on working with designers 148, 159–60
set models *see* models
Sevy, Bruce
  on actor commitment 31, 70
  on analysis 117, 125
  directing credits 69
  on rehearsal 264, 276–7
sexism 92, 97
Shaker meetings 152
Shakespeare & Company 76
Shakespeare Behind Bars 22
Shakespeare Memorial Theatre 10
Shakespearean Negotiations (Greenblatt) 315
Shakespeare's Metrical Art (Wright) 256
shaping in rehearsal 281–2
Shenandoah Shakespeare Express 64, 66
Shephard, Scott 13
Sher, Bartlett 14
Shine, Stephanie
  on actors' role 31
  on context of story 20
  on developing an approach 93, 103–4
  directing credits 67

on limitations of concept
approaches 105–6
original practice views
67–8
on rehearsal 183, 188, 263
on research 117
on table work 198–9, 214
on tech rehearsals 298–9,
304
Silva, Vilma 15, 26
sketching 225–6
Smith, Keith Randolph 166
source texts 130–1 *see also* text
of Shakespeare
Soviet Union 154–5
speaking skills 249–53
specificity 191
speed-throughs 319
Spolin, Viola 32, 76, 251
spondees 256
stage directions 101
staging
blocking 218–20, 223–5, 238
improvisation in 230–4
overview of directors'
approaches 217–21
sketching structures 225–30
from table work 221–3
transitions 235–7
Stern, Tiffany 185
story, interpretive contexts 20
story analysis 208–9
storyboards 98
storytelling 222, 273
stresses in language of
Shakespeare 243, 254–5,
257
Stuhlbarg, Michael 84
stumble throughs 273, 283,
284, 285

subtext 264, 278–81
Sullivan, Daniel
on casting 167, 170–1
on complexity in
Shakespeare 29
on concepts 93–4, 106
directing credits 46–7
on language of Shakespeare
47–8, 242, 243–4, 247,
255–6
*Midsummer Night's Dream,
A*, production 166
on preparing the production
text 132, 139
on previews 310, 311, 313,
316
on rehearsal 262, 264, 265,
268, 280–1, 285, 289
on research 117, 121
on staging 220, 233
on subtext 264, 280–1
on tech rehearsals 299, 305
on transparency in directing
30, 47
on working with designers
147, 148, 157–8
Sullivan, J. R.
after openings 312, 323
As You Like It production
218
directing credits 45–6
on invisible directing 29–30,
46
on openings 311, 321
on rehearsal 263, 265, 266,
271–2, 284, 291
on staging 217, 218–19, 225
on table work 200, 210
on tech rehearsals 298,
301–2

table work
- comprehension and scansion 204–8
- image chains and 214–16
- overview 197–200
- returning to 214
- scene-by-scene vs. full cast 201–4
- story analysis 208–9
- studying structure 210–13
- transition to staging 221–3
- unifying purpose 209–10

Taming of the Shrew, The
- contemporary challenges 91, 96
- Kate Buckley's production 15, 149

Taylor, Nancy 12–13
Taymor, Julie 13, 14, 20–1
tech rehearsals
- challenges and opportunities 300–2
- honing performance with 299, 300–1, 305–6
- *Merchant of Venice, The* example 307–8
- in original practice productions 302–4
- varied approaches 297–300

Technical notes 287

Tempest, The
- contemporary challenges 96
- image clusters in 127
- imagery 216
- McSweeny's production 100–1, 161, 182, 239
- music in Zipay's productions 303
- Webster's production 8

tension, exploring 268–9
text of Shakespeare *see also* language of Shakespeare; table work
- authentic communication in acting 72–4
- condensing 111
- cutting 134–40
- directors' views 30–1, 66–7
- discoveries in rehearsal 194–5
- effect of overemphasis of design on 160
- interpretive contexts 20–1
- punctuation 131, 133–4
- reading aloud 117, 123–4
- replacements and adaptations 142–4
- revising in previews 316
- transposing scenes 132, 140–2
- version and editing considerations 129–32

theatres as interpretive contexts 21–2
theatres performing Shakespeare in US 1
Thompson, Kent
- on analysis 117, 124–5
- on context of language 20
- on developing an approach 91, 95–6
- directing credits 57
- on language of Shakespeare 30, 57–8, 263, 275–6
- on previews 311, 315
- on staging 219, 227
- on table work 199, 200, 204–5, 214
- on tech rehearsals 298, 301

on working with designers
147, 155
time management 289–93
Timon of Athens
  Gaines's production 90, 94, 109–11
  Metropulos on editing 140
  Packer's performances 102
Tommy 194
tracking charts 266, 289
traditions 24
transgender characterizations 107
transitions
  in Elizabethan theatre 103
  importance in Shakespeare 220, 235–7
  using to continue story 318–19
  in Victorian theatre 7
transposed productions 12
transposing scenes 132, 140–2
Tresnjak, Darko
  on casting 168, 176–7
  directing credits 54
  Hamlet production 116
  on interpretive directing 30, 54–5
  on preparing the production text 131, 132, 133, 134, 137–8
  on previews 310–11, 315
  on rehearsals 264–5, 282
  on research 117, 122–3
  on staging 218, 223
  on table work 199, 200, 201, 206, 211
  on working with designers 148, 162

trial scene, *Merchant of Venice, The* 228–9
trochees 256
Troilus and Cressida 50, 298
Tucker, Patrick 10, 17
Twelfth Night
  Kulick on editing 141
  MacLean's comment on themes 43
  music in Zipay's productions 303
  table work to examine 204–5
  themes 278
  Webster's production 8
Two Gentlemen of Verona 137
Two Noble Kinsmen, The 176–7

Ur texts 134

Venora, Diane 177
verse 58–9, 138, 255–8 *see also* language of Shakespeare
veteran actors 170
Vickery, John 253
Victorian staging conventions 7
visceral directing 68–74, 93
vocal technique, overemphasizing 171
Vogel, Paula 84
voice 242, 245, 246–7

Wadsworth, Stephen 172
Wanamaker, Sam 10, 135
Warren, Jim
  after openings 312, 323
  on developing an approach 92
  on following text 66

Macbeth, production 16
original practice views 31, 66–7, 102–3
on preparing the production text 131, 132, 134–5, 136, 138
on rehearsal 265, 286
on table work 200, 212
on tech rehearsals 298–9, 304
Washington, Denzel 47, 55
Wasserstein, Wendy 47
Webster, Margaret 8–9
Welles, Orson 13, 140
Wetherall, Jack 130
What Peter Sellars Did to Mozart 54
Whitney, John O. 77
Wiles, Magan 198
William, Clifford 102
Wilson, August 107
Winter's Tale, The 127
Wolpe, Lisa
 casting approach 33, 83–4, 168
 directing credits 82–3
 on directing Shakespeare 25
 Othello production 23
 in *Women Direct Shakespeare in America* 13
women
 interpreting in Shakespeare 97–8
 non-traditional casting 33, 82, 83–4, 168
Women Direct Shakespeare in America (Taylor) 12–13
Woodard, Charlayne 47

word choices 249–50
working as equals 26–7
Woronicz, Henry
 on design 145
 directing credits 55
 on interpretive directing 56
 on language of Shakespeare 30, 56, 243, 255
 on preparing the production text 131, 135
 on previews 310, 313
 on rehearsal 261–2, 266
 on research 116, 117, 119
 on staging 219, 226
 on table work 200, 210
 on working with designers 148, 160
Wright, George 256

Zimmerman, Mary
 on casting 167, 168, 169–70, 177
 on complexity in Shakespeare 29, 44–5
 directing credits 43–4
 on language of Shakespeare 242, 249–50
 Pericles production 19, 22, 44, 45, 119, 152, 236
 on preparing the production text 131, 136
 on previews 310, 313–14
 on rehearsal 181, 184, 191–2, 193–4, 265, 266, 283–4, 288, 290
 on research 115, 118–19, 151
 on staging 219, 220, 226, 236–7
 on subtext 264, 279–80

on table work 198, 202–3
on tech rehearsals 299, 305
on working with designers
147, 151–2
Zipay, Joanne
on casting 33, 81–2, 168,
177–8
directing credits 81
on language of Shakespeare
243, 253–4
on original practices 18
on staging 219, 231
on table work 197
on tech rehearsals 298–9,
303–4
'zones,' Payne's use of 8